Yvonn

D1685425

MIND AND PERSONALITY

MIND AND PERSONALITY

AN ESSAY IN PSYCHOLOGY AND PHILOSOPHY

BY

WILLIAM BROWN, M.D., D.Sc.

WILDE READER IN MENTAL PHILOSOPHY IN THE UNIVERSITY OF OXFORD.
HON. CONSULTING PSYCHOLOGIST, BETHLEM ROYAL HOSPITAL, LONDON.
PSYCHOTHERAPIST TO KING'S COLLEGE HOSPITAL, LONDON.

LONDON
UNIVERSITY OF LONDON PRESS, LTD.
10 & 11 WARWICK LANE, E.C.4
1926

"Thy body at its best,
How far can that project thy soul on its lone way?"

Printed in Great Britain for the UNIVERSITY OF LONDON PRESS, LTD.,
by HAZELL, WATSON AND VINEY, LD., London and Aylesbury.

TO

MY WIFE

PREFACE

IN the following pages an attempt is made to obtain a synoptic view of personality, as considered from the standpoints of the various sciences—especially from those of psychology, psycho-pathology, and philosophy. It is in the nature of an interim report on the subject, since the material furnished by psycho-pathology continues to flow in an abundant stream, and the working out of its philosophic implications is a task that cannot be hurried. The results of prolonged or " deep " analyses of relatively normal individuals are also needed, to correct the balance and to serve as a standard by which the pathological may be more justly estimated. But enough is now known, under both heads, to justify provisional and tentative generalizations.

The book is the result of several years' work, while carrying on simultaneously my duties as an academic psychologist, and as a practising psychotherapist, and I find no excuse for further delay in its publication— apart from its obvious shortcomings, of which I am only too vividly aware, but which I am unable at present to rectify. I hope to be able to deal more fully in a later publication with the relation of value to temporal experience, and the bearing (if any) which the modern Theory of Relativity has upon the degree of reality attributable to the time-series within personal experience.

My thanks are due to the editors and publishers of *Problems of Personality* (Kegan Paul), *Science, Religion and Reality* (Sheldon Press), *Psychology and the Sciences*

(A. & C. Black), *Experimental Psychology and Child Study* (Sir Isaac Pitman & Sons, Ltd.), and of the journals "Psyche," "The Practitioner," "Journal of Neurology and Psycho-pathology," and "Health and Empire" for permission to make use of articles of mine appearing in their pages, and also to the National Baby Week Council for permission to include a lecture on Child Psychology given under their auspices. But all this material has been subjected to a thorough revision with reference to the central theme, and forms but a small proportion of the entire book. Finally, I owe a special debt of gratitude to Mr. W. Stanley Murrell, the manager of The University of London Press, for his help and encouragement, and for his unfailing courtesy in the preparation of the book for the press.

W. B.

OXFORD,
    October 10th, 1926.

CONTENTS

MIND AND PERSONALITY

PERSONALITY AND PSYCHO-PATHOLOGY

PERSONALITY AND ETHICS

PERSONALITY AND EVOLUTION

PERSONALITY AND RELIGION

PERSONALITY AND VALUE

SURVIVAL OF BODILY DEATH

MIND AND PERSONALITY

CHAPTER I

INTRODUCTION

THE problem of Personality is dealt with in the following pages along special lines. In one sense, Personality may be discussed in such a way as to make the exposition simply a textbook of Psychology, but that has not been my object in this volume. I wish rather to devote the whole space at my disposal to a consideration of Personality as such, that is, to a consideration of *the unity of the mind* from every point of view. It is a fact that, when one turns to the literature of the subject, one finds that little has been written on exactly these lines. There are textbooks on Psychology and Philosophy galore; books on Psycho-pathology, too, are extremely numerous, as well as books on Physiological Psychology and Experimental Psychology. But it does not seem to have occurred as yet to any author to bring together the various points of view, or, rather, to consider the general problem of personality from all these various points of view, and to attempt to adjust them one to another. If we turn to almost any standard textbook of psychology we find that far more than half the book is concerned with the study of lower forms of mental process, and that only a few concluding chapters are devoted to the consideration of the highest forms of mental activity, such as deliberation, choice, volition and character-formation. The ways in which these higher, or more

I

complicated, problems are solved depend, of course, upon the general line of thought developed in the earlier part of the book, and it naturally happens that in different books quite different lines of thought are followed. It has therefore occurred to me that something useful might be done by taking the developed human mind in its unity, and considering this mind scientifically from various points of view; from the points of view of biology and physiology, of the various schools of psychology, psycho-pathology, logic, ethics and metaphysics, and finally from the point of view of the theory of religious experience; always with the object of working out some sort of harmony from these conflicting opinions. In doing so I hope I may be forgiven if I neglect as far as possible to quote actual names; for, if one undertakes to describe the theories of individual people, one is committed to a very faithful following of them, and this easily leads one aside from the main question at issue. Only in certain special cases do I propose to mention names in any systematic way.

I might be expected to commence my discussion with a definition of Personality. That would be really impossible* : different schools of thought hold decidedly different views as to the nature of what the general public call personality. Only after considering these various views and relating them to one another could we even attempt such a definition. But it is only fair at the commencement to consider at any rate the derivation, and to remind ourselves that *persona* in Latin is supposed to mean a mask; so that, according to this derivation, personality is the part we play in this drama of life, and the use of that word personality emphasizes the fact that we all of us play many parts;

---

* A general guiding thread in the discussion is given by the concept of *mental unity*.

as we say in different terms, we are each of us many selves. We come into contact with the world at many angles and see it from many points of view, and we are different in accordance with the differing environments in which we find ourselves.

And yet, although the word itself, *persona*, suggests drama, even melodrama, pretence, hypocrisy and the like, nevertheless when we come to consider the ordinary use of language we find that people who are regarded as having personality are just the opposite of this. They are not people who play a part. They are people who are genuine, who really believe in what they work and live for. They are people who have taken a definite line of their own. They work out and achieve a certain degree of originality; they do not wear a mask, they are themselves. But once they have created their personality, if that personality is sufficiently strong and striking to impress others, there will be a large number of people ready to model themselves on that personality, to wear that mask; so that in this sense one might say that personality is something that in itself is worked out by the individual, but that it can be copied with a more or less degree of faithfulness; others can take it as a model. This dramatic sense of personality is, of course, the popular sense and is generally left aside by strict science. If one opens any textbook on psychology and expects to receive enlightenment on the subject, one is doomed to severe disappointment. Drama and the science of psychology seem to fall apart from one another. In the past they have kept rigidly clear of one another,* but I think we can truthfully say that in recent years a *rapprochement* has occurred, and on the

* As a striking exception to this generalization I would refer my readers to the late William Archer's study in the psychology of acting, *Masks or Faces?* London: Longmans, Green and Co., 1888.

one hand professional psychologists are more ready to learn from dramatists and novelists, and on the other the dramatist and the novelist are more ready to turn to psychology for information and general points of view.

We are led to ask what has been the cause of this change of attitude, because it is a distinct change of attitude characterizing the present generation, within the last 10 to 20 years. I think we can reply with perfect confidence that it is the advance made in so-called " individual psychology," and that this advance is definitely linked up with the name of one man, viz., Sigmund Freud. However extensively we may disagree with him in the details of his theory, we must all agree that in his original method—which he has gradually modified and improved—we have a means of getting at the soul of man, the essential individuality and personality of man, more powerful than any previously devised. His method of psycho-analysis is, as is well known, a method of persistently following up what the individual is ready to say about himself. It is not unlike confession ; such written confessions as those of St. Augustine or Rousseau remind one to some extent of self-analysis, but they do not go far enough to be justifiably called psycho-analysis. In ordinary confession one simply describes what thoughts are at the moment in one's mind, and goes over one's past life in that way, just stating what one remembers. That by itself is not psycho-analysis. It is the beginning of psycho-analysis, but for adequate analysis, which is to carry us any further than this, we have to follow up these memories, and encourage the individual, when being analysed, to say just what comes into his mind, *à propos* his various memories of the past, his various attitudes towards the present, all the various problems in his life, in which he has had to adapt himself to his environment.   Instead of the psycho-analyst explaining and solving his problems for him, the psycho-analyst should endeavour to encourage and make him solve them for himself, in this faith, that the solution will be reached by a still more thorough-going self-scrutiny.   In the end the aim is for the patient to acquire self-knowledge, but that self-knowledge is a matter of considerable mental labour and effort, a matter of over-coming " resistances," and the effort must be on the part of the person analysed and not merely on the part of the analyst.*

This form of analysis, on which we shall have much more to say in later chapters, brings us nearer to human nature than we have ever got before—brings us especially near to the more dramatic aspects and elements of human nature.   We find in the course of analysis that things that are important, the experiences that have had special bearing on the development of the patient's life, are conative and emotional in their nature.   They are related to the most fundamental instincts and impulses of the human race.   In a way they represent a sort of interaction between the primitive instinctive tendencies and the actual past experience of the individual.   The individual's mind may have become tangled up to a greater or less extent through the persistence of these instinctive tendencies in relation to special experiences of the past, which are preserved in memory.   These memory-traces are themselves in some way or other connected with primitive instinctive tendencies, such as those of self-preservation, self-assertion, and sex ; and through their interaction with these instincts they them-

---

* There is also, of course, the important factor of the " transference " (*Uebertragung*), which the analyst has to deal with and eventually " resolve."   *S. Freud: Collected Papers*, vol. ii., chap. **xxviii.**, " The Dynamics of the Transference."   Hogarth Press, 1924.

selves remain active, although they are no longer within the circle of the patient's conscious life. His memories are not like pictures that have been stored away or hung on the walls of some museum, but are actual forces, still making themselves felt in the background of the mind, still influencing the conscious mind, although themselves remaining unconscious, or outside the field of awareness.

This, then, is one way of approaching the mind; the analytic way, which is dramatic, which does justice to the conative and emotional nature of man, to the mental conflicts that inevitably accompany him on his path through life, and so in its description is more convincing than earlier description. With what may we contrast this modern outlook? We may contrast it, first with the outlook of the introspective psychology of earlier times and, secondly, with the outlook of physiology. The first was introduced into modern thought by, and it had its beginning in, John Locke. It was a method of just looking into one's mind and seeing what was to be observed there.* The task was undertaken mainly for the purpose of obtaining fresh insight into the nature of *knowledge*, and all the earlier work of modern psychology was concerned primarily with this question of knowledge —especially as to how the individual could get to know the external world. Locke introduced this " new way of ideas " ; Berkeley found the method so convincing that he denied the existence of anything beyond mind. Hume with his sceptical temperament found that he could go even further than Berkeley and abolish even the individual self, and reduce experience to a sequence of sensations, or impressions, and ideas linked together

* Introspection, according to John Locke, is " the notice which the mind takes of its own operations." Essay Concerning Human Understanding.

by laws of custom or habit. All three were primarily concerned with the problem of the intellectual side of human nature, the problem of knowledge.

The physiologists, on the other hand, being impressed by the fact that all mind is embodied in a brain, and is in relation to physical change somewhere or other in the organism, worked along entirely different lines. They sought to correlate mental processes of one kind or another with physiological processes and so eventually reached the theory of cerebral localization, according to which there was held to be a correspondence between mental processes and physical change in special parts of the nervous system. For Locke, Berkeley and Hume the unity of the mind, the personality, was mainly of an intellectual nature, and whereas Locke assumed a subject of experience, regarding his "ideas" as the object of that experience,* of that understanding, Hume explained away the subject of experience itself, and so seemed to destroy any essential unity of the mind. Physiology put in the place of psychological unity a physiological unity, and taught that the unity of the mind was merely the correlate of the unity of the body and especially of the nervous system, which co-ordinates the working of the different parts of the body.

But a consideration of the more general biological aspects of physiology has led psychology back to something between the extreme intellectualism of the earlier philosophers and the materialism of the earlier physiologists. It has made us see that the mind, like the physical organism, has had a history, and has an environment with which it interacts, so that we look upon psychological accounts of mental reactions to the environment as the completion—as it were, the fulfilment—

---

* For John Locke, an idea is " whatsoever is the object of the understanding when a man thinks."

of more strictly physical and physiological modes of reacting to the environment. And for a time, just as it was held in physiology that the physiological reflex action would serve as the starting point for a systematic explanation of the way in which the brain and mind works, so in biology it has been hoped that the study of the various instinctive tendencies will suffice to give us a systematic explanation of mind in its conative and emotional aspects as well as in its intellectual aspect.

We shall see later that, although all these are good beginnings and true as far as they go, they do not suffice. They do not carry us far enough, although they are very useful in enabling us to write the earlier chapters of psychological textbooks. Thus we can write about the awareness of an external world, the problem of perception, the nature of attention, etc., along the lines of Locke, Berkeley, Hume and their more modern representatives. We can also write descriptions of the central nervous system, and its connections with the sense-organs on one side and with the muscular system on the other. We can thus go a certain way towards explaining the issues of life. Further, we can enumerate the various primitive fundamental tendencies, show their relation to the various fundamental emotions and their inter-relations, and thus obtain the beginnings of a systematic explanation of the conative life or the life of active striving. But along each of these paths we soon find apparently insurmountable difficulties, and are thus led to recognize that they do not carry us far enough. And when we come to consider the more explicitly active side of the mind—deliberation, choice, volition—and the higher forms of æsthetic and religious experience, we can obtain no help from them at all.

I believe that the latest method of analysis, that of " deep analysis," will carry us further. I prefer to use the phrase " deep analysis " for the simple reason that the word psycho-analysis has now become a technical word, belonging to a particular school of thought. Just as Freud was the first scientist to use the word, so now the strict followers of Freud claim that word as their own. Their method is psycho-analysis, and the method used by any who refuse to accept Freud's theories in detail should perhaps not be called psycho-analysis, so that we need a more general term. The followers of C. G. Jung have suggested the term "analytic psychology"; but the objection to that is that it has already been used in the history of the subject with a very different connotation. It is the title of one of G. F. Stout's books on General Psychology, and is not sufficiently distinctive. It does not indicate the special kind of analysis that is meant. Another term sometimes suggested is mental analysis or psychological analysis, but perhaps the more expressive term, that Freud himself has on occasion used, is analysis of the depths, or deep analysis. This analysis really is deep in the sense of (metaphorically) going below the surface of the mind, going behind what is immediately apparent, in the faith that in psychology things are not always what they seem. To dig down deep—this is a metaphorical phrase ; the mind is not something solid into which one can dig, but it has layers or strata as it were, layers of mental activities into which one can penetrate from more superficial layers.

This method of deep analysis is more likely to help us because it does not need invariably to simplify its data, as other methods in psychology have had to do. Psychological textbooks generally quote as a merit of scientific method that it works from the simple to the complex and makes sure of its ground in that way. But actual experience in the use of these various methods makes one inclined to doubt the universal truth of this.

It is extremely probable that psychology has over-simplified itself in the past, and has allowed itself to be held up too much in the matter of words, in defining terms and getting certain fundamental problems solved, when it had not yet adequate material to solve them. The mind seems different from other realities of the world in this respect, that the more complex, the later developed forms of mental activity, though super-imposed upon earlier forms of mental activity, explain the latter quite as much as being explained by them. If one starts with the opposite assumption and tries to explain the later in terms of the earlier, one is adopting a method of very doubtful validity. It is no doubt valid in the case of the physical world ; there it is shown to be true by the way in which it works. It is quite true that our engineers would never have reached the point of inventing aeroplanes unless they had previously established their knowledge and power over nature in more simple forms of mechanism. But this is not necessarily the case with regard to the mind. In the more complex forms of mental activity one has an explication of phases implicit in earlier forms.

One may illustrate this by taking the most extreme instance, namely, religious experience. Attempts have frequently been made to explain civilized religious experience in terms of more primitive religious experience ; and, as a matter of fact, we have offered to us a whole sequence of developments from, perhaps, the use of magic spells through primitive forms of petitionary prayer, thence through idolatry of different kinds, to the purified religions of the highest form, such as the Christian religion. But it has become very apparent that no real explanation has been achieved in this way, and that the simpler forms of religious experience are much more adequately understood through our know-

ledge of later forms. This is the question that I shall
be dealing with fully in a subsequent chapter, but, inci-
dentally, I may refer to an important book on the
subject which has recently been translated into English,
Das Heilige, *The Idea of the Holy*, by Rudolf Otto.
This book contains an effective criticism of the
ordinary historical method, and of the conclusions often
drawn from the historical treatment of the subject.
So it is equally with questions of volition. If one starts
off with merely impulsive and conative tendencies and
tries to work up to volition from them, one will never
reach volition. One has to start with volition and work
downwards, or rather start at both ends or anywhere
you like and keep moving back and forth until one
gets a more and more adequate appreciation of mind
in its length as well as in its cross-section. In analysis
that is what one is doing the whole time. I doubt
whether anyone can realize what a powerful instrument
deep analysis is until he has used it himself. To those
of us who are engaged in this work it is simply astounding
to find certain psychologists and other scientists taking
the trouble to write critical books about it, and rejecting
it for the reasons which they see fit to bring forward.
It cannot be criticized or adequately dealt with apart
from itself. Many years ago C. G. Jung compared the
method with the telescope of Galileo; and just as
Galileo refuted his critics best by claiming that they
had not used his telescope, so modern analysts can quite
well give an adequate reply to their unqualified critics
by pointing out that these critics have not used their
methods.*

The method deals with personality as such the whole

---

* As regards the *inferences* drawn by psycho-analysts in the course of
their use of the analytic method, there is room for very serious and far-
reaching criticism.

time, and although Freud's own theory is the most
thorough-going theory based upon deep analysis, the
writings of another analyst, Alfred Adler, who has broken
away from the Freudian school, shows how important
this line of approach is to the inmost essential problem
of individuality and personality. In his books, *The
Neurotic Constitution* and *Individual Psychology*, he introduces a new point of view in psychology, setting
himself the task of working out what he calls the " *life-
line* " of the individual. He takes the individual, the
person in his present state of physical and mental
evolution, and analyses him back, showing how certain
forms of behaviour and trends of mental activity reveal
themselves again and again, year after year, in his life.
He traces the individual's more detailed likes and dislikes, hopes, fears and aspirations, back to more fundamental likes, dislikes and aspirations, not necessarily
explaining the later and more complicated in terms of
the earlier, but gaining thus a clearer and more detailed
view of the articulation, as it were, of the personality—
the way in which various parts of the personality work
together in producing the final psycho-physical reaction.
Even the most pathological individual does face the
world as a unity. He reacts in definite ways to his
physical and social environment. But there is one
fundamental trend or tendency which is most prominent
in him, and other tendencies less prominent which are
subordinated to this one. The kind of description and
appreciation of personality for which we can look to
psychology in the future is of that nature. It will aim
at telling us something of the individual's personality
in terms of a main tendency, a main life-line, showing
itself, not only at the present time, but throughout the
past years, with subordinate tendencies, some of them
conflicting with the main tendency, others co-operating

with it and supplementing it. William McDougall's doctrine of the " master-sentiment " is in place here.

If we then turn back to general psychological problems from such a systematic description of the individual mind as this, we shall perceive much more reality in such problems as those, for instance, of evolution, and freedom, and faith. We shall be able then to realize more adequately the creative aspect of consciousness ; for, as Henri Bergson has said, consciousness is creative from moment to moment. So far as the mind is a conscious mind it is always producing something new. Nevertheless, we cannot from this general vague freedom of Bergson get to a definite view of volitional freedom, unless we take into account the structure of the mind of the individual. What psychology does, then, is to explain the mind as a structure, a system of tendencies—but a system superimposed upon a still more primitive system. The individual, so far as he is a man, comes into the world provided with a certain system of mental tendencies, but superimposed upon that system there are further differentiations of tendency, distinguishing one man from another. From this point of view, the significance of the term personality is again that implied in the word whence it is derived, viz., *persona* or mask. Personality is the final differentiation which the individual has made, as it were, and produced in himself and superimposed upon all that he has inherited from past generations and lower forms of mental evolution. The term has been used by Jung to illustrate the contrast of what he calls the " personal unconscious " and the " collective unconscious." Speaking metaphorically one may compare the mind to a pyramid or mountain ascending to an apex. Corresponding to the apex there is the conscious personality, which has below itself the personal unconscious ; and still below that, stretching out indefinitely, there is the collective or racial unconscious, merging in the general unconscious of the entire physical universe. Thus far psychology. But when we pass to a philosophical consideration of the problem we shall find that personality has a *universal* element that contrasts it with the individual and the singular, and that in this respect it is an ideal never completely achieved by finite minds.

PERSONALITY AND PHYSIOLOGY

(I)—MIND AND THE NERVOUS SYSTEM
(CHAPTER II)

(II)—MIND AND THE PHYSICAL ORGANISM
(CHAPTER III)

CHAPTER II

LET us first consider the problem of Personality from the point of view of the physical organism. In one sense it might be argued that, considered in connection with the general problem of the relation of mind to body, personality is distinctly a matter of the mind. For, when we speak of personality we are thinking in the first place of something mental, namely, its unity ; even though we may admit that it has other characteristics also which may be, indeed certainly are, dependent in some way or other upon the body. Our problem is to ascertain to what extent and in what way these characteristics are so dependent.

On the one hand it is possible to regard the human body as a physical mechanism—after the style of a physical machine. Certain theorists in biology and physiology, indeed, consider that the only solid knowledge we have hitherto obtained is that of the structure and functioning of the human body ; the knowledge, in short, that is based ultimately upon the facts and concepts of chemistry and physics. Their hope is to explain the body as a very complicated machine, such that its functions depend upon its structure and its structure depends upon previous functioning of a material nature. Well, at any rate, if it is a machine it is a self-regulating, self-feeding and self-propagating machine, and the problem is whether such a machine is, or ever can be, explicable in mechanical terms.

Our problem here is not the problem of vitalism. We can only just refer to it in passing; we have to pass beyond that. We can say at any rate that, at the present stage of knowledge of biology and physiology, the mechanistic view has proved itself to be insufficient. Although the body does obey physical and chemical laws, processes nevertheless go on in it which are inexplicable in those terms; the total reaction of the body upon its environment cannot be explained in that way. The total reaction of the body—not only the human body, but the bodies of animals, right down to the protozoa themselves—shows certain characteristics that cannot, in my opinion and in that of a large body of scientific observers, be fitted into a mechanical scheme.

Let me enumerate a few of these characteristics* : one is that which we call spontaneity, another is persistence of action after the stimulus producing that action has ceased. A third characteristic of vital activity, as we observe it in ourselves and in others, is the coming to an end of the activity after a certain purpose has been achieved. Another characteristic is the tendency to alter and modify behaviour in the light of previous results, the so-called power of learning by experience. Another characteristic of behaviour is that the organism acts as a whole, and not simply and merely in its various parts, although this characteristic really includes all the rest. In a few words we can sum up these various characteristics by saying that all animal behaviour is *purposive ;* it occurs with a view to an end, although the end may not be clearly imagined or conceived by the individual. This purposiveness of vital activity is not explicable in terms of the laws of physics and

---

* See W. McDougall, *An Outline of Psychology*, pp. 43–49, Methuen and Co., 1923, for an illuminating discussion of these characteristics of purposive behaviour.

chemistry, although attempts have from time to time been made so to explain it by bringing in various conceptions, such as those, for example, of tropisms and conditioned reflexes.

The word tropism, which was first introduced into the vocabulary of psychology by Jacques Loeb,* denotes a tendency to turn towards or away from certain stimuli —a tendency supposed to be completely explicable in terms of physico-chemical activity. Examples of such tropisms are helio-tropism, geotropism, and photo-tropism. Tropism may be positive—a turning towards, or negative—a turning away from. When, e.g., a number of protozoa in a water tank with glass sides are subjected to the stimulus of a beam of light passing through the tank, we may find these protozoa all clustering in the course of the beam, showing positive photo-tropism, or we may find them getting out of the way of the beam of light, clustering together in any dark part of the tank, showing negative photo-tropism. But even these examples of tropism appear on closer examination to show a variability which is not in complete harmony with a physico-chemical or mechanical hypothesis. The investigator who has studied these lower forms of life most closely is H. C. Jennings,† and the conclusions he has come to are that protozoa such as the amœba or paramecium show all the marks of behaviour that I have enumerated ; so clearly, indeed, that if the amœba were magnified a large number of times we should unhesitatingly attribute to it consciousness—a conscious life. Its activities are varied in relation to the changing stimuli so closely that we are irresistibly impelled to believe that it is working under the influence of a definite purpose, such as the pursuit of prey, or food, or whatever the

* *The Mechanistic Conception of Life.* Chicago, 1912.
† *The Behaviour of Lower Organisms.* 1906.

purpose may be. Thus the continuity of life from the highest to the lowest forms is one of supra-mechanical purposive activity.

The other attempt to maintain the mechanist's point of view is that which is based upon the theory of reflex activity, and especially of what are called conditioned reflexes. In reflex activity the stimulation of a sensory nerve fibre is propagated through a nerve centre or series of nerve centres and eventually down a motor nerve to bring about a certain muscular reaction. In animals deprived of their brain these reflexes can be studied in isolation from one another. Reflexes, especially of the spinal cord, can be accurately studied in the frog. After the brain has been destroyed the frog still lives, and these reflexes are found to show a mechanical regularity of response. They do not show the characteristics of behaviour, as such, which is purposive, yet they are in another sense purposeful. The response is appropriate to the stimulus and seems to deal more or less adequately with the stimulus. The reflex theory of vital activity is that more and more complicated forms of reaction to environment can be explained as complexes of reflex activities. Whole series of reflexes are built up in the animal, which responds in relation to outside stimuli in such a way as to show an adaptation to its environment. These characteristics of mechanical reflex activity are apparent in such a lowly organism as the frog deprived of its brain. Even in animals highly placed among the mammals, such as the dog, if the cerebrum is destroyed, leaving all the lower centres intact, all sorts of very complicated reactions can be elicited by appropriate stimuli.* But the most significant fact

* Henry Head: "The Conception of Nervous and Mental Energy," *Brit. Journ. of Psychology*, vol. xiv., pp. 126–147, Oct., 1923 (his doctrine of " Vigilance ").

observed is that all *spontaneity* has disappeared ; all the
characteristics of behaviour are wanting, and the animal
responds like a machine. As soon as the response has
occurred the machine returns to its original condition.

On the other hand, the intact animal can be shown to
manifest what are called conditioned reflexes. The dog
secretes saliva under the influence of the visual appearance
of a piece of meat. Now experiments can be carried
out of this nature : simultaneously a bell is rung when
the meat is being shown, and subsequently, after a course
of training of this nature, the dog will be found to display
a tendency to secrete saliva whenever the bell is sounded,
even though the meat is not shown. Originally, of
course, no such reflex would have followed the sounding
of the bell. This seems to show that the bell has acquired
a *meaning* which is connected with the meaning previously
carried by the appearance of the meat. That is an
example of conditioned reflex.

Many modern enthusiasts for reflex activity, especially
J. B. Watson† and his disciples, consider that the true
science of the mind is the science of behaviour—a science
of reflex action, or, in other words, a purely physical
science. They lay very great stress upon the class of
conditioned reflexes as enabling us to pass from the
merely mechanical aspects of vital activity to the more
purposive. But, as McDougall has recently pointed out,‡
decerebrate animals which show reflex activity do not
manifest conditioned reflexes. The conditioned reflex in
its nature seems to be purposive, and the behaviourists
are begging the question when they say that conditioned
reflexes are to be explained otherwise than in terms of
purposive activity—meaning by purposive activity a
general urge or drive in the animal towards a certain

† J. B. Watson, *Behaviorism*.   Kegan Paul, 1926.
‡ *An Outline of Psychology*, pp. 55, 56.

end, and the use by the animal of certain means towards that end.*

We come back from the physical side to the conception of the organism as a unity manifesting laws of chemistry and physics in the various material processes which go to make up that unity. But, nevertheless, the unity is such that it cannot be explained merely in terms of chemistry and physics. A new principle has emerged, the principle of self-regulation, assimilation and propagation. Further attempts have been made to bring this within the realm of more definite physical thought by the neo-vitalists. In earlier days vitalism was a flourishing doctrine, and according to this doctrine there was such a thing as " vital force," which accounted for the unity of the organism and its power of self-regulation. The neo-vitalists do not hold this theory of a vital force, although they emphasize the self-regulative power of the organism. The more philosophic of them, such as J. S. Haldane, do not look for any special force or any special factor in addition to chemical and physical factors. But in the publications of the philosopher Hans Driesch, a well-known neo-vitalist, we do seem to find a positing of such additional factors, such as the " entelechy " and the " psychoid," which, though not themselves forces, exert a *directing* influence upon the living organism which produces the appearance of an adaptive unitary activity. According to Driesch's terminology, the entelechy is " the natural agent which forms the body," the psychoid is " the elemental agent which directs it."† Although the word psychoid seems to suggest mentality, Driesch explicitly denies to the psychoid anything mental, and refuses to speak of " psycho-physical " interaction. Yet

---

* For a full discussion and refutation of Behaviourism, see A. A. Roback: *Behaviourism and Psychology*, University Bookstore, Inc., 1923.

† Hans Driesch : *Science and Philosophy of the Organism*, vol. ii., p. 82.

he says " the psychoid or entelechy uses the conductive and specific faculties of the brain as a piano-player uses the piano."‡   The entelechy " does not act in space, it acts into space ; it is not in space, it only has points of manifestation in space."§   The entelechy and the psychoid are factors which control the alteration of potential into kinetic energy, and vice versa, in the course of activity of the individual.

But if we look into this expression more closely, we see the cloven hoof of the older vitalism—of the theory of occult forces.   It is difficult to conceive of entelechy or psychoid as other than an occult force, not reducible to the forces with which we are acquainted in physical sciences, but nevertheless a force of its own nature added to the others.   Such a conception is logically and philo-sophically unsatisfactory.   It is more philosophical to hold that purposive activity is a new and additional category, or phase of activity which is *sui generis*, and not to be explained away by material processes, being quite distinct from them although it leaves room for them, and is not in conflict with them.

Just as the fundamental physical and chemical processes cannot be ultimately explained away, but have to be merely accepted, so this quality of purposiveness in all vital activity has to be taken as an ultimate, that works in conjunction with these forces.   It does not compete with them or interfere with them ; none of the laws of physics and chemistry are broken by vital activity. There is, e.g., conservation of energy throughout, but the total reaction is not the same as that which one would find in a machine.

I have so far confined my remarks to the individual organism and have only just touched on the process of

‡ Op. cit., vol. ii., p. 97.
§ Op. cit., vol. ii., p. 235.

propagation. But there is also the process of inheritance, by which the unity is handed on from one generation to the next ; and no doubt the true unity of the individual is not adequately understood unless we take it in relation to the unity of the species to which the individual belongs. So eventually we arrive at a unity of the whole range of organic life, and of this unity the individual is to a certain extent an abstraction. Certainly he cannot be considered as entirely self-sufficing. He is a link in the sequence of generations, the characteristics which he manifests are characteristics which have been handed on to him from previous generations, which he will in his turn hand on to later generations ; and this self-regulating power, of which we have spoken, is a power which is in a still greater degree characteristic of the species and eventually of the race.

The more closely we examine this category of the purposive, the more we find that we can only get a satisfactorily clear impression of it if we think of it in mental, psychological terms. We can, of course, infer it from our observation of the behaviour of other organisms. Nevertheless, we find that this behaviour is more adequately explained if we take it in relation to what we ourselves, as individuals, are aware of. Whenever we observe that our own conduct is showing various characteristics of behaviour, we always find that certain definitely psychological factors are in operation. Thus, in the ordinary way, whenever we think of the behaviour of animals, we most naturally think of them as conscious beings. If we object to think of them as conscious individuals, preferring some purely biological alternative with no psychological implications, we find ourselves left with a conception (namely, that of a unitary self-regulating entity) which is not self-explanatory. We have to take it merely as a fact, as a statement, whereas, when we consider our own life we find that it has this added, psychological, side as well, which does make it self-explanatory. We have conations or tendencies towards certain ends which are at first not clearly imagined or conceived, and later on by further experience may become more and more explicitly distinct from the tendencies themselves. We feel that here we have something as self-evident as any of those facts of chemistry, physiology or biology which we observe from the outside.

Our conclusion, then, would be that psychology and biology do not deal with different data. From a biological point of view one might regard psychology as a part of biology, as completing biological science, as giving it a fuller meaning; we should probably be nearer the truth if we held that all vital processes are mental in nature. The degree or the nature of consciousness may vary according to the complexity of the organism, but as regards actual mental experience, there is probably no break in fact all along the line from the lowest organism to man himself. The real gulf probably lies between the inorganic and the organic. Later on we may find that within the domain of the mental lies a chasm or gulf of another nature which would distinguish a certain form of conscious experience from simpler forms of conscious experience.

The problem of the relation of mind to body is often set out and dealt with in rather a different way. Taking the highly developed form of human organism, we point to the fact that conscious experience seems most closely related to a very special part of that organism, the nervous system, and especially to its highest levels in the cerebral cortex. According to ordinary doctrines consciousness is related to change in various parts of the cerebral cortex, a thin layer of grey matter covering the

two cerebral hemispheres. The work of certain neurologists of an earlier generation, about the end of last
century (Ferrier, Hitzig, Munk, Golz and others), has
shown that there is a localization of the physiological
functions corresponding to the different kinds of conscious
activity ; and that functional activity of certain areas
of this cerebral cortex is correlated with consciousness
of a sensory nature, while activity of other areas is
correlated with consciousness of a motor nature. Thus
the occipital area of the cerebral cortex is correlated
with visual consciousness, the temporal area is correlated
with auditory consciousness, the post-central convolution
is correlated with cutaneous sensibility, while the pre-
central convolution is correlated with voluntary movement of the various muscles of the body.

Bundles of association fibres link up these various areas
with one another. The physiological theory of the
activity of the mind in relation to that of the brain is the
theory of integration—the association, that is, of the
sensory experiences among themselves and with movements, grounded in the integration of their physiological
correlates.* This leads us to a form of the question which
is very general and indeed ultimate in its nature. What
exactly is the relation between any particular change in
the cerebral cortex and the corresponding alteration in
the individual's conscious experience ?

Let us take a definite example—that of visual
experience. Physiology tells us that when we are aware
of the sensation of red a physiological change is taking
place in a certain part of the occipital cortex. That
change is physiological, a physico-chemical change in
protoplasmic substance. That change is something
quite different from the experience of red *per se*. The

---

* Sir C. S. Sherrington: *The Integrative Action of the Nervous System.*
London, 1906.

problem is, how are the two related to one another ?
Or, again, when one wills to move one's arm, physiology
tells us that material change is occurring in a very
definite part of the pre-central convolution of the brain,
a definite change which is essential to volitional movement of the arm. If that change cannot take place
through injury of one kind or another, the experience,
the consciousness of volitional movement of the arm,
does not take place.

There are three alternative explanations. The first
is that the physiological change produces the conscious
experience. Another is that the physiological change
interacts with something distinct from the brain, which
we may call the soul, and elicits from the soul the
conscious experience. The third alternative is that
physiological change and the change of conscious
experience occur simultaneously. These three theories
are the theories of materialism or automatism, interactionism, and parallelism respectively.

According to the first theory, then, mental process
is simply a result of physiological change in the organism.
The general objection to such a theory is that it denies
mental activity. It can be refuted quite generally and
easily as follows. If the brain is the real agent, and the
mind as we know it is never an agent and only appears
to be active, then mental activity is illusory ; if mental
activity is illusory then intellectual activity, which is
one particular form of mental activity, is illusory ; if
intellectual activity is illusory the products of intellectual
activity are illusory. Now this particular theory is one
such product of intellectual activity, therefore this
theory is illusory. Thus, the theory of materialism as
applied to the mind contradicts itself. Another objection
to materialism is that it explains an effect (consciousness)
in terms of a cause (brain activity) entirely different in

nature from that effect ; the effect, say, is the experience
of a red patch of colour, the cause is physico-chemical
change in the posterior part of the brain, in the occipital
cortex, a change we can only think of in terms of the
dance of molecules, atoms and electrons. What similarity
is there between those two things ? They are so distinct
from one another that one cannot pass continuously in
thought from one to the other.

We turn to the second theory—the theory of interaction. According to this theory the mind is relatively
passive in sensory experience and relatively active in
volitional experience. I say " relatively " because,
according to the theory of interaction the mind is, to
a certain extent, always active. Even when receiving
impressions, it is reacting to the outside world. According to interactionism, when we experience a sensation of
red what is happening is this : a physiological change,
initiated in the retina and propagated along the optic
nerve and its sub-cortical connections to the occipital
cortex, has produced there a certain kind of physiological
change, and that change elicits from the soul, which
can be regarded as something distinct from the brain,
the experience of a red sensation. As soon as we bring
in the conception of the soul, a psychical entity, we
find the disproportion in nature between cause and effect
to which we have already referred less of a difficulty.
We might argue thus : if you say that the physical
change causes the sensory experience, as certain inter-
actionists do, you are faced with the same difficulty as
the materialists are, but if you maintain that it is an
interaction with some other substance that produces the
sensory experience, then you have something not quite
so apparently inconceivable. Physical change of a certain
kind interacts with the soul producing as effect sensory
experience. A possible objection to this, of course, is

that we are assuming an entity, the characteristics of which we are not otherwise aware of. According to interactionism, when a movement of the arm follows upon the will to move the arm, the mind, as the result of mental activity, forms the determination to move the arm, that determination brings about a physical change in a certain centre of the pre-central convolution, and so nerve fibres are stimulated which conduct the nerve-impulse down the pyramidal tract across to nerve centres in the opposite side of the spinal cord and thence to certain muscles of the arm which bring about the movement. The general objection to interactionism is that if one does not assume the soul as distinct from the brain as another substance, one has all the difficulties of materialism. If one does assume such a soul one is making an assumption that takes one beyond the evidence, and consequently should not be resorted to unless all other modes and forms of explanation prove unsatisfactory. We shall return to the question of interactionism later. We must now consider parallelism.

According to the theory of parallelism there is no causal relationship between the activity of the cerebral cortex and consciousness, or mental activity. They are two sides of the same reality. Thus, when we are aware of the patch of red, our experience of it is the other side of certain physiological changes, especially those in our occipital cortex. When we will to move our arm, the process of willing, and of being able to move the arm, is the other side of the physiological change in the pre-central convolution, so that the two occur simultaneously. They are two sides of the same process. According to this theory, which has subsidiary forms, one may consider the reality as something different from physical and mental alike. The real events going on are not merely physical, not merely mental, but they are

events that reveal themselves under these two forms or
" attributes " of extension and thought (Spinoza).

Another form of the theory is that reality is the
mental side, while the physical process is simply the way
in which that reality appears to another " centre of
consciousness." According to this theory—the theory of
so-called psycho-physical idealism—one's consciousness or
mental life is the reality of one's brain. Let me explain
it by a special example. At this moment imagine that
I am receiving an impression of yellow from the electric
light above me. I know from physiology that a change
is occurring in some particular part of my occipital cortex ;
I am not aware of that change, I am aware of the electric
light at which I am looking. But conceivably it might
be possible for my skull to be opened and a hyper-
microscope, such as Jules Verne would conceive, fitted
to the back of my head, and another observer might be
able to look down that miscroscope and, by means of
a special form of illumination, be able to see exactly what
physical changes are going on in my occipital cortex
corresponding to and correlated with my experience of
that electric light. The situation then would be that
I should be seeing the electric light and the other person
would be seeing the physical change in my occipital
cortex. But just as I cannot see the change in my
occipital cortex, so he cannot be aware of my experience
of the electric light ; all that he can see is this particular
dance of molecules in my brain. I am aware of the
visual experience simply because for me there is only the
visual experience. But my visual awareness appears to
the other person in the form of physical change in my
brain. Brain change and visual experience are related to
one another as appearance and reality, respectively.

But you may say, that is all very well, but could not
a microscope be devised by which you might see your

own brain ? Imagine a special microscope, an invention of a few thousand years hence, an arrangement whereby you could look down the microscope and by reflection through a series of mirrors look at the brain change, corresponding to what you are looking at. Then you would be looking at your own brain, and conceivably you could look at that part of your brain which is active, just that part of the occipital cortex correlated with your visual experience. Surely then the two would come together, one's experience and the physiological correlate of one's experience would be present to the same percipient. No, they would not, because you have to take account of the velocity of light. What you are looking at is the state of your brain, corresponding to an immediately antecedent visual experience. Even in that specially assumed case you would not be experiencing both sides of the correlation simultaneously. One argument in favour of psycho-physical idealism is that nowhere and under no conceivable conditions can one see both sides of the relationship at the same time. So far as each individual's experience is concerned, there are not two sides, there is only one.*

This theory can be further generalized, as follows : Just as the cerebral cortex of an individual is the form in which his immediate experience appears (or might conceivably appear) to another individual's experience, so the totality of the material universe (including all individual organisms and their physical environment), the *facies totius universi* of which Spinoza speaks, is the manifestation, the appearance to any one finite per-cipient of an all-inclusive mental activity, viz., the Soul of the Universe. The Absolute is the reality of the totality of the physical universe, just as the individual mind is the reality of the physiological correlate of

* C. A. Strong : *Why the Mind has a Body.* Macmillan, 1903.

individual mental activity. Thus one may conceive the universe as a supra-personal existence, manifesting itself for some inscrutable reason in and to finite " centres of consciousness," creating personalities of varying degrees of unity and complexity. These finite persons see the Absolute and one another from the outside under the form of physical nature, but experience themselves directly, as mind. In mystical experience they have direct awareness of the Absolute. This theory is the theory of pan-psychism. Despite its apparent simplicity, it is none too satisfactory when we look at it more closely.

The theory of parallelism relieves us of some of the difficulties of both materialism and interaction, but only at the cost of leaving us with still more serious difficulties. In fact one can say of parallelism that it is no explanation. It is merely a statement of the problem, and not its solution, to say that consciousness runs parallel with physiological change without interaction. For after all it is a miracle that they should run parallel. I have already stated one attempted answer to the problem, in the metaphysical theory of pan-psychism, but towards the end of our discussion we shall find serious psychological as well as metaphysical difficulties in the way of accepting that theory.

CHAPTER III

MIND AND THE PHYSICAL ORGANISM

It will have become apparent to readers of the previous chapter that by extending the conception of teleology, or purposive activity, to lower organisms, and in fact to all forms of life, we tend to cut the ground from beneath the feet of some arguments in favour of inter-actionism. One of the great arguments in favour of interactionism, as against automatism on the one side, and parallelism on the other, has been the argument from the unity of consciousness. Consciousness is a unity at any one moment, although it has a plurality of aspects. It is essentially unitary, and, as R. H. Lotze argued, a unitary resultant can only arise among physical forces if those forces act at a point. There must be something unitary in order to give rise to a unitary result. One of the most fundamental laws of Mechanics is the law of the parallelogram of forces. This law states that if two forces acting at a point can be represented in magnitude and direction by the two adjacent sides of a parallelogram passing through that point, then their resultant is repre-sented in magnitude and direction by the diagonal of the parallelogram passing through that point. Two or more forces can combine and give a unitary effect only if they act at a point, or what reduces to the same thing, on some rigid body. It is exactly the same with the working of the mind itself. It has a plurality of aspects, but all its various aspects are aspects of a unity. Neverthe-less, when one turns to the physiological side and studies any of the brain changes correlated with these changes

3

in consciousness, one does not seem to find a corresponding unity. Therefore, said Lotze, there must be a unitary soul, upon which these various physiological forces can act in order to elicit or call out a unitary resultant—forms of consciousness having unity in themselves.

According to modern theories, the reply advanced by physiology and biology to that argument is simply that there *is* also a unity on the physiological or biological side ; namely, the unity of the organism itself. It is therefore contended that the unity of consciousness may very well be the mental correlate of this unity of the organism ; so that, from this point of view, parallelism, or the doctrine that mental process runs parallel to physiological process in certain parts of the organism, remains untouched.

Another argument in favour of interactionism, as distinct from parallelism, is that which may be termed the " utility argument." This asserts that, according to the principle or theory of natural selection, only those functions are developed and preserved which are of benefit to the organism in its struggle for existence with its rivals and with the world in general. Now we have to believe that consciousness has developed in the course of natural evolution in greater and greater degrees of complexity. Therefore consciousness must be of use to the organism, and it can only be of use to the organism if it is able to interact with the organism in order to bring about actual movement in the outside world. A consciousness that was entirely inactive would be useless, and therefore, one would assume, not likely to be developed in the course of evolution. The counter-argument to this is simply that it involves the assumption that mental process is distinct from corresponding cerebral process. If, however, the two are identical with one another, as the psycho-physical parallelist

maintains, then it is intelligible that, in the process of
evolution, more and more complicated brain events
occur which are more and more adequately adapted to
the needs of the situation, and these brain events have,
as their mental correlate, consciousness ; so that consciousness becomes more and more complicated in the course
of development because it is merely the other aspect of
physiological activity.   The view is not necessarily a
materialistic view, because, as already explained in the
last chapter, it may well be that the mental process is
the reality, and the brain change merely the way in which
that reality appears, or can appear, to another reality,
another part of mental reality ; so that, according to
this theory,—the pan-psychist theory,—the course of
development of the organic world, the progress of
development in time, is really a progress and development
of mind or mentality, of individual " centres of consciousness," or " monads."   This development shows itself
objectively under the form of physiological processes.

According to this conception of psycho-physical
parallelism, the fate of the mind is bound up with the
fate of the body.   Now it is possible to observe what the
fate of the body is.   We know that at death the body
disintegrates, and that the brain, the cerebral cortex, is
involved in this process of disintegration.   Therefore,
according to the theory of parallelism in any of its forms,
the individual mind as such disappears.   Parallelism
leaves no hope for personal survival of death, and that is
the serious objection on the scientific plane, since it is
always possible that the theory may at any moment be
overthrown by the discovery of additional facts.   From
time to time many investigators in the field of psychical
research have claimed to have discovered such facts
proving the survival of individuality after death.   Such
a survival cannot be harmonized with parallelism ; the

only general theory with which it is in harmony is that of interaction. For this reason, among others, I personally would prefer the interaction theory. Nevertheless, as regards actual evidence, we may say that at the present day most of it can be harmonized with either theory. The one theory that must be definitely rejected is the theory of materialism or automatism.

There is, however, a further possibility ; the *impasse* which we reach here may be due to the inadequacy of our concepts. After all we are attempting to explain and to solve the greatest riddle of the universe, the relation of the mind to the brain, of the soul to the body, in terms of concepts that have been of considerable help to us in other branches of science, but may very well be inapplicable to this, the greatest problem of all.*

I do not think that this problem of the relation of mind to brain is so essentially linked up with the problem of personality as may have appeared from writings of the last generation. The tendency nowadays in psychology is to leave this question of the relation of mind to body severely alone, to regard it as a question of metaphysics rather than of psychology. At any rate, so far as it is a problem of psychology it has to be faced at the end of our investigations and not at the beginning. But before I leave the subject I may say a few words about the relationship of certain parts of the body, namely, the endocrine glands or glands of internal secretion, to personal consciousness.

For many years now, it has been known that adequate functioning of the thyroid gland is essential to a normal

---

* I leave on one side the important doctrine of *emergence* (see C. Lloyd Morgan : *Emergent Evolution*, London, 1923), as it does not seem to me to contribute greatly to a solution of the psycho-physical problem. So far as it is not a merely verbal explanation it is akin to one form of the parallelist hypothesis. Bergson's theory of the relation of mind to brain is considered in Chapter XIX.

consciousness ; and it was found that if the thyroid gland became relatively or absolutely feeble in function, or failed altogether, the consciousness of the individual was blunted, his powers of concentration diminished, and initiative and spontaneity almost disappeared. Physical changes, such as the falling-out of the hair, the thickening of the skin, etc., likewise occurred ; and, in this form of illness, called myxœdema, it was discovered that, if extract of thyroid glands were given to the patient, he recovered, though he had to continue taking the extract for the rest of his life. In more recent years, it has been found that other glands of internal secretion also play a great part in preserving the normal aspect of personality—the parathyroids, the adrenals, the pituitary, and the sex glands. All these seem to produce internal secretions that pass into the blood-stream or the lymph-stream and are carried by it to different parts of the nervous system, and thus through the nervous system influence conscious life. Nevertheless, it still remains extremely doubtful what exact contribution to consciousness is made by each one of these glands. In the first burst of enthusiasm about these new discoveries, it was thought that the problems of personality had received a final solution here. One well-known book is L. Berman's *Glands Regulating Personality*, which discusses the effects on consciousness of modifications of activity in these glands. Berman and others are very ready to believe that many of the idiosyncrasies of personality can be explained in this way. But, if we turn from these instructive and intriguing hypotheses to the facts, all we find is that *disturbances* in the functioning of these various glands produce a *disturbance* in consciousness ; a disturbance, however, which can be recognized as pathological, not normal. In other words, though we may concede that many of the pathological alterations and changes of personality can be partially explained in terms of disturbed activity of the endocrine glands, this is quite a different thing from claiming that normal personality is to be explained in a materialistic way by the normal activity of these glands. The endocrine glands are no more essential to a normal personality than the brain itself or any other part of the body. There is no doubt that any sort of alteration of the body will produce alteration in the personality, and there are thousands of facts proving to us at every moment of our existence " how at the mercy of material happenings our spirit is." Nevertheless, this is no proof of the complete dependence of mind upon body. The theory of interaction still remains possible. If we are impressed by the fact of the modifications of thyroid activity upon personality, should not we be still more impressed by the fact, for instance, that a blow upon the head will abolish personality altogether for a time, or that fever will alter personality ? These are pathological questions. One cannot argue from a fact of the pathological order to an explanation of the normal mind.

For medicine, no doubt, these facts about the endocrine glands are of extraordinary importance, and I can briefly indicate along what lines they are important. Much* of the disturbance of conscious life in mental illness seems to be explicable in terms of auto-intoxication, or septic infection. This view of septic infection has been held for many years. What is of more recent discovery is that the intoxication often affects the personality through the intermediation of the endocrine glands. A septic appendix, septic tonsils, septic teeth, a septic intestinal tract—all will involve the absorption of toxic products which in their turn may affect the thyroid gland. When this happens the thyroid

* But by no means all. See later chapters on this subject.

gland may not function so adequately,* and the patient becomes dull and heavy and unable to concentrate. The patient may be helped by thyroid extract, but, of course, the real or radical cure is to get rid of the foci of infection —the diseased teeth or tonsils, etc.—and to banish indigestion, constipation, and accumulation of waste products in the intestinal tract. As the patient improves, his endocrine glands are able to function more adequately, and they in turn induce adequate amounts and proportions of secretions, and stimulate and nourish the nervous system so that it becomes more healthy, and consequently less disturbing to the health of the personality.

All this we may admit ; but what we are concerned with here is merely to insist that the argument is not reversible. Because pathological disturbance of consciousness, and of personality itself, can be explained in terms of pathological disturbance of the body, it cannot reasonably or with justice be inferred that the healthy mind is a mere product of the functioning of the healthy body. Indeed, even on the pathological side, we find that the causal process often works the other way. Mental conflict, mental difficulties, produce disturbance of activity of the endocrine glands, disturbance of the intestinal tract, lowering of vitality of the organism, so that it is more susceptible to infection ; and in that way a vicious circle may be set up, starting from the mind and ending in the mind again. Great grief will in this way lower the vitality of the organism, diminish the activity of the endocrine glands, disturb the balance of functioning of the organism, and in short produce physical depression. Physical depression in its turn will produce or intensify mental depression. If a person is depressed he gives way to grief. Grief depresses the vital functions, and the vital functions produce further

* Or it may be over-active, making the patient irritable and emotional.

depression in his mind ; a circle is set up and he goes on downhill mentally as well as physically. In treating such a patient, one naturally considers his mental as well as his bodily health. One does all that can be done to combat infection, and to regulate the functions of the body ; but at the same time one analyses the patient's mind and endeavours to help him to retrace his steps mentally, and get back to his mental state prior to this great shock of bereavement, or whatever the shock may have been.

In spite of myself, then, I have here been brought to consider the bearing of pathology on personality, a question that I had hoped to postpone to a later chapter ; but it is so intimately related to the bodily aspect of personality that it cannot be passed by here. Indeed, there is a whole school of thought which would explain all mental illnesses, including those known as the insanities or psychoses, in terms of physical disease. The majority of physicians who work in mental hospitals where most of the cases are chronic, see how regularly insanity runs in families as a form of heredity, and they tend more and more to look for a physical explanation of these diseases. On the mental side, since the majority of the cases are chronic, they are not very amenable to treatment by methods of psycho-therapy. And although for that matter physical methods of treatment are no more successful, yet the general aspect of the patient and the course of the disease seem to bear out the physical view of its causation. There is one particular mental disease, known as general paralysis of the insane, in which the symptoms are predominantly mental, although the cause is known to be a physical one, namely, degeneration of certain parts of the cerebral cortex caused by a specific micro-organism, which brings about the softening of the brain. This disease is a progressive one and the patient eventually dies. The mental symptoms become more and more marked, the memory is enfeebled, the powers of concentration are diminished. Meanwhile, intensified feelings of self-value—delusions of grandeur, as they are called—may become very evident. The patient believes that he is a millionaire, that he is the incarnation of Napoleon, or even the Messiah Himself. On the intellectual side, the power of the autocritical sense is greatly diminished. The patient loses his moral sense, is less and less able to live according to ethical standards, and eventually ends his life in the hospital. Here is a case, then, where the symptoms are mainly mental, though the disease is a physical disease of the highest levels of the nervous system. Another mental disease is that called manic-depressive insanity. In this disease the patient will live for weeks or months, sometimes for several years, in a state of acute depression, depreciating himself, wishing for death, and taking no joy in life at all. Then suddenly one morning, or at any other time of the day, a change will occur. He begins to feel happy again and passes into a state of exaltation where he is conscious of exceptional mental and physical powers. In this state he commences all sorts of undertakings, he is ready to accept all sorts of responsibilities, and perhaps spends money at a much greater rate than he can afford. He is, indeed, just as unable to assess his real mental power as he was in the opposite direction when he was in a depressed state. I have said that this change occurs suddenly. It may, in fact, occur very suddenly, in a single day, for instance, but in other cases it comes more gradually, though still with relative suddenness compared with the slow progress of the depressed or exaltation stage. Within the course of a few days his friends say that he is a different person, and then he will pass back into the depressed stage, and, in some cases, pass from one stage to another and back again with extraordinary regularity. The exaltation may last for three, four, or five months, or longer, the depression may be for about the same length of time (though not necessarily so), and then once more the stage of exaltation sets in and runs the same course. In other cases the alteration is nothing like so regular, the person may be depressed for months or years, and then pass into the exalted stage for days or weeks and once more plunge into melancholia, from which he does not recover. Now it is sometimes easy to demonstrate certain alterations of a physical nature accompanying this disease in its depressed state. There may be evidence of auto-intoxication, evidence of bacterial infection, etc., but that in itself does not suffice to prove the disease to be solely or primarily a physical one. For mental depression will result in a reaction of a depressing nature upon the body, the colon will not work so vigorously, the waste products of the body will accumulate and not be got rid of so regularly, and toxic absorption will occur. Under these conditions bacteria will flourish, and in their turn will produce toxic substances ; which, being absorbed, will pass into the blood-stream and so into the nervous system, depressing that system still more. Theoretically, therefore, it is conceivable that the depression may be mentally caused, although it has these physical effects. Up to quite recent times, the experience of alienists dealing with these causes has emphasized the apparently inevitable course taken by this disease. Patients become and remain depressed, whatever is done for them, and then suddenly, or more gradually, become well again or pass to an exalted state, independently of what is being done for them. You try to cheer them up in every possible way, for instance, by altering their environment, mental and physical. All this has no effect upon them, until one day they seem to recover of themselves and get excited. You try to repress the excitement, in fact to treat them in the opposite way ; that has no effect, whatever you do, until the hour strikes when they once more become depressed, and that is the reason why alienists feel that the disease is a physical rather than a mental one. But in quite recent years some of us have had the opportunity of treating some of these patients mentally, by analysis ; going very closely into their past histories, the conditions under which they first fell ill, their illusions, the constellations of ideas and emotions that have been working in their minds. As a result of such analysis, we think we have observed in some cases an amelioration of the condition ; that is, the analysis (by which I mean an analysis not of a few hours merely, but of dozens of hours) in the depressed state will in some cases, though not in all, produce an improvement in definite relation to the degree of analysis. It will shorten the period of depression, and afterwards when the period of exaltation sets in, this will not be so intense or prolonged. In other words, the patient will have more insight into his own mental condition than on previous occasions, and will be better able to control himself. We also find that the state does not last so long.

What conclusions are we to draw from these facts, for facts they are ?   I think the conclusion is not that the disease is a purely mental one. We are not justified in assuming that, but must rather accept the more moderate conclusion that some of the factors of the disease are mental and that those mental factors can be dealt with in a mental way. At the same time we still hold that there are physical factors concerned, and so that brings me back to the still more general question of mental illness in relation to physical illness.

Up till quite recent times a distinction was made within the domain of neurology (or the science of the diseases of the nervous system) between organic or structural nervous disease and functional nervous disease. Organic nervous diseases were curable only by physical methods, if at all. Functional nervous diseases benefited by mental treatment. Hysteria was the stock example of a functional nervous disease. According to this view of functional nervous disease, the structure of the nervous system is normal or intact but the system is working abnormally. As against that view, we are faced with the fact that hysteria is an hereditary disease, or at least shows signs of hereditary incidence, just as so many other diseases do. Therefore, it is dependent to a certain extent upon a preformation which is physical in nature. But the still more fundamental objection is the *a priori* argument that it is inconceivable that the nervous system, or any other system, should remain structurally normal if functioning abnormally. As soon as a nervous system, or any delicate machine of whatever nature, beings to function abnormally, its structure must alter. It is impossible to conceive anything else, of which the structure could remain exactly as before with the functions altered. On the other hand, all disease is functional for the simple reason that matter itself is functional. Matter is not something inert, it is not merely a structure. We know that it has a function. Even the electrons within the atom are assumed to be moving very briskly in relation to one another—that is their function. Atomic structure and atomic function are correlative. One can make such distinctions in thought, but one cannot separate them in drawing conclusions about facts. We may, therefore, say that all disease of the nervous system is functional disease—it can always be recognized by some functional alteration. How then can we distinguish that special class of mental diseases called functional nervous diseases from the others ?

Well, we can distinguish them in another way altogether. We can say that they are psychogenic, that is, that they are produced or originated by mental factors. Hysteria, so far as it is not an organic nervous disease, is a psychogenic nervous disease, originated on the mental plane. It arises through maladaptation—that is to say, it results from the failure on the part of the individual to adapt himself to his environment, physical and mental. And now we can explain and widen this point of view, and bring a wider group of facts within it. We can now say that in all disease in general there may be physical or mental initiation, or both. In most of the physical diseases recorded in medical textbooks the initiative comes from the material world, bacterial infection, actual physical lesions of blood-vessels, bones, muscles, etc., or disturbances of chemical metabolism, and other changes in the body. In most groups of mental diseases the initiative is mainly a mental one. The individual finds difficulty in adapting himself to his fellows, and to the physical claims on his life; he becomes depressed or worried, or disorientated, or shows many other symptoms of a mental order. At the same time his physical organism works less and less efficiently, so that secondarily he becomes ill on the physical side; just as secondarily the person suffering from physical illness may become ill on the mental side, although as a rule he does not tend to do so.

The difficulty at the present day in dealing with mental disease is that physicians fall so readily into one or other of two opposing factions. Either they emphasize the physical factors to the exclusion of the mental, or they become so enthusiastic over recent advances in medical psychology that they ignore or neglect the physical aspect. It is quite clear that both sides should be dealt with. Indeed, even on the extreme assumption that all mental disease is physical, that the initiative is originally physical and is wholly sustained by physical alteration in different parts of the nervous system or elsewhere—even though we adopt this extreme view, psychotherapy or mental treatment is not thereby ruled out, because psychotherapy can, and does, produce physical changes in the nervous system. In psychotherapy one gets the patient to speak to one, and in speaking he is passing through physical changes. He speaks with great emotion about some earlier incident, and that working-off of emotion seems to have a definite physical effect upon him. It certainly can have the effect of overcoming a functional paralysis. A person who is functionally paralysed in the lower limbs, and describes to one with great vividness the experience of the shock which originated the paralysis, may show a sudden disappearance of the paralysis. The disappearance is a physical thing, is a breaking down of resistance in the paths of nerve fibres conducting impulses from the brain to the muscles.

We can even consider most education from the physical point of view. When a boy is taught algebra he is gaining a certain physical dexterity in the manipulation of symbols ; that dexterity is a physical alteration of his brain, but it is an alteration brought about by mental means, by the interference of the teacher. That influence takes place through physical channels, because the sense-organs themselves are physical channels. The spoken word, the exhibited diagram, the printed page—all are physical means of getting at the individual. In the same way, a person who is depressed, and whose depression is almost, if not entirely, due to physical factors, may conceivably become a little less depressed if worked upon mentally. What you are doing is, as it were, producing a physical change in the highest levels of the nervous system through the channels of the sense-organs. You

are doing this more surely than if you gave him a drug.
For the drug has to reach the brain *via* the circulatory
system, and this is not very selective, as it affects a large
number of sets of nerve fibres. When you speak to him
kindly and get him to talk out his past troubles and
recapitulate the conditions under which he fell ill, you
are setting in vibration special parts of the nervous
system, making them work again as they worked before,
and to that extent you are producing a physical change
which is beneficial to him. For this reason I, as a psychotherapist, would not alter my methods, even if materialism
were proved to be true. I consider that the methods
fit in with materialism, not as well, but almost as well,
as with any other theory. On the other hand, the facts
of psychotherapy itself are facts throwing light upon the
question. It possibly makes little practical difference in
psychotherapy whether materialism is correct, or whether
voluntarism is more correct; though one finds such
a distinguished neurologist as Dejerine saying in his
book on psychotherapy that belief in freedom is essential
to the more successful application of the methods of
psychotherapy. He claims, practically at any rate, that
we must believe in freedom if we are to hope to influence
our patients on the mental side. Without going so far
as that, I am inclined to say that a belief in freedom,
in self-determination, on the physician's part, strong
enough to sustain or originate a similar belief in the
patient's mind, is a very important factor in mental cure.

PERSONALITY AND PSYCHOLOGY

(I)—EXPERIENCE AND THE ORGANIZED SELF

(CHAPTER IV)

(II)—INSTINCT, EMOTION, AND SENTIMENT

(CHAPTER V)

(III)—VOLITION

(CHAPTER VI)

(IV)—RESPONSIBILITY AND MENTAL DISEASE

(CHAPTER VII)

CHAPTER IV

CONSIDERATION of the problem of the relation of the mind to the body has shown that it is impossible in this way to get a satisfactory view of personality. Personality is not a matter of the body as such, even of the conscious organism ; it is essentially a psychological matter, or, in other words, it is certainly something mental. (We shall find in later chapters that it is much more than merely psychological, but we need not enter into these deeper problems at present.) In previous chapters we turned from a consideration of the unity of the body as a purposive unity to the consideration of the unity of the mind, which is likewise purposive ; and we saw that mental activity in all its forms shows a number of characteristics which can be regarded as marks of purposive activity, or of what W. McDougall has called " behaviour." We noticed various characteristics of this order, as, for instance, spontaneity, as contrasted with mere mechanical reaction to external stimuli ; persistence with varied effort, so long as the end which is consciously or subconsciously aimed at is not actually secured ; and, thirdly, a cessation of the activity as soon as the end is achieved. We also noticed a prospective attitude, a tendency to lie in wait for and look out for stimuli which, when they occur, are reacted to in a special way. Again, the factor of modification of behaviour or activity in relation to the results of previous activities of a similar nature. We also saw that another mark of purposive behaviour is the fact that the organism behaves as a whole, as a unity. And from this view of the purposive nature of behaviour, we can pass very simply to definitions of two important general forms of mental process or activity.

One of these is instinctive activity, which is purposive activity independent of previous experience ; for we know that purposive activity can be carried out independently of the animal's previous experience and practice. On the other hand, what we call intelligence is the power of modifying instinctive or purposive activity in the light of individual experience. Instinctive or purposive activity, which the animal or human being brings into the world with him independently of his individual experience, may be explained in terms of the experience of his ancestors. Intelligence, on the other hand, is shown in the modification of this purposive activity in the light of individual experience.

Now we find that psychologically the problem of personality falls under two main heads : There is first the problem of the nature of the subject as experienced at any particular moment. In the life of the conscious individual we can discriminate between the process of experiencing and that which is experienced, between the subject and the object of experience. We find this duality running through all experience ; one cannot point to any form of experience or consciousness which does not show implicitly or explicitly this duality of subject and object. Psychologically, therefore, we have a special problem in deciding what is the nature of the subject of this experience. The other general problem, which forms the basis of our discussion of personality, is the problem of the structure of the mind and the way in which individual minds are differentiated from one another, and so vary in their individual experiences from moment to moment by virtue of such structure. The mind is not a *tabula rasa*, not something which merely receives external impressions or mirrors them. We know that it reacts to things in the outer world according to its own nature, and that this nature is gradually changing from the cradle to the grave, in virtue of various sensory experiences and also of mental activity going on within, or, as we say, subjective activity. It is in this way that the mind of one person comes to differ from that of another, and the difference is psychological —a difference of mental structure.

We may decide that it is paralleled by a difference of anatomical structure, and a corresponding difference in physiological process and activity. But, even if we can believe in a complete parallelism between one and the other, in accordance with the theory of psycho-physical parallelism, we shall have to wait a very long time yet before physiology gives us much helpful insight into the structure of personality. In psychological observation we have an additional line of approach, and a method of observation which cannot be dispensed with at the present time, nor for many generations to come. Even if, theoretically, we do believe that the body produces everything, yet the way in which individual minds work throws light on this bodily activity of the organism, which can be adequately gained in no other merely physiological way. But we shall see that such a theory of parallelism is an extremely improbable theory, and we need not stop to go into it in much more detail now.

There are these two general problems we have now to consider, the subject of experience and the problem of the organized self. Let us consider a number of experiences, such as, for instance, the visual experience of seeing a set of electric lights in front of one. Analysing that experience we find that we are faced with a duality.

There is the act of perceiving, the visual perception, and there is also the object which is perceived. The object is what we call the cluster of electric lights, which may be explained in its context as a part of the physical world around us. We may or may not consider that object as we see it to be mental rather than physical. That is a problem of metaphysics. But, even if we hold, with the realist, that it is physical or non-mental, we have no doubt whatever about the other side of the relation. The visual experience is certainly mental and belongs to the subject. Or, take another experience, that of pain in a diseased tooth. There the subjective side of the experience is the process of being in pain in a particular part of the body, the object of experience is the pain sensation. Here there is also, in addition to the pain sensation, a feeling of discomfort, a tendency to move away from the object.

This feeling or feeling-tone seems to belong to the subject rather than the object side. In seeing the electric light there is a feeling-tone also. One may wish to turn one's eyes away if it is unpleasant, or one may have a pleasant feeling-tone after being too much in an unilluminated room. Here again the pleasure or displeasure falls on the subject, rather than on the object, side. In another experience one may be working out a mathematical problem, e.g., considering a theorem in geometry. Here again, we distinguish between the subjective side of the experience, the process of thinking, and passing from one stage in the proof to the next, and the parts of the proof that one is thinking about. When the proof is completed there is, on the one side, the process of thinking this geometrical truth, and on the other, the geometrical truth that one has thought. For example, the truth that the square on the hypotenuse of a right-angled triangle is equal to the sum of the squares on the other two sides,—this truth itself has no physical reality. Unlike the case of the cluster of electric lights it is difficult to conceive of it independently of mind ; it is something that seems to be essentially related to mind, much more than the electric light cluster, in the way that it is made by the mind. If one thinks it out, one finds that it shows the nature of the mind— the mind works just in that way. To a certain extent that is so with the electric light cluster too ; the colour and the shape are mental characteristics. They may be regarded as mental characteristics, but as having an independence of one another and also relations with other objects in space, in a much more pronounced degree than the truths of geometry. We may feel that geometrical truths are not independent of mind, as such, and that physical facts may be independent of mind, as such. The idealist position is that not even physical facts and theories are independent of mind. But if I continued this line of thought, I should be dealing not with psychology but with epistemology, with meta-physics.

To return to the consideration of the subject. Throughout individual consciousness, we find from moment to moment subjective acts of experience succeed-ing one another in a continuous series. We are active from moment to moment, reacting to objects. In each one of us there is this continuous stream of experience or thought going on. The question arises, " What degree of unity, as well as of continuity, can be attributed to this sequence or stream of individual experience ? What is the nature of this unity ? " As regards the outside world, there is a tendency to think of different things as having their own substance and essential nature. The facts that we observe about them are called their qualities, primary and secondary, and we have learned from philosophy that the external object is really the law of its states and activities. It is useless to ask or to look for some kernel, or central reality, distinct from the various qualities. These qualities as shown by external bodies are parts of it, and so far as we know these qualities we know *it*. We know only a very small portion of these total qualities, which are infinite, because they vary in relation to other things and to the experience of individuals, and these relations are theoretically infinite. Anyhow, these qualities vary in relation to one another and obey certain laws, or rules of uniformity.

Here the question naturally arises : Can we argue in the same way about the individual mind in successive moments of its subjective experience ? If we think of an internal subject of experience, distinct from every moment of its experience, we hold the theory of a soul, a metaphysical entity distinct from its manifestations. We have a view similar to that which regards the external object as being something distinct from its states or properties. Similar argument may be advanced to show that, as psychologists, we have no right to postulate such a metaphysical entity. William James has endeavoured to get over the difficulty by the statement that the unity of experience is carried by the passing thought or experience. He says somewhere " Thought is born an owner and dies owned." At any given moment the passing thought (using the word thought in the wider sense as corresponding to any mental process with its object or content at the moment) owns what has occurred just before, takes it up into itself, welcomes it, feels its " warmth and intimacy," a relationship of warmth and intimacy that it does not feel towards the experience of other mental entities. All this it gathers up into itself and goes on growing, representing all that has previously occurred. Then each " thought " in its turn dies, or

melts into the next moment of consciousness. James
has claimed that this is all that we can say of the unity
of consciousness, or of the subject of experience, from the
psychological point of view. According to this account,
then, the subject of experience is a part of a system of
consciousness which sums up in itself all precedent
experiences in the order of their sequence ; it is not
a very satisfactory theory if we can only get something
more convincing ; and we find that James Ward holds
a different view entirely.

Ward rejects William James's view with scorn, and
considers that unbiased analysis of experience shows
that we must distinguish the process of experience from
the content of experience. William James has confused
the two. When William James talks of the passing
thought he means the process-content, and he speaks
as if it were just a pulsation of experience, which takes
up into itself preceding experience, not distinguishing
the subject from the object side. James Ward contends
that any moment of experience shows three aspects, viz.,
attention, feeling, and what he calls presentation.
Presentation is the object of experience at any moment
or in any one " concrete state of mind." We can better
illustrate this by an example. Take the electric light
cluster again. As we see it, that is the presentation,
the momentary modification of our consciousness through
which we become aware of the light. That presentation
is associated with, and perhaps produces, a feeling of
pleasure or displeasure and, so far as the presentation is
in existence, it is associated also with the process of
attention. We are attending to the electric-light cluster,
the presentation is the object to which we attend.
The feeling-tone is the result of the attention, or it may
perhaps be the cause of the attention—it may be either
the one or the other. We may open our eyes and happen

to fix them on the electric-light cluster for a moment and notice it, because it is too disturbing, too bright. Otherwise, we take much less notice of it. In this case the feeling-tone determines the attention. Or we may attend to see why one of the globes has gone out, and then we find that the feeling-tone may follow the attention process. That attention process, Ward says, is certainly subjective, the feeling is likewise subjective, while the presentation is objective. What is associated or organized in the case of experience is the successive presentations which are related to one another through rules of association and other forms of unity.

Thus for James Ward acts of attention belong to the subject and are manifestations of the subject's existence. He postulates a subject as such, which is to be a subject of experience, but the experience itself is on the object side. So one's criticism of James Ward is that he goes to the other extreme of William James's theory, and makes the subject of experience far too abstract, something which is quite otiose except in so far as it serves the purpose of explaining experience. We would urge that what is associated in successive experiences is the various acts of experience rather than the presentations. We find, for example, that in learning-experiments, words become associated together, and can be memorized in accordance with a sequence of acts of attention. It is the movement of attention from one to the next which links the one to the other, for the reason that one process of attention is linked to the next, and this, of course, gives greater reality to the subject side. This is not what we get in Ward's doctrine. The truth, probably, as usual, lies between the two extremes. Speaking purely psychologically, we regard the conscious mind as a sequence of mental processes in time ; which sequence obeys certain laws, or shows certain uniformities, due to the organization of acts of experience with their corresponding contents in systems.

And this brings us to the second of our problems, the problem of the structure of the mind. The mind in its general nature is purposive; and its purposive factors may be classified under the two headings of those inherited and those developed in the individual life. Inherited purposive manifestations are the various, instinctive activities,* those acquired are modifications through individual experience, through the working of so-called intelligence. Accordingly, we can best begin our consideration of the structure of the mind by considering what are the various instinctive tendencies in the human mind. McDougall has drawn up a list of fourteen such instinctive tendencies,† which he considers primary and fundamental. He has given us an important theory as to the relation between instinct and emotion. He considers that these are objective and subjective aspects of the same thing. We speak of instinct when we are thinking biologically, that is, in terms of the individual's reaction to his environment. We speak of emotion when we are thinking psychologically, that is, considering the individual's subjective experience. The instinct of escape is an inherited instinct to a set of actions favouring escape. On the subjective side, we may find‡ that, when that instinct is thrown into activity, the emotion of fear is produced. McDougall correlates escape with fear. The instinct of pugnacity

---

* McDougall defines instinct as " an inherited or innate psycho-physical disposition which determines its possessor to perceive, and to pay attention to, objects of a certain class, to experience an emotional excitement of a particular quality upon perceiving such an object, and to act in regard to it in a particular manner, or, at least, to experience an impulse to such action." (*Introduction to Social Psychology*.)

† *An Outline of Psychology*, p. 324.

‡ But see next chapter for a criticism of this.

shows on the subject side the emotion of anger ; the instinct of repulsion has for its subjective emotion disgust, and so on down the whole list of the fourteen instincts.

McDougall writes : " The two lists would run in my opinion as follows, but others might arrange the lists in a slightly different order :—

Names of Instincts (Synonyms in Parentheses).	*Names of Emotional Qualities Accompanying the Instinctive Activities.*
1. Instinct of escape (of self-preservation, of avoidance, danger instinct).	Fear (terror, fright, alarm, trepidation).
2. Instinct of combat (aggression, pugnacity).	Anger (rage, fury, annoyance, irritation, displeasure).
3. Repulsion (repugnance)	Disgust (nausea, loathing, repugnance).
4. Parental (protective) ..	Tender emotion (love, tenderness, tender feeling).
5. Appeal	Distress (feeling of helplessness).
6. Pairing (mating, reproduction, sexual).	Lust (sexual emotion or excitement, sometimes called love— an unfortunate and confusing usage).
7. Curiosity (enquiry, discovery, investigation).	Curiosity (feeling of mystery, of strangeness, of the unknown, wonder).
8. Submission (self-abasement).	Feeling of subjection (of inferiority, of devotion, of humility, of attachment, of submission, negative self-feeling).

9. Assertion (self-display).	Elation (feeling of superiority, of masterfulness, of pride, of domination, positive self-feeling).
10. Social or gregarious instinct.	Feeling of loneliness, of isolation, nostalgia.
11. Food-seeking (hunting)	Appetite or craving in narrower sense (*gusto*).
12. Acquisition (hoarding instinct).	Feeling of ownership, of possession (protective feeling).
13. Construction . .	Feeling of creativeness, of making, of productivity.
14. Laughter	Amusement (jollity, carelessness, relaxation).

The minor instincts of scratching, sneezing, coughing, urination, and defecation, are so simple in their bodily expressions that we cannot recognize as specific qualities the excitements which accompany their exercise ; though the impulse of each may on occasion be excited in great strength." (*An Outline of Psychology*, pp. 324, 325.)

McDougall considers that these various primary instincts and emotions are fundamentally inherited ways of reacting to changes of environment. In the course of individual development and experience complex emotions may be aroused through the simultaneous activity of two or more fundamental instincts ; so that admiration, for example, in his view, is a complex emotion, a fusion of wonder and negative self-feeling ; due to the simultaneous activity of the instincts of curiosity and of self-abasement shown subjectively in the emotion of admiration. However much doubt we may feel about the actual analyses which he gives us of complex emotions, he is undoubtedly on the right track in his general theory as to their nature.

But, besides these straightforward examples of complex

emotion, where we have two or more dispositions aroused simultaneously in the mind, there are other, more complicated, emotional states and processes that can only be explained in terms of a higher degree of structure of the mind ; that is, if we take the primary instincts as corresponding to the basal emotions of the mind. The simplest form of structure is manifested in the simultaneous activity of two or more independent tendencies, but this occurs very seldom ; more frequently it is activity of the basic tendencies in the light of previous experience of all kinds. Still keeping to this instinctive-emotional level, we see that a certain class of complex emotions only occur in specially developed minds in relation to what are called " sentiments." The word " sentiment " is now used in a technical sense in psychology. It was first suggested by A. F. Shand in 1896. Sentiment, according to him, is an organized system of emotional dispositions, centred about the idea of some object*. It will be clearer if we take an example. Friendship is a sentiment in this sense. Our feelings towards our friends are not crude primary emotions ; their formation and occurrence are, at any rate, more complex. Our feeling of friendship is not a summation, a complex of emotions, but it is the law according to which different emotions are aroused in different circumstances. As Shand says : " We feel joy in our friend's presence, sorrow in his absence, anger towards those who do him an injury, gratitude towards those who help him." We feel different emotions in different circumstances. This is because in past experience our emotional dispositions have become organized about the idea of our friend. So it is with hostility and hatred.

---

* Ribot, in his *Essai sur les Passions*, uses the term " passion " in a similar sense. He defines passion as a prolonged and intellectualized emotion dominated by a " fixed idea."

Hate is a sentiment rather than a simple emotion. We feel sorrow in our enemy's presence, joy in his absence, gratitude towards those who injure him, and anger towards those who help him. Hate and love seem to be systems composed of the same emotional dispositions, but each reacting in opposite circumstances in the two cases ; and that may be one reason why Love can easily pass into Hate, and often Hate, in a curious unaccountable way, pass into Love. In both cases there is intense interest in the object. The word " interest " is, perhaps, a better general term than sentiment. We may say that emotional dispositions are organized in different systems, systems of interests. These sentiments of which Shand speaks are interests not only in persons, but in things, and in abstract qualities, causes, ideals. We may have abstract sentiments, or sentiments about abstract objects, as well as concrete sentiments, and in this way one may visualize the structure of the mind as a whole ; first the lowest level of the various instinctive dispositions, and then a series of higher levels. From these merely instinctive dispositions—able to function simultaneously in twos, threes, or any number, but having cross-connections between them—one passes to systems of individual emotions and their psycho-physical dispositions corresponding to concrete objects, and later on to systems corresponding to more abstract objects ; and at the top of the pyramid one has one overshadowing object, the object of the most lasting and general interest, to which all other interests are subordinate. So one may conceive a mind as a system of interests, with emotional reactions, showing different degrees of unity in the systems of subordinate unities ; these systems being incorporated in wider systems, and these wider systems again being incorporated in still wider systems, till at last one has a total system dominated by one all-satisfying interest. In the philosopher one finds the love of Truth as that dominating influence. In the case of such a philosopher as Spinoza, this dominating interest, to which everything was subordinated, was his desire to find something, love for which would fill the mind with complete satisfaction. Spinoza set out with that feeling in his mind, and the result was his system of philosophy—his intellectual love of God was his master-sentiment. His whole life was organized with reference to that.* In the case of Napoleon, the love of power was the most central interest, all subsidiary interests, loves, hates, likes and dislikes, showed reference in his life to this dominating interest. The miser has the love of gain, of money as such, as the master-sentiment, which controls all his other interests.

In McDougall's general scheme of mental organization, the master-sentiment, which forms the basis of character, is the self-regarding sentiment—the love of self in the widest sense of that term. Character is strong or weak, according as this self-regarding sentiment is strong or weak. Even if we take care not to confuse the self-regarding sentiment with crude self-love, we yet feel that this theory of McDougall's is not entirely satisfying. It is too individualistic. We all of us know and have read about characters who show master-sentiments of a much more impersonal nature. We cannot help feeling that love of Truth as such, or of Goodness as such, is higher than mere love of the Self, even in its highest form. McDougall goes so far as to use this self-regarding sentiment as his principal concept in explaining volition. He considers that in cases of hard choice, which are

---

* It is interesting to note how certain thinkers, whose master-interest may have been determined by the hazards of their own lives, tend to generalize such master-interests in the race as a whole, e.g., the exclusively economic view of life maintained by Balzac and Marx, perhaps partly in consequence of their individual struggles.

crucial cases, where we seem to act along the line of greatest resistance, cases where we follow an ideal in the face of temptation of a crude physical nature, this result is achieved precisely because the ideal which we follow is linked up with our self-regarding sentiment, that is to say, with the organization of our emotional disposition about the idea of ourselves. In other words, it corresponds with our ideal of ourselves as we wish to be, which we take as the standard of value for ourselves. McDougall argues that the seemingly more powerful physical temptation is overcome through the use of energy derived from these various emotional dispositions, and that the energy which they supply is more than sufficient to prevent the temptation from being realized. We may find that this general scheme advanced by McDougall of the organization of the mind is in need of supplementation when we extend our view to the consideration of the ethical and metaphysical aspects of personality.

CHAPTER V

W. McDougall's recent book, *An Outline of Psychology*, to which we have already so frequently referred, may be regarded as the latest and best of a series of expositions of the structure and functioning of the mind, but despite its manifest excellences there can be little doubt that in the future systematic psychologists will have to take very much more account of so-called " deep analysis " than they have hitherto been able to do. In his *Outline* we have the most complete analysis of the mind up to date along the lines of ordinary normal psychology, using material and data obtainable by anyone who restricts his attention to the study of his own consciousness and of the behaviour of other normal human beings and animals.* Deep analysis, however, is not content to observe the surface of the mind, but pushes enquiry further and further back ; and, in pushing that enquiry back, obtains by its own methods a greater and greater wealth of material, and draws conclusions from that material according to certain rules, comparing it also with material obtained by close and prolonged studies of pathological cases. Such a method of deep analysis may throw a somewhat different light on the whole matter. It is not that we wish to explain the normal in terms of the abnormal, but these great experiments made by nature upon the human mind do magnify certain lines of functioning, and so make them observable, whereas in the past they have been overlooked.

---

* McDougall has himself supplemented this in his still more recent book, *An Outline of Abnormal Psychology*, Methuen and Co., 1926.

It will be remembered that McDougall's general conception of the structure of the mind is that it is built upon a foundation of instinctive dispositions. These dispositions are conative in nature, they show characteristics of purpose, and reveal themselves in consciousness as different forms of emotional activity; so that we have, corresponding to various fundamental instincts, various fundamental forms of emotion. After these fundamental instincts have been discovered and enumerated, McDougall proceeds to describe what he calls secondary emotions, which are due to the simultaneous activity of two or more instinctive dispositions. As an example of such an emotional compound we may take the anger and disgust felt towards anyone who has been guilty of a mean action. That feeling carries with it two corresponding impulses : anger—to destroy or injure the person ; and disgust—to keep clear of, and have nothing to do with, him. And then McDougall proceeds in his latest book to improve upon the system of emotions he gives in his *Social Psychology* by bringing in derived emotions ; and this is a very important class, because it shows that he is not unaware of modes of production of emotion which psycho-pathology has forced upon our notice for some years past.

These derived emotions are, for example, such emotions as hope, expectation, anxiety, surprise, despondency, despair. Such emotions do not seem to follow his rule of being the subjective aspect of instinctive activities. If you look closely, you see they are all related to one fundamental form of mental activity—desire. In fact, they have been stated by A. F. Shand† in his *Foundations of Character*, under the heading " Prospective Emotions of Desire." These emotions are aroused in relation to the degree of success or failure of any desire in achieving

† A. F. Shand: *The Foundations of Character*, 2nd Edit., London, 1921.

or attaining its end. If the end seems likely to be attained, hope springs up in the person's mind ; complete attainment brings joy. With the possibility of failure there arises a feeling of anxiety ; when the prospects of failure become more pronounced, despondency ; when failure seems inevitable, despair. Now, compare these emotions with that of anger, which accompanies the combative instinct. Here in regard to the emotion of anger, McDougall himself admits that it is related to or results from the thwarting of other instinctive activities. If these activities are thwarted or hindered the feeling of anger may be aroused or stimulated. But he will not admit that a similar situation is to be found in regard to the emotion of fear. He correlates the emotion of fear with the instinct of escape, and he considers that it is fully explicable in terms of the instinct of escape.

The obvious objection to such a view is that, so far as the instinct of escape is working according to plan, the individual does not experience fear. The man escaping from his pursuers is concentrating his attention on what he is doing, e.g., leaping from crag to crag ; he has no time to experience fear. In a way McDougall admits that he may not really feel fear at that time, but insists that the fear is there if he had the opportunity to look more closely into his mind. But it is not a question of not noticing the fear ; it is not there at all. When a man is successful in his escape he may not find any trace of fear. Soldiers have often verified this in the course of a war. They have been so busy carrying out their job that they have not had time or occasion to feel fear. But if they are in a tight corner where no means of escape offers itself, they do feel fear. Fear, as such, in the main is similar to members of this class of derived emotions. It arises from the thwarting of the instinct of escape. Besides that, I have no doubt that it tends to be aroused when danger threatens, when the instinct of escape is also aroused. A certain amount of fear arises as a danger signal. The mind is thus woken up, but it passes into much more extreme forms of fear and terror when the means of escape are cut off or are problematical.*

Further, if we look down McDougall's list of primary emotions, opposite to the gregarious instinct we find that he puts, not the emotion corresponding to the gregarious instinct, whatever that may be, but the various emotions that arise in the mind when the gregarious instinct is thwarted or interfered with. If the gregarious animal is separated from the herd or flock, that animal feels restless, lonely and greatly disturbed ; and this emotion seems to be what McDougall has in mind as the emotion accompanying the functioning of gregariousness. I think it would be rather the pleasant feeling that people seem to experience in going, e.g., to a political meeting or attending a theatre or concert, a feeling of union with their fellows ; but the fact that he has to emphasize in his list just the contrary emotions—those that arise when the instinct is not satisfied—gives us a further hint of a kind of classification which is different from his own, and which is more in harmony with the usual view of emotion—the view that it is a kind of friction in the mental machinery. This, no doubt, was at the back of the minds of the philosophers of old who considered the state of being free from emotion (ἀταραξία) as the happiest state ; otherwise we have not complete control of our mind ; it is a nuisance to feel emotion.

---

* We may also note that in the training of character it is desirable, and possible, to diminish or abolish the proneness to anger and fear, while preserving the instinctive activities of combat and of escape and making them more prompt and precise in their response.

Probably the truth lies between the two extremes. A great deal of emotion is undoubtedly the result of mental conflict, although we must admit that, even where there is no conflict, in certain cases there is emotion. Of course, in psycho-pathology this factor of mental conflict is all-important. The symptoms of the psycho-neurotic can be expressed in general as a perverted or inadequate means of solving, overcoming, or escaping from the stress of mental conflict—of saving the patient from himself. We shall have to consider that more fully later. Keeping to our task of dealing with McDougall's system, we pass from this important class of derived emotions to the emotions that are aroused within a sentiment. A sentiment is an organized system of emotional dispositions centred about the idea of some object, and certain emotional experiences can only be felt when a sentiment of that kind is present. For example, the emotion of reproach is different from the emotional experience of anger, and yet it is not a blending of anger with any other specific emotion. It is the arousing of the emotion of anger within the sentiment of love. If a stranger does us an injury or displeases us in any way, we simply feel anger towards him ; but, if a dearly loved friend does something to hurt our feelings or disappoint us, we feel reproach. There is the feeling of anger, but softened by the sentiment of affection or love, which involves the potentiality of a large number of different emotions experienced under different circumstances. Only where a sentiment is present would such feelings be experienced.

Our present purpose, however, is not to enumerate the different forms of feeling, but to consider general principles of mental organization. McDougall has applied the doctrine of the sentiments in dealing with the difficult problem of volition, particularly in cases of so-called hard

choice, where the individual is moved simultaneously in
two directions ; in one direction by the very intense
native propensity of a fundamental instinct accompanied
by a strong feeling-tone, and in an opposite direction
by an impulse of a more ideal nature, which seems to
carry less energy with it, and yet may win the day.
William James, faced with this problem, explained it
in terms of a *fiat* of the will. His view was that, if this
propensity on the one side was stronger in itself than
the motive to act according to an ideal of conduct, the
ideal motive being accompanied by a much less vivid
feeling would be overwhelmed by this strong native
propensity ; but that the man of strong will over-
comes such native propensity by bringing in also something additional, a fiat of the will. McDougall is not
satisfied with this solution. He asks whence comes the
energy of this effort of the will, and considers that he
can find it in the energy represented by a fundamental
sentiment which he calls the " self-regarding sentiment."
A man has strength of character in so far as he has
organized his emotional dispositions about the idea of
himself in the form of the self-regarding sentiment ;
and in a case of hard choice, he brings this self-regarding
sentiment into activity. This is the source of the energy
which, as an effort of will, reinforces the individual's
ideal impulse in its conflict with native propensity.

This is perhaps a more detailed and accurate explanation
of volitional activity than has hitherto been given in
psychological textbooks. It certainly goes one better
than James, and at any rate it has the courage of entering
into detail ; but yet it strikes one as being rather too
mechanical to be a worthy description of such a complicated organization as that of the human mind. The
truth probably is that the will—volition—is the entire
mind in action in its most complete development as

a harmoniously working unity, and that within this unity of the mind there are various levels corresponding to different successive stages of development of mental power. The lowest level is the animal level of instinct and appetite. Above that one comes to the level of intellectualism, or generalization of wishes and desires; and, through the interaction, as it were, of knowledge on the one side and various individual conative systems of the mind on the other, there develops an organization possessing and showing a greater and greater degree of freedom in that it becomes more and more relatively independent of external events as such. That is to say, the mind becomes more and more self-determined in the course of its development and thus manufactures freedom. Freedom is a characteristic that develops. The mind starts with a minimum of freedom which is present in the simplest form of mental reaction, i.e., in the purposiveness which is to be seen in all behaviour. It develops this in its own way, and, when one has a case of so-called hard choice occurring, one really has one of the lower levels of organization struggling against the higher organization; and, though on the surface, in consciousness, it may make a great deal of fuss, as it were, and may seem to have a great deal of power at its disposal, yet actually it is very much weaker than the rest of the mind. The latter has reserves of power which deal with it; just as after a wound, although the bodily organization shows a rise in temperature and the wound itself looks ugly and attracts attention, nevertheless the rest of the body, the healthy part, is destined to win the battle with it.

We must now turn to another side of the structure of the mind—the cognitive side. Here we have a further very illuminating suggestion from McDougall. He cogently argues that an individual's knowledge accumulates in the form of cognitive dispositions. Just as the active side of his mind arises from the better organization of the conative dispositions of instinct, so on the side of knowledge the individual gradually builds up an organized system of cognitive dispositions. He does this, not so much by observing different individual objects in space, comparing them with one another and so getting more and more general ideas, as we say, of objects ; passing, for instance, from different kinds of dogs to a conception of dogs in general, then from dogs, cats, horses, etc., on to the idea of animals in general. Rather, he begins in the other way with a generalized experience, and learns to differentiate that experience by noting in the course of his life more and more carefully the points of difference between objects. The tendency in the young child is to generalize, but not in the logical sense. It is inclined to overlook differences at first and to classify different things together ; then gradually, by noticing differences in relation to its needs (because it only notices owing to its interest in the object), it learns to appreciate variety. But besides this process of differentiation there occur assimilation and apperception, where resemblances are observed between different objects ; so that by slow degrees the total system of knowledge of the individual takes a form analogous to that of a tree with its main trunk, branches, twigs and terminal leaves, corresponding to the general conception of objects, and the existence of the different kinds of laws in different sciences. This is merely to say that this systematic knowledge is a systematic arrangement, as it were, of cognitive dispositions ; and the way in which the individual acquires this systematic arrangement of cognitive dispositions is through the processes of differentiation, comparison, abstraction, apperception, and association.

Nevertheless, in addition to this kind of system, one

finds also the historical system. The individual lives his life from day to day, various incidents occur, these incidents are in a certain sense retained in memory, and knowledge is laid down, as it were, in that form. This historical kind of experience is not, however, wholly unrelated to the other form, which is not itself historical, but, as it were, *sub specie æternitatis*—the general knowledge of laws and properties, etc., of things and objects, animate and inanimate, and not the actual working of the mind at any point which it has reached. Take an individual at the age of twenty-six or so. He has these various cognitive dispositions laid down in the course of his life, and his reaction to his environment has reference to both these systems. He reacts according to his own individual experience, and also according to his scientific knowledge, which has been acquired partly by himself, by experiment, etc., and partly from what he has read in books. It is essential to note that both systems of cognitive dispositions have become linked up with conative dispositions. He has acquired likes and dislikes for different branches of knowledge and also in relation to incidents in his own life. And it is when we consider the relation of the cognitive dispositions to conative dispositions that we are facing the real problem of voluntary action.

Individual acts, then, occur with reference to knowledge, on the one side, and wishes, desires, strivings, etc., on the other. These are the sentiments, to which we have already referred, examples of interorganization of cognitive and conative dispositions. But we find that in the individual, besides these healthy sentiments, which are normal features of the mind, there is a tendency for abnormal, unhealthy mental systems to be produced in the mind corresponding to painful experiences of the past. The individual may have had, e.g., a painful experience of a frightening nature. He has been disturbed by a certain event in his life, and later on his whole mind tends to react to analogous situations with reference to the previous fright. Such abnormal systems are called complexes, and the word complex should, I think, be restricted to abnormal systems. We should not use the term complex if we mean the normal systems, for which the technical term would be sentiment. But where we find pathological disturbance of the individual's judgment, which puts him out of harmony with his environment and prevents him from reacting adequately to a situation, then we would call it a complex. He has had an unfortunate experience, and has developed, let us say, a complex against a certain type of individual, so that he does not do himself justice later on when he meets individuals of the same profession or class as the one who has thus disturbed his mind. A complex is essentially of the nature of a fixation, anchoring the mind down and preventing it from moving onward, whereas we can look upon a sentiment as a healthy growth of the mind. Likes and dislikes with reference to adequate experience, i.e., the various sentiments, grow by including a larger and larger number of objects within themselves, and by being adjusted more and more adequately to these objects. Through them the mind gains greater and greater freedom, a wider scope of activity, and a greater and greater degree of harmonious working. A complex, on the other hand, ties the individual down to the incident that aroused the complex; it is a kind of precipitation of the mind. The mind is held down and cannot develop further. Other parts of the mind do go on developing, but that particular part is fixed in such a way that when the complex is struck on, as we say, that is, stimulated through association by some chance event, the whole mind reacts just exclusively and explosively to that complex. The individual may, e.g., explode with anger without clearly knowing why he is angry.

We may now ask : why should there be this difference between complexes and sentiments ? It is the difference between repression and unrepression—the complex is repressed experience. It is not normal, not healthy, not fully justified ; it has not been adequately faced by the individual but has been held in check in a quasi-mechanical way. He has lost the power of normal integration of consciousness. A sentiment can, under appropriate conditions, produce the various emotions according to rule ; but in the case of a complex what is repressed is, not so much the emotion, but rather the cognitive disposition, i.e., the original experience is withdrawn from attentive control. The mind has lost the faculty of recalling the original experience, although the corresponding emotional reaction can be re-aroused. In certain situations, a person flies into a rage and does not fully realize why. He acts mechanically, like an automaton, instead of like a free human being. One analyses his mind in order to overcome the repression, to bring these forgotten experiences into full consciousness, and in that way the complex is got rid of.

And then the interesting question arises about the relationship of complexes to sentiments as regards analysis. Complexes can be dealt with by analysis ; one can resolve a complex. Can the same thing be done with our sentiments ?* Theoretically it might be possible. We might look upon sentiment as a much more fundamental, thoroughgoing, deeply-founded system of interests, a strong organization which needs very deep and prolonged analysis for disintegration. Friendships for different

* See T. H. Pear : "Complex and Sentiment," *Brit. Journ. of Psychology*, vol. xiii., 1922.

people, and interests which we have formed in different kinds of subjects or causes or ideals, ethical, æsthetical, etc.—all these are of the nature of sentiments. In a long analysis they might possibly be interfered with. I think we must leave it as a possibility which will be decided empirically in the course of further experience of long analyses. We know that a number of people have been analysed for a very long time, and some are still being analysed ; and it is quite probable that, in their enthusiasm for psycho-analysis, some psycho-analysts will persevere with analysis of their clients—subjects who are not necessarily patients—for longer and longer periods of time. Short analyses may extend over six months or more, deeper analyses may go on for two or three years or even longer, and it would be interesting to see what the effects of such analyses upon sentiments are. One meets with special cases from time to time where the analysis has proved to be extremely disturbing, where the individual has needed further help to restore the balance of his mind. We know also, and are prepared for, the possibility that, where patients are on the verge of severe mental breakdown, an analysis might suffice to push them over the border. It is an obvious danger that every psycho-analyst would admit. It is possible that there are limits to analysis, though on the face of it, this seems fairly improbable. A person analysed may have derived a certain amount of benefit, not only as regards the symptoms which he may have shown, but also in getting a deeper insight into his mind, and learning to use it more and more adequately by getting rid of the effects of chance incidents of the past, i.e., his various complexes ; and then, with a continuation of the analysis there might be a danger of interfering with his healthy sentiments. As far as one can make out, such a question as that does not seem to interest the enthusiastic followers of Freud. They speak of complete analysis, as if an individual could go right through with the analysis and come out, as it were, on the other side a stronger and better man, and yet they bring forward no conclusively satisfactory reasons for this view.

As regards terms, therefore, we can look upon complexes as pathological formations analogous in structure to sentiments of the normal mind. In both cases there is a union or systematization of cognitive and conative dispositions, and they both point forward to the general problem of freedom or self-determination of the mind, and the general problem of volition. McDougall's theory of volition in terms of the self-regarding sentiment is clearly a very important generalization which, to a certain extent, does fit in with what can be said about disturbance of volition in pathological cases through the existence of complexes ; but when we come to deal with the mind from the point of view of ethics and metaphysics, as distinct from the merely psychological point of view, we may feel more firm in our suspicion that the explanation is somewhat too mechanical.

CHAPTER VI

VOLITION

It will be convenient at first to recapitulate and restate some of the observations and arguments of the preceding chapter. We have seen that psychologically the mind can be regarded as a system of subsidiary systems of conative and emotional dispositions, organized in relation to a hierarchy of cognitive dispositions. In general terms the mind has achieved the power of knowing or getting into intellectual touch with facts concrete and abstract, and of feeling emotions of different kinds, and instinctive tendencies towards action in relation to such facts. Starting with primitive instinctive-emotional dispositions, such as the instinctive emotions of fear, anger, etc., these become organized round various objects in which the mind " takes interest," and each of these organizations of emotional dispositions about objects is called a sentiment. So the mind first acquires a series of concrete sentiments, and these concrete sentiments can in their turn give rise to sentiments of a more abstract nature. By different acts of justice we acquire not only the virtue of justice but the sentiment of justice as such ; learning to be loyal to individual people and groups of people, we eventually gain the general abstract sentiment of loyalty. In this way various interests become organized in systems which thus control the conduct of the individual. The individual becomes more and more capable of regular consistent conduct—conduct according to rules that can be predicted with more or less accuracy. And this tendency towards the production of wider and more general systems strives towards an ideal aim of one all-inclusive system or sentiment, to which all others are subordinated.

The unity of activity of the mind and its freedom are dependent upon the extent to which an all-inclusive system of this sort is achieved. It is a commonplace to say that we are each of us many selves, different in different circumstances. We seem sometimes to be actuated on different occasions by wholly different motives. However true that may be, there is the more fundamental truth that we are more or less at one with ourselves in all these subsidiary selves. They are not unrelated to one another except in disease. So far as the mind is healthy the subsidiary selves are organized in one all-inclusive self. And it is to the organization of this all-inclusive self that we must look for a solution of the problem of volition or will.

Will is not a form of mental activity that arises suddenly full-blown at a particular point in the development of the individual mind. It has a developmental history of its own, and rudiments of it are to be found in the earliest beginnings of consciousness. So far as there is system at all and subordination of particular to more general tendencies, so far one has the beginnings of will. One has the raw material of will in what is known as conation, the active aspect of consciousness, the striving towards an end (implicit or explicit) that is to be realized at every moment of conscious life. Conation as such is the lower limit. It becomes more clearly defined and organized as intellectual development proceeds. It progresses in relation to the development of knowledge, and is thus made more and more precise. On the perceptual level there is direct instinctive perception of objects. Instinctive reactions to objects also occur at the higher level where memory and ideation become possible. There are conations directed towards ends not themselves yet actualized, ends that can be imagined but are not at the moment actual. These ends are first, individual events in the outer world and individual actions. At a later stage of mental development ends of a more abstract nature can be pursued, purposes of a general nature such as to help others, to be true in word and deed, to seek always the highest good. The mind can set these abstract ends before it.

The question is, whence comes the energy that sustains the pursuit of these ends ? The ends themselves can be discovered by observation, and by reasoning on the basis of observation. It is in the conative part of the mind that we must look for the energy, the driving force which carries us on to achieve these ends. The various instincts themselves have their own driving force, and among these instinctive tendencies one would include the tendency to observe, question, classify, to acquire fuller and fuller knowledge of the world around us. One cannot entirely agree with McDougall when he says that the intellect as such merely fixes the end to be aimed at, without itself supplying any energy for achieving that end. Intellect does furnish a certain amount of energy, and the self-denying way in which scientists will put everything second to the pursuit of truth in their particular domain is to my mind an illustration of the inborn tendency to develop energy along these particular lines, which other people do not possess to the same degree. While recognizing that fact, however, we must proceed to admit with McDougall that the energy of volitional activity comes for the most part from another source. If we compare people with one another as regards will-power, we see that to a great extent it is a question of degree of development of the self-assertive instinct. If the self-assertive instinct is strong, there is

6

a possibility of great strength of will eventually arising. If the self-assertive instinct is weak, one is more likely to find vacillation and lack of tenacity. If, in the place of a strongly developed self-assertive instinct, there is a pronounced development of the instinct of self-abasement, there is still greater probability that the powers of volition will not be high. Volition is not self-assertion, it is something much more than that, in that it is the work of the mind at its highest level, and since the highest level cannot work by itself, but draws other levels into itself, volition is the entire mind and the entire character in action. What makes that character one is partly, at any rate, the presence of the self-assertive instinct, whether from the active point of view, or from the point of view of contemplation and of æsthetic appreciation. Emotional dispositions, various tendencies towards taking interest in various ways, are organized about the idea of the self to produce the self-regarding sentiment. This self-regarding sentiment subordinates to itself the other sentiments, concrete and abstract, that have been gradually developing *pari passu* with it, and so introduces discipline and a hierarchy of government which is most effective in bringing about harmonious activity, producing an individual adequately adapted to his environment.

We can test this theory that volition is the whole character in action with the sentiment of self-respect in command, within which the self-assertive instinct bulks large, by considering special cases of volition. Although volition occurs wherever the mind acts as a whole, acting on the highest level even when the individual is not aware of any conflict or stress, yet it becomes more pronounced in cases of mental conflict where the individual seems to act in the line of greatest resistance. There are two general levels of mental conflict, the analytic and the synthetic. In the first, there are alternative

solicitations of sense on the same level of mental development. A person feels tempted to do one thing, feels an
impulse to carry out one line of action, to follow up one
desire, and simultaneously to follow another desire, and
there arises a conflict of the two on the same level. This
is called analytic choice. But in so-called synthetic
choice the two sides that conflict are at different levels
of mental development. On the one side there may be
a so-called native propensity, and set against it there
may be some ideal aim or purpose. In such a case as
that the nature of volition comes out most strongly.
As William James said, when a patient under the surgeon's
knife checks the cry of pain, or when a man in the face
of temptation, as, e.g., the reformed drunkard tempted
with the desire for drink, crushes those feelings and turns
away, these people seem to act in the line of greatest
resistance. James's solution might be put in the form of
two equations :—

$$I \text{ (ideal impulse)} < P \text{ (native propensity)}.$$
$$I + E \text{ (effort of will)} > P.$$

What is needed in psychology, however, is to get
a more complete analysis of the nature of this effort of
will. McDougall has faced this problem, and in his
theory has argued that the effort of will represents
a store of energy furnished by the self-regarding sentiment
—that the individual who is passing through these
temptations and putting up an adequate resistance is
able to do so because he is not merely in a momentary
state of consciousness, but in his past life has organized
his conative and emotional dispositions in a particular
way around the idea of self. He has developed a strong
feeling of self-respect. This feeling of self-respect, which
has at its command the energy of the whole system of
those emotional dispositions, can furnish energy sufficient
to turn the scale in favour of the ideal impulse. The

efficiency of volition, according to this description, turns partly upon the degree of harmonious development of the self and partly upon the strength of the self-assertive instinct. After the personality has passed through a course of smooth development from the lower to the higher form in adequate adaptation to its environment, one would expect to find a person of strong volition, with strong powers of will. But actually, of course, each individual has his own special difficulties to surmount, and although struggling with difficulties often increases strength and tenacity of will-power, the result may be less fortunate where the struggle is unsuccessful, especially if initial difficulties occur in early years when the character is least developed. If the formation of these great fundamental sentiments—these more primitive systems of emotional dispositions—is interfered with, one would expect to find later on a defect in the power of volition. And so we come to the problem of the pathology of will.

There is one other aspect of volition, represented by the contrasted theories of free-will and determinism. We can at once dismiss any doctrine of free-will of indifference. If we are to be psychologists, to believe in the possibility of giving a scientific account of the mind and its development, we must believe in the general principle of *relevance*. Whatever occurs in the mind is relevant to what has occurred before and what is occurring simultaneously. As the mind, if not in itself always rational, looked at from the outside is a rational organism in which the different elements are related to one another in ways that can be understood by reason, so it obeys the principle of sufficient reason (Leibniz). When anything occurs in it there is a sufficient reason why it should occur rather than not occur. That is not the same thing as saying that every moment of consciousness is mechanically determined by preceding events in consciousness. We have to take account of the nature of consciousness itself. We find that it is never passive; even in its simplest form it is active, and has its own peculiar nature, and because of its own peculiar nature it is removed from the realm of explanation that would apply to material phenomena observed from the outside. It has a degree of spontaneity which is, perhaps, more pronounced at its lowest levels. In the child at play the spontaneity seems most obvious, because relevancy is least apparent. A child's life is spontaneous in that it is *irrelevant;* different moments of consciousness are not closely linked with one another in accordance with a general plan. As the mind progresses, and development proceeds, the plan becomes more pronounced, and the mind becomes more and more determined by its own inner nature; and if we follow up that development from the beginning to the end we see what after all is meant by the freedom of will. As soon as the will itself has conquered, then comes its action in accordance with character. A man acts freely so far as he is true to himself and so far as he is acting in accordance with the principles developed in his individual life and according to his own personality. So that in the theoretically normal person responsibility is a self-evident fact. A person is responsible to himself, therefore he is responsible to others. But in most people's lives instances occur where one cannot impose full responsibility upon them. In such cases one feels that there has been a disturbance of the unity of the mind, and certain tendencies have been called out so strongly that the rest of the mind has not been able to oppose them adequately.

Experiences during the first few years of childhood may have a profound influence upon the development of the will. The young child living in a normal household, with normal parents, and in congenial surroundings, tends to develop normally, happily, and harmoniously, because the various persons and things present before it, which it can admire and imitate, are in harmony with one another. If the parents feel affection for one another and live in harmony, and the brothers and sisters live in harmony, the little child observes all this and becomes more harmonious in itself, because it has a strong tendency to identify itself with those around it. On the other hand, if the parents are at enmity with one another, however hard they may try to conceal it, the fact becomes apparent and exerts its baneful influence upon the child. The child sympathizes with both parents, and so internalizes in itself the outward conflict. The child really is each of the parents to some extent, and is torn different ways whenever there is outward conflict. The conflict becomes implanted in the child's mind, and is a source of serious weakness later on. It has often been observed that children of parents who do not get on well together are unhappy and frequently neurotic, and the explanation sometimes given is that the absence of love in the parents really affects the young child before it is born. That may or may not be so, but quite apart from this the observed conflict is sufficient to explain the bad effect on its character.

If certain instinctive tendencies in a child are called out too strongly as compared with other instinctive tendencies, and are developed prematurely, if a child at an immature age is subjected to experiences that hurry up the development of instinct—I am thinking especially of the sex instinct—there arises another very serious source of disturbance. Recently a patient (a girl of 18) came to me complaining that she was obsessed by certain sex thoughts and was incessantly tempted to use certain words. Investigation of her case revealed that her father was alcoholic, and that when she was as young as seven or eight he would use in her presence all sorts of objectionable language, which she half understood and which evidently stirred up sex feelings prematurely, with the result that there was an impulse to use these words and to think along these lines ; and in spite of her best endeavours she was unable to control it adequately. In a case like this one cannot consider the patient as fully responsible as another person who had had a normal childhood and normal protection from adults around him.

The instincts of self-assertion, self-abasement, and self-preservation (fear) may be unduly stimulated in early years, and in each of these cases there may arise a certain type of character which is defective in a definite direction, and defective volition occurs. If a person is frequently frightened in childhood, and his fears are played upon— such cases are constantly occurring—later on he may find it very difficult indeed to stand firm in the face of fear-inspiring incidents. In particular, if a young child is frightened with water, if the nurse is careless in dashing water over the child, and it gets frightened, although perhaps quite a courageous child in other respects, it may find great difficulty in learning to swim and dive. Children are sometimes injured through carelessness in putting on and taking off clothes. One child had a horror of suffocation, traced back to the age of four or five, when he used to wear a tight jersey, and the jersey was pulled over his head by his nurse slowly, just for the fun of teasing him and hearing him cry out.

As regards the self-assertive instinct parents can do their children a disservice by being too ambitious for them. By encouraging the spirit of rivalry too strongly in early years they may disturb the balance and harmony of the developing character. A child may be led, as the result of over-stimulation of the self-assertive instinct, to take on more than he can adequately achieve. Failure brings feelings of self-dissatisfaction and self-depreciation, and in that way he may become the victim of what is called an "inferiority complex."* This has two aspects, and may in some cases be quite as accurately called a superiority complex. Often if such people do not go on being ambitious they feel that they are untrue to themselves. On analysis, one finds that what they are untrue to is the ideal which their own mother or father has put before them, and with which they have identified themselves. In analysis they can get free from that, and they are only too glad to do so.

To my mind the most pronounced result of analysis, carried out carefully and without undue interference on the part of the analyst, is *liberation from false personality*. The impression one gets as one analyses is that the patient has had imposed upon him a personality different from his own; he has had to wear strange clothes, as it were, that did not entirely fit him. Analysis strips them off and the true character emerges. The patient learns to understand himself, but he can only understand himself adequately if he considers in the analysis not only the facts of the situation through which he passed in early years, but also his various instinctive reactions to them. One may find that he has been unduly strained in certain ways, certain instincts have been stimulated too intensely as in the examples just quoted. Instincts can in this way give rise to very clear-cut symptoms, e.g., the instinct of disgust. A young child comes into the world almost free from this instinct, which first shows itself between the first and the second year. If a child is well brought up, this instinct has no opportunity in early life of coming out in an intense form, but through careless-

---

* The more usual cause of an inferiority complex is a direct over-stimulation of the instinct of self-abasement or self-depreciation.

ness occasions may occur which arouse it intensely just at the time when it is beginning to make itself felt, and it becomes "sensitized," as it were, and may give the child a great deal of trouble later on. The obsessional fear of dirt and infection can be traced back to faulty development with regard to this instinct, to a revulsion of feeling in connection with it, and also to the suppression of other primitive tendencies in early life.

Further consideration of the question of responsibility must be reserved for the next chapter.

CHAPTER VII

RESPONSIBILITY AND MENTAL DISEASE

IT has been suggested that modern doctrines of psychology are tending to weaken the sense of moral responsibility both in those who commit crimes and in those who pass judgment upon them. The truth is that psychology as such is not concerned with the central problem of responsibility at all. Its task is the more modest one of attempting to trace antecedent factors of wrongdoing in the criminal's heredity, in his previous mental constitution, and in the conditions of his environment.

Roughly speaking, most wrongdoing may be psychologically described as failure of social instincts to control merely self-regarding instincts, where such control is called for in the interests of the community. Such disorder of conduct may be due to excessive strength of impulses needing control, or to exceptional weakness of controlling factors, or to a disturbance of the intellectual life preventing the individual from knowing what he is doing. In some cases all these factors contribute to the resulting action.

If we turn to the legal definition of responsibility we find the intellectual factor alone explicitly mentioned. An individual is to be regarded as legally responsible if he is aware of the nature and quality of his act, or that what he is doing is wrong.* But even on the intellectual

---

* The exact wording of the M'Naghten rule is: "To establish a defence on the ground of insanity it must be clearly proved that at the time of committing the act the accused was labouring under such a defect of reason from disease of the mind, as not to know the nature and quality of the act he was doing, or, if he did know it, that he did not know he was doing what was wrong."

plane it is clear that the application of this criterion must be accompanied by the two provisos (1) that knowledge itself is a matter of degree, and (2) that effective knowledge of the act must include knowledge of the circumstances in which the act is done.

There are many forms of mental illness to which this criterion satisfactorily applies. Alcoholic mania, post-epileptic automatism, paranoia, mania and melancholia are all obvious instances. A crime of violence may be committed by a certain class of epileptic in a dream state, or possibly in a state of complete unconsciousness, in which knowledge and control of his act are both in abeyance. Such an act may occur either immediately after a fit or as a substitute for one. It is generally an act that has become habitual to the individual, or it may be a sort of caricature of an habitual act. Thus a butcher or a soldier may commit an apparent crime of violence in such a state of mind, whereas citizens following more peaceful occupations are not so likely to have acquired habitual modes of reaction which would lead to deeds of violence.

A person suffering from paranoia is under the influence of systematized delusions of persecution and jealousy, which may impair his judgment so far as to move him to deeds of violence against people of his immediate environment for which there is no objective justification whatever. A melancholic may be so weighed down with grief and so convinced of his own unworthiness that he may look upon suicide as a duty. His illness may cause a further delusion that some awful fate is in store for those near and dear to him, and under the influence of this fear he may kill wife and children with the object of saving them from a much more awful doom.

But in addition to such cases as these there is a whole class of individuals who suffer from overwhelming

compulsion to acts of a criminal nature, a compulsion
sometimes so strong that the powers of control even of an
otherwise normal man would be inadequate to hold them
in check. Kleptomania is a familiar instance of this. In
this disease a patient steals not for personal gain but
under the influence of an uncontrollable impulse to collect
a certain type of object; like a jackdaw, he may collect
objects of no intrinsic value to himself however valuable
they may be to their original owners, and, having collected them, he loses all further interest in them. Thus
one patient, a woman, was discovered to have collected
130 parasols from various shops and hidden them in an
attic. It is quite obvious that such a person could not
be held responsible for a crime of theft in the same
sense in which an ordinary thief is responsible.

Analysis may show, however, that the patient is not
entirely free from guilt, although the guilt is to be found
elsewhere. In some cases of kleptomania one finds that
the patient has a bad conscience in another direction
altogether (e.g., in the domain of sex), and, as it were,
relieves his conscience by purloining some small article.
The bad conscience comes from disturbances of mental
development in early years. The patient sometimes
knows that he is criminally disposed, and instead of
becoming a great criminal he makes himself a petty
criminal. One mentions this as a possible explanation;
absolute certainty in such matters is impossible—all that
one can be sure of is the genuineness of the cases.

The uncontrollable impulse may sometimes be of a
much more serious nature, and the patient may feel
impelled to commit murder or some other deed of
violence. Such patients are clearly aware of the serious-
ness of their condition and come to a physician in the
hope of being relieved from it. Psychological analyses
of such cases as these often show that the events and

phantasies of early childhood, and strong repression of infantile tendencies are responsible for these impulses, so that although the patient is not fully responsible for the act to which he at the moment appears to be impelled, he is in a sense responsible for the mental tendencies of earlier life which he had not at the time adequately faced. Often such responsibility is extremely slight; far less than the responsibility of the people concerned with his upbringing.

These cases of impulsion are especially good illustrations of the advance of modern psychology in the problem of moral responsibility. The result towards which such investigations tend is not the abolition of responsibility but its redistribution. Responsibility must be put on the right persons. In a sense each one of us is his brother's keeper. Collective responsibility is often as real as personal responsibility, and often much more ruthlessly exacted in the world-process.

In conclusion, let it be repeated, modern psychology does not contest the reality of moral responsibility. It holds the view that criminals suffering from certain forms of mental disease are less fully responsible for their acts than are normal people. But it certainly does not countenance the view that all criminals suffer from mental illness, nor that mental illness is an invariably sufficient excuse for crime.

PERSONALITY AND EXPERIMENTAL PSYCHOLOGY

(I)—EXPERIMENTAL PSYCHOLOGY

(CHAPTER VIII)

(II)—THE MIND AND MATHEMATICAL ABILITY

(CHAPTER IX)

CHAPTER VIII

EXPERIMENTAL PSYCHOLOGY

WHEN G. T. Fechner published in 1860 his *Elements of Psycho-physics*, he imagined that he was founding a general theory of the relation of mind to matter and propounding a new system of philosophy. His immediate purpose was to establish definite mathematical relations between physical sense-stimuli and the intensities of sensation following thereon, and so to build up a system of mental measurement which should be the psychical counterpart of the science of mathematical physics. His ultimate aim was to sketch out a new theory of the Universe, centred in the nature of the psycho-physical relation. In neither of these attempts has his work stood the test of time, and the ideals he pursued have been shown to be unrealizable. Yet his labours were not in vain, for in the course of his researches he developed a technique of experimentation, summed up in the so-called " psycho-physical methods," which formed the starting-point of a new science, the science of experimental psychology. In its earliest development it was the work of one other man, Wilhelm Wundt, who published his *Physiological Psychology* in 1874, and opened the first laboratory for experimental psychology, in Leipzig, in 1879. There is now hardly a university in Europe or America which does not possess a psychological laboratory, and the position of the science is so well assured that its methods and spirit are exerting a profound influence upon the course of development of kindred sciences such as Education, Medicine, Philology, Æsthetics, and Criminology.

7   97

Starting out from the definition of Psychology as the science of the mind, with introspection as the fundamental method whereby it acquires its data, we have in experimental psychology not so much a new science as rather an improved technique, in which introspection is carried out under pre-arranged conditions.* In the performance of a psychological experiment, the co-operation of two persons, an experimenter and a subject, is generally necessary, although in certain special cases their work may be done by one and the same person. The experimenter arranges the external conditions of the experiment, manipulates apparatus, etc., whereby modifications are produced in the subject's consciousness. The subject then observes these mental changes in himself by careful introspection, and records them with as much detail as possible. In this way, both objective and subjective conditions of mental change can be accurately controlled, and the experiment can be repeated as often as is necessary, not only by the same two workers, but also by other workers in other laboratories, so that results can be compared with one another and general laws of mental reaction finally deduced.

THE PSYCHO-PHYSICAL METHODS.—In the early days of the science, experiment was used mainly for the purpose of elucidating the relations between sensations and their corresponding physical stimuli. The attribute of sensation to which attention was chiefly devoted was that of intensity ; and, working on the assumption that sensation intensities could be measured in terms of a unit of intensity, Fechner and his followers deduced the general law that within any realm of sensation, sensation

---

* The best general description of the position of Experimental Psychology at the present day is given in C. S. Myers and F. C. Bartlett: *A Textbook of Experimental Psychology*, Cambridge University Press, 3rd edition, 1926.

intensity varied as the logarithm of the stimulus. It is now universally agreed that sensation intensities are not in themselves measurable magnitudes, but that "contrasts" between one intensity and another, or "sense-distances" as they may be called, are measurable. If these sense-distances are taken as the measurable magnitudes on the psychical side, the logarithmic law still correctly expresses the relation between them and the stimulus values of the pairs of contrasted sensation-intensities. Just noticeable differences of intensity which figured so prominently in the earlier work as the "difference threshold" are merely a limiting case of such contrasted intensities.

It was in the course of experimental work on sensation-intensities that the so-called psycho-physical methods were developed, as we have already mentioned. These methods are three in number :—

1. *The Method of Minimal Change*, or the method of limits, in which a standard sensation stimulus is compared with regularly increasing or decreasing values of a variable stimulus in the following ways. That value of the variable is chosen which gives an obviously more intense sensation than the standard stimulus gives, and is then reduced by successive small amounts until it ceases to elicit from the subject the answer "greater." It is diminished still further and then increased until it again just gives the answer "greater." The mean of these two values gives the upper difference threshold. By choosing values of the variable less than that of the standard, and proceeding in an analogous way, the lower difference threshold can be similarly determined. The order in which the standard and variable are presented is found to influence the result, and therefore separate determinations are made for the cases where the former or the latter is presented first. In this way, a quantitative measure of the influence

of the time-order on the subject's judgment of difference
is determined, and is known technically as the "time-
error." In similar fashion, where the standard may be
presented either to the right or to the left of the variable
(as in the case of lifted weights), a "space-error" occurs
and can be measured.

2. *The Method of Average Error,* or the method of
production. Here the subject himself adjusts the size of
the variable until it appears to him equal to the standard,
and makes this adjustment a large number of times
under varying conditions (e.g., in one series of measurements with the variable to the right of the standard, in
another with the variable to the left). By averaging
these measurements separately and comparing them,
a "space-error" can be quantitatively determined.
There is no time-error in this method. One important
measure that may be obtained by the use of the method
is the "mean variation" of the different values of the
variable which the subject has judged equal to the
standard. This is obtained by first finding the average
of all the values and then finding the average of all the
deviations of the individual values from this average,
counting all the deviations as positive. It is a general
measure of the reliability of the subject's judgment, and,
although not identical with the difference threshold,
varies directly with it.

3. *The Method of Right and Wrong Cases,* or the
method of constant stimuli. In this method there is
a graduated series of variables, with each of which, in
quite irregular order unknown to himself, the subject
compares the standard a large number of times. The
standard is sometimes to the right, sometimes to the
left of the variable ; sometimes presented first, sometimes second ; and the subject gives as his answers the
judgments "greater," "equal" or "uncertain," and

" less " with reference to the last-presented stimulus. In this way, a series of percentages of each of the three kinds of answers is obtained corresponding to the different variables used. The value of the variable corresponding to 50 per cent. of answers " greater " gives the size of the upper difference threshold. From the series of answers " less," the lower threshold can similarly be determined. The values are most accurately determined by the method of interpolation (i.e., by fitting smooth frequency-curves to the obtained values).

These methods admit of a more extended application than that for which they were originally devised. They have, for example, been employed in the investigation of optical illusions ; and the different results obtained by varying the length, inclination, etc., of the lines forming the illusion-producing figures and by observing the figures under conditions of momentary as well as prolonged exposure, throw much light upon the factors underlying such illusions. Even in the realm of sensation-intensities, a more careful comparison of the subject's introspective record with the various numerical results obtained has in recent years added greatly to our knowledge of the psychological processes involved in the comparison of sense impressions. The effects of the experience of " absolute impression," " side comparison," and similar factors have been worked out, and furnish a valuable psychological supplementation of an otherwise merely quantitative result. Shorter methods of measurement are sometimes used, but in principle they are variations or abbreviations of the classic three. A thorough training in the use of the latter is an indispensable part of the mental equipment of every experimental psychologist.

Head's Experiments.—In a short review like the present, it is impossible to do more than merely refer to a few selected topics, and to indicate in an impressionist way the type of problems with which experimental psychology attempts to deal. Passing over the enormous amount of detailed work that has been done on the sensations of vision and hearing, and the psycho-physiological theories that have been propounded to explain the large number of facts known about these forms of experience, we may with advantage mention some recent work on cutaneous sensations which is of considerable theoretical importance. An experimental investigation was made by Henry Head, who cut through one of the cutaneous nerves of his own forearm and then observed the gradual recovery of cutaneous sensibility which occurred in the course of time. It was found that immediately after the operation there persisted sensibility to heavy pressure, and that the experience of deep-seated pain could also be elicited. If, however, the skin supplied by the severed nerve was lifted up in a fold and pressed between the fingers of the experimenter, no sensation was experienced. In course of time, cutaneous sensibility returned in two stages. The first comprised sensibility for heat and cold, localized in definite spots on the skin ; and to pain. The temperature and pain-sensations aroused radiated widely, and showed no precise localizability. The two points of a pair of compasses, simultaneously placed on the skin, could not be discriminated as two, however widely apart they were separated. This condition of the skin was named by the investigators *protopathic* sensibility. At a much later stage, sensibility gradually returned for light touch, warmth and coolness (not localized in definite points of the skin), and the discrimination of two points simultaneous'y touched on the skin when at a sufficient distance from one another. This form of sensibility was named *epicritic* sensibility, and on its return the previous radiating and vaguely localizable character of the protopathic sensations disappeared, and was replaced by definiteness and restriction. It would seem as though the cutaneous sensations of the normal skin, which to introspection appear simple and ultimate, were the result of a complex physiological mechanism whereby a later form of sensibility is superimposed on a more primitive form ; and that the simplicity and definiteness are a result of this synthesis. There is evidence that the areas of protopathic and epicritic sensibility do not completely correspond, the conclusion to be drawn being that they are supplied by different sets of nerve fibres. Sensations from the viscera, which give rise to " referred " pain, are probably to be classed with protopathic sensations.

Experiments dealing with Visual Experience.—In the domain of perception, experiment has added greatly to our knowledge. By employing conditions of momentary as well as prolonged exposure in the case of visual perceptions, not only has a deeper insight been obtained into the nature of optical illusions, but also the processes of reading and of the apprehension of number have become better understood. The tachistoscope in its various forms, whereby visual stimuli such as dots, lines, words, and other visual objects can be presented to a subject for a brief interval of time (e.g., $1/10$ sec.), is an apparatus of great general usefulness in analysing the apperceptive processes that take place in all acts of perception (i.e., the bringing to bear of past experiences, either in the form of memories or of unconscious dis-positions, upon the given impression). By presenting a succession of momentary impressions of words or sentences, and observing the mistakes which the subject makes in apprehending them, inferences can be drawn as to the processes of apperception aroused, such inferences being confirmed or corrected by appeal to the intro-spection of the subject. In visual perception under conditions of prolonged exposure, the record of eye movements, either by photography or by a system of levers joined up to one writing on a revolving smoked drum, gives interesting results. It is found that in the apprehension of optical illusions and æsthetic diagrams or objects, the eye movements have no relation to the illusory or æsthetic character of the perception, and are therefore to be ruled out as possible factors in its production. On the other hand, in the process of reading the eyes move discontinuously from fixation point to fixation point along a line of print, the fixation points being only three or four in number, in the case of a line of about a dozen words, and the two terminal ones being some distance within the two ends of the line. This sequence of eye movements is found to correspond with the processes of attention and apperception involved in the reading.

Long series of experiments have been carried out with children and adults to determine the character and accuracy of their observation processes. The psychology of testimony has become almost a science in itself, and many types of the observing process have been distinguished. The importance of all this work for the estimation of scientific and legal evidence is obvious.

Experiments dealing with Memory and Association.—In the domain of memory and association of ideas, the possibilities of experiment are well nigh unlimited. Single words may be presented to the subject and he may be asked to reply as quickly as possible with the first word that comes into his mind, the time elapsing between the stimulus and the reply being measured correct to fifths of a second by means of a stop-watch. The replies may be classified according to the kind of association that has occurred, and full introspective records from the subject give valuable information as to his type of association process. The association-time, as the interval between stimulus and response is called, varies from association to association and from individual to individual; but, if it exceeds three or four seconds, as it sometimes does, it is regarded as significant of something abnormal in the association. In such a case, the reaction is usually of an emotional nature, a whole system of ideas and memories tinged with a particular emotion being aroused by the stimulus word. Where no conscious emotion accompanies a prolonged reaction time, it is sometimes assumed that the emotion is unconscious. But a state of fatigue or distraction may in some cases adequately explain the anomaly.

In experiments on memory, the material used has been for the most part nonsense syllables, each consisting of two consonants and an intervening vowel not making sense. These syllables have no preformed associations, and therefore the process of building up associations between them can be studied from the beginning. Lists of such syllables are learnt in definite ways and under definite conditions, and then relearnt after the lapse of definite intervals of time; or the memory for them is tested in other ways. There are many different memory methods, but the most reliable is the scoring method. In this method a series of nonsense syllables, say, sixteen, is presented to the subject's view one by one at a definite rate of sequence through an aperture in a screen. The subject sees only one syllable at a time, and he learns the series in trochaic rhythm (i.e., accenting every odd member). This helps to divide the series up into associated pairs of syllables. The series is thus presented a definite number of times, a number insufficient to produce complete learning. The strengths of the individual associations are then tested, either immediately after the learning or after definite intervals of time, by presenting through the aperture the odd members of the series in quite random order. The subject is asked to reply with the first nonsense syllable that occurs to his mind, and the time elapsing between stimulus and reply may be measured by a chronoscope connected up electrically with the apparatus. The percentage of correct replies and the lengths of the association times are approximate measures of the extent to which the syllables have been memorized.

Among the many results obtained by the use of this and other memory methods are the following :—

1. The rate of forgetting is high immediately after the learning, but becomes less and less with further lapse of time.

2. The learning of a list of syllables immediately after a previous list has been committed to memory tends to weaken the association of the previously-learnt series— a phenomenon known as " retro-active inhibition."

3. A given number of repetitions are more effective the greater the number of days over which they are distributed.

4. Repetitions of a series from beginning to end are more effective than an equal number of repetitions of sub-sections of the series ; in other words, the " whole " method is more efficient than the " part " method.

5. The strongest associations are formed between successive syllables in a series, acting in a forward direction ; but associations are also formed between non-contiguous members of a series, and also between contiguous members acting in a backward direction.

6. Of associations of equal strength but unequal age, the younger associations suffer more at the hands of time than the older.

The learning of rational material, of course, takes place with greater ease than that of senseless material, but the laws above mentioned are merely supplemented, not superseded, by the effects of rational connection.

It is found that as many as twenty sentences, each expressing some definite thought and read slowly in pairs, can be reproduced correctly as regards their thought-contents, although not necessarily in their original verbal form, after a single reading; whereas, the number of nonsense syllables that can be correctly reproduced after a single reading is usually not greater than seven or eight. This brings us to the question of the nature of thought as distinct from mere association, and the comparative experiment just mentioned illustrates the kind of experimental evidence upon which the existence of definite but imageless thought-elements is based. In other experiments a number of sentences are read out to the subject, and shortly afterwards a number of other sentences expressing analogous thoughts but arranged in a random order, and comprising also one or two irrelevant sentences as "catches," are read out, and the subject is asked to state the thoughts of the earlier sentences which correspond to each of the second series. The task is satisfactorily performed by most subjects, and introspection shows that there is awareness of the thoughts and of their relations to one another more or less independent of the verbal sensory material in which they are clothed.

Association experiments have also been devised which indicate the existence and throw light on the nature of definite volitional elements distinct from the sensory elements ("sensations of strain," etc.) of consciousness. A series of nonsense syllables is read a number of times in trochaic rhythm, as in the scoring method; but when the odd members are presented later, the subject is asked to reply, not with the spontaneously arising second syllables, but with syllables which contain the same letters of the presented syllables in the reverse order;

or, in other experiments, with syllables rhyming with the presented syllables. An effort is needed in overcoming the mechanical tendency built up by the initial repetitions, and detailed introspective accounts of this effort have been obtained which prove definitely the existence of a non-sensory volitional element. The technique of all this experimentation on processes of thought and volition is still somewhat crude and immature, but a great deal of work is being done along these lines which will undoubtedly produce results of far-reaching importance for the science of psychology, and possibly, too, for those of logic and ethics.*

Pleasure and Pain Experiments.—Experiments on feeling have till recently been almost entirely limited to a registration of the physiological changes accompanying experiences of pleasure and pain. The plethysmograph, sphygmograph, and pneumograph have been used to give tracings on a moving smoked surface of the alterations of volume of blood vessels, rate of pulse, and rhythm of breathing corresponding to variations in feeling tone. This general " method of expression " is now being supplemented more and more by the " method of impression," in which æsthetic preferences are observed under varying conditions of presentation of the stimuli, and fuller and fuller introspective accounts are demanded of the subject. The word-association test, to which we have already referred, is very useful in the exploration of emotionally-tinged systems of repressed ideas, i.e.,

---

* N. Ach (*Über den Willensakt und das Temperament,* 1910) analyses the phenomenal aspect of the act of will as follows : The act of will shows four " moments," (1) the " *anschauliche* " moment (sensations of strain), (2) the " *gegenständliche* " moment (means and ends), (3) the " *aktuelle* " moment (the activity " *ich will wirklich* "), (4) the " *zuständliche* " moment (*Bewusstseinslage* of strain). The essential factor is the third, which is independent of all forms of imagery and is unique. Other work on similar lines and with similar results has been carried out by Michotte, Prüm, Aveling, etc.

" complexes," and is finding a wide sphere of application in psychiatry. It is often used in conjunction with the psycho-galvanic reaction test (described in a later chapter).

The Measurement of Fatigue.—Methods of investigating mental efficiency and mental fatigue can be but barely referred to here. The ergograph and æsthesiometer have given reliable results in skilful hands, but great care is needed in drawing conclusions from them. Direct mental tests of efficiency and fatigue have been coming more into favour during the last few years. The addition or multiplication of figures, the erasing of certain letters in a page of print, the filling-in of blanks in an otherwise continuous piece of prose, all give quantitative results, and can be used either as continuous tasks producing mental fatigue and measuring its progress at the same time, or as interpolated tests applied at regular intervals in the course of mental work of another kind. Work-curves can be obtained by either of these methods, showing change of mental efficiency with time. The various factors affecting the shape of the work-curve, such as practice, fatigue, incitement, and adaptation, have been investigated in great detail, as well as the effect of rest-pauses of varying lengths upon the total amount of work done.

The Science of Mental Variation.—Finally, we can but touch the fringe of a field of psychological research in which exceptional activity is being displayed at the present time. This is the psychology of individual differences, better termed the science of mental variation. Individuals differ from one another in every form of mental ability, and a precise statement of these differences can in many cases only be obtained by quantitative determinations. In the various forms of mental tests, some of which we have already mentioned in connection with the problem of mental fatigue, we have means of getting a many-sided view of these variations. The psycho-physical methods, adapted and simplified to meet the exigencies of the case, have a new value and furnish the basis of a more general scheme of mental measurement than that sketched out by Fechner. And when we go further and consider the question of correlative variations of mental capacity in groups of individuals, we find that the modern mathematical theory of probability admits of application in its fullest extent to the elucidation of the problems of the mind. The extent to which any two mental abilities show a tendency to vary concomitantly within groups of individuals is measurable by the so-called " correlation coefficient," if the concomitance is linear, or by the " correlation ratio," if it is non-linear. These values form the starting points of mathematical investigations which are at present still in the process of formulation, but which, when developed, will throw a flood of new light upon the dynamics of the mind, and will bring appreciably nearer that ideal towards which Fechner strove—the ideal of an all-inclusive science of mental measurement.

The work on scholastic and mental tests by C. Spearman, G. H. Thomson, Cyril Burt, P. B. Ballard and others in England, as well as that by numerous investigators in America and in Europe, has already laid sound and firm foundations for a quantitative science of mental ability ; and in the researches of C. S. Myers, G. H. Miles and their coadjutors of the National Institute of Industrial Psychology, we have important advances in knowledge and practical application of knowledge in the domain of industrial efficiency, vocational guidance, etc., which is a complete vindication of the scientific status of Experimental Psychology and of its indispensableness within the circle of the sciences.

In the following chapter I have singled out the problem of mathematical ability to illustrate the use of objective methods (statistical, etc.) in dealing with such questions.

CHAPTER IX

MIND AND MATHEMATICAL ABILITY

THE psychological problems involved in any detailed consideration of the nature of mathematical reasoning are numerous and complex, and it is impossible in one short chapter to do adequate justice to all of them. The more important of them, those which can alone be considered, fall naturally under two heads, and the discussion will therefore consist of the following two sections :

A. A brief consideration of the nature of mathematical ability in its most general aspects, its connection or lack of connection with other forms of mental ability, its hereditary transmission, the conditions which favour its exercise, and similar problems.

B. A description of one or two statistical investigations which I carried out some years ago on the interrelations of different forms of mathematical ability and elementary mathematical processes among themselves. This will entail a brief explanation of the meaning of the terms " correlation " and " partial correlation " as used in their mathematical and technical sense ; and the feeling may possibly arise in the mind of the reader that he is being given a " mathematics of psychology " rather than a " psychology of mathematics."

A.* The relation of mathematical ability to general

---

* In this section I have derived much help from a very interesting chapter, " Die Anlage zur Mathematik," contained in W. Betz's monograph entitled *Ueber Korrelation*, Leipzig, 1911.

intellectual ability is a very difficult problem. Some psychologists would deny the existence of any such entity as general intellectual ability entirely. Without going so far as this, we may well ask for a much more complete psychological analysis of it than we at present possess before committing ourselves to any views as to its relation to other forms of ability. The truth is, we are still very far from clear as to the exact manner in which the *process of thinking* goes on. We do not yet possess any satisfactory psychological account of thought. One fact that has been definitely placed beyond doubt by recent experimental investigation is that men do not as a rule think syllogistically. In this respect therefore the logical systems of Aristotle and his modern representatives give us little help, and may even be misleading. It also seems clear that thought may occur without mental imagery of any kind. But what exactly are the positive psychological characteristics of thought we do not know.

In the view of the " plain man," an intelligent person is one who is able quickly to adapt himself to new circumstances, especially to adjust his ideas in relation to new objects, one who possesses in a marked degree the power of analysing a new and complex situation and discovering its more important implications. There remains the question whether this power is a general one, functioning with approximately equal facility (*ceteris paribus*) in relation to all kinds of objects and situations, or whether it is in its very nature specialized and tied down to definite objects and situations. The solution of this problem will most likely be obtained, if at all, through *objective* methods of enquiry, especially those statistical methods now so much in vogue among psychologists. In any case, we can say that our objective knowledge of the nature of intelligence is more satisfactory than our subjective knowledge. We are more clear as to *what* intelligence does than as to *how* it does it.

Current opinion is in favour of a close relationship between mathematical ability and general intellectual ability. In school the former is generally considered a reliable test of intellect, and even in after-life it is regarded with respect. Nevertheless there have been many men of exceptional mental ability (quite apart from their genius), such as Kant and Goethe, who have experienced the greatest difficulty in learning mathematics, and conversely many eminent mathematicians have been markedly deficient in intellectual ability in other directions. Again, as Betz points out, great mathematicians seem always to have been more numerous than great historians, politicians, or philosophers, so that the ordinary view is probably too extreme.

There is good reason for thinking that school-mathematics and higher mathematics relate to different forms of ability and should be clearly distinguished from one another in reference to our question. The former is probably a better measure of general intelligence than the latter. Even in the former, the unmathematical and mathematical boys of equal general intelligence, although perhaps equally successful in mathematical routine work, apperceive it in different ways. In working problems in geometry and algebra, it is neither syllogistic argument in the one case nor a mere permuting and combining of symbols in the other that mark the procedure of the genuine mathematician. It has even been suggested that " school-mathematics would be taught more mathematically, had Euclid been a better mathematician and a less acute logician." Typical mathematical reasoning is better exemplified in so-called " Higher Mathematics," involving the Differential and Integral Calculus. The well-known German mathematician,

8

Felix Klein, of Göttingen, has defined mathematics as essentially "funktionales Denken," or thinking in terms of functions, which is identical with the reasoning of the Calculus. One quantity is thought of as varying continuously with another or a number of others according to a certain rule. I am myself inclined to think that this is true only of algebraical or analytical reasoning, and does not apply to the more intuitional methods of geometrical reasoning. That the two forms are distinct has been held by many mathematicians, especially by the late Henri Poincaré,* and experimental evidence for it will be adduced in a later section of this chapter. I should, however, agree with Betz in the more general view, which he holds, that mathematical talent probably consists in an exceptional ease in carrying out certain thought-processes, which need not be identified with a special and, as it were, fundamental ability, though it does not exclude such a view. Betz writes : " The mental situation shows a certain similarity to the case where one seeks in a visual memory-image to seize and hold fast certain details of which there is at first only the slightest trace visible, only in mathematical thinking it is not a question of visual memory-images but of peculiar presentations or ideas which are felt rather than seen and which in another connection† I have called *minimal ideas*. I believe I can show that the mathematical type of mind is characterized by a special clearness of these minimal ideas, and by the ability to vary them with precision ; whether this also involves a special logical ability cannot be decided, so long as the psychology of inference remains shrouded in obscurity."‡

---

* *La Valeur de la Science*, Paris, 1908, pp. 11–15.

† " Vorstellung und Einstellung," *Archiv. f. d. ges. Psych.*, 1911.

‡ Op. cit., p. 74.

As a point of some interest, it should be noted that many good mathematicians have been weak in arithmetical calculation.

An extensive enquiry has been made by the German psychologist Möbius§ into the relations between mathematical ability and the shape of the head. According to this investigator the relation is a definite one, mathematicians showing prominences over the outer parts of the eyebrows, that on the left side being as a rule the more pronounced. Möbius publishes portraits of distinguished mathematicians which show this characteristic clearly marked, but it has been reasonably objected that his argument could only lay claim to cogency had he also given portraits of non-mathematicians of high intellectual ability and been able to show that the prominences were absent in these cases.

Even if the correlation were satisfactorily demonstrated we could not infer from it the existence of a " mathematical organ " in the brain corresponding to the prominence. The known facts of cerebral localization are all against such a view. We could only regard the relation as the result of correlated variations, accumulating in the course of evolution.

An interesting investigation into the method of working, etc., of mathematicians was carried out some years ago by H. Fehr.‖ He employed the " questionnaire " method, sending out a list of thirty questions to about one hundred eminent mathematicians. Among the results he obtained are the following :

1. Interest in mathematics generally appears before the sixteenth year (84 per cent.), although it may develop as late as the twenty-sixth year.

2. In two-thirds of the cases mathematical ability ran

§ P. J. Möbius : Franz Joseph Gall, Leipzig, 1905.
‖ H. Fehr : *L'Enseignement Mathématique*, Paris, 1905, 1906.

in the family, being inherited four times more frequently on the father's than on the mother's side.

3. Preferences for geometrical and analytical methods occur with almost equal frequency.

4. "Inspiration" often occurs among mathematicians, especially after sleep, but is not a universal occurrence.

5. Mathematicians are as a rule very fond of walking, and take a great interest in music and in religious questions.

6. With one single exception (Boltzmann) the mathematicians interrogated found alcohol more of a hindrance than a help in their work.

In concluding this section, I may say that the balance of evidence seems to be in favour of the existence of a special capacity or faculty underlying mathematical ability, distinct from, and with no essentially close connections with, other forms of intellectual capacity.

B. *Statistical Investigations (Correlation)*.*—In its technical sense, correlation may most adequately be defined as a tendency towards concomitant variation exhibited by two series of measurements. When the two series tend to vary in simple proportionality, either direct or inverse, the correlation is said to be linear, and is conveniently measured by the " correlation coefficient," r. When the concomitant variation is not one of simple proportion, the correlation is said to be non-linear or skew, and in such a case r is meaningless, and the only adequate measure of the correlation is the " correlation ratio," η. r may range in value between 1 and -1, η between 1 and 0. When r$=1$ (or -1), or $\eta=1$, the correlation is said to be complete. Such cases occur, with close

---

* For full details of these researches, see the following articles of mine : " An Objective Study of Mathematical Intelligence," *Biometrika*, vol. vii., 1910 ; " Some Experimental Results in the Correlation of Mental Abilities," *Brit. Journ. of Psychology*. vol. iii., 1910.

approximation, in physics. Thus the relation between length and temperature of a metal rod is a linear one, and consequently the correlation coefficient, r, between series of measurements of the length and corresponding measurements of the temperature is $=1$. The relation of the pressure and volume of a given mass of gas, for constant temperature, is non-linear, the curve expressing the relation being not a straight line but a rectangular hyperbola. Here r is meaningless, but the correlation is satisfactorily measured by η, which again $=1$. The cases, however, where the general theory of correlation is more useful are those where, owing to the number and complication of the factors involved, the correlation is not complete. Measurements exhibiting definite and pronounced variability, such as those of biology and psychology, are those that tax the full resources of the theory. Here, owing to the variability, the proportionality is not complete and r (or η) measures the *tendency* towards concomitance of variation.

To make this clearer by a special instance : suppose one hundred boys are measured for their ability in geometry and also for their ability in algebra, then if the boys above the average in one ability tend as a group to be above the average in the other ability the correlation will be positive, somewhere between 0 and 1, but if they tend as a group to be below the average in the second ability, the correlation will be negative. This tendency is what is measured in correlation. It may be continuously and evenly in one direction throughout the group, as you pass from the worst to the best boys in either of the abilities. In this case the correlation is " linear," and is satisfactorily measured by the correlation coefficient, r. But it may change in direction, either once or any number of times as you pass from the worst to the best in either of the abilities, *i.e.*, if the boys are classed into groups according to their varying excellence in one ability, and then the *average* excellence of each group in the other ability is calculated, these averages may be found not to rise (or fall) continuously throughout the whole of the main group, but after rising may definitely fall (or vice versa), and then perhaps rise again. Or the rise may be continuous throughout the group but not uniform ; it may be more rapid in one part of the group than in another. Either of these cases would be a case of " non-linear " or " skew " correlation. The correlation would not be satisfactorily measured by r, and so the correlation ratio, η, would have to be calculated. When the correlation is linear, $\eta=r$, within certain limits, so that a good way of deciding whether this is the case is to calculate both values. In cases of non-linear correlation η is always greater than r.

For methods of calculating r and η, I must refer my readers to my book on *Mental Measurement*,* as the subject is far too complicated to be treated adequately in this short chapter. I will just quote the formulæ here and pass on. The *correlation ratio*, η, is the ratio of the standard deviation of the means of the sub-groups above-mentioned to the standard deviation of the entire group, the measurements being in both cases of the *same* ability. The *correlation coefficient* is given by the formula :

$$r = \frac{S\,(xy)}{N\,\sigma_1\,\sigma_2}$$

where x and y are deviations from the mean values of the two abilities measured, σ_1 and σ_2 are the standard deviations of the two abilities measured, and N is the number of individuals in the group.

If ability is represented by order of merit, as is fre-

---

* *Essentials of Mental Measurement.* Cambridge University Press, Third Edition (with G. H. Thomson), 1925.

quently the case in school subjects, the following two formulæ give r, viz. :

$$\rho = 1 - \frac{6 \, S \, (d^2)}{N(N^2 - 1)} \, , \text{ and } r = 2 \, \sin\left(\frac{\pi}{6} \, \rho\right)$$

Here d is the difference between the rank of an individual in the one series and his rank in the other, and S ( ) is the symbol for summation. Correlation between two abilities in a group of individuals may be regarded as evidence of partial identity of the factors involved in the two abilities. This may mean partial identity of the two abilities themselves, but we must constantly bear in mind, when interpreting correlation results, that the identity may be an identity of external factors, an identity of the external conditions under which the abilities are exercised, or under which they have been evolved in the history of the race.

Using the method of correlation, I attempted some years ago (see Biometrika, 1910) to make a quantitative analysis of mathematical intelligence by determining the closeness of inter-relation of the various forms of such intelligence that are logically distinguishable. For this purpose I examined 83 boys of a public school by papers in geometry, arithmetic and algebra, and in marking the papers kept the marks separate for the following performances :

Geometry.—A. Memory of definitions and general principles (*e.g.*, principle of superposition). B. Memory of constructions. C. Memory of preceding propositions and power of applying them. D. Recognition of necessity of generality in proof, and power of recognizing general relations in a particular case.

Arithmetic.—E. Accuracy. F. General memory of rules and power of applying them. G. Power of doing sums in percentage and proportion.

Algebra.—H. Accuracy. I. General memory of rules and power of applying them.

Far more detailed distinctions were at first made, but they were found to be statistically unsatisfactory, owing to the small size of the group (83) examined. The total marks for geometry, arithmetic and algebra were also noted.

Correlations were calculated between these twelve series of measurements. The coefficients thus obtained were of course crude values and had to be "corrected" for the irrelevant conditions, age and difference of form or class,* the method used for correcting being the method of "partial correlation," which will be briefly explained later on, in another connection. For further details, I must refer my readers to the Biometrika article. From this article I quote the following list of finally corrected correlation coefficients :

Alg. Arith.	·76±·03	BD	·27±·07	FG	·41±·06
Geom. Arith.	·28±·07	CD	·69±·04	BG	·11±·08
Geom. Alg.	·18±·08	Arith. G.	·65±·04	DG	·11±·08
AB	·42±·06	Alg. G.	·45±·06	CF	·20±·07
AC	·64±·05	Geom. G.	·39±·07	CI	·05±·08
AD	·31±·07	CG	·28±·07	EH	·33±·07
BC	·57±·05	IG	·00±·08	FI	·04±·08

Many interesting results may be deduced from these coefficients by using the method of "partial correlation," which I will now explain in connection with the particular case of Geometry, Arithmetic and Algebra. These

* The influence of "age" was very small, as measured by correlation, and was practically negligible. The influence of "difference of form or class" was considerable, and due mainly to the difference in the extent of syllabus covered in the five different forms which made up the entire group,—and this in its turn was partly due to the difference of mathematical ability of the various sets of boys. Hence the uncorrected or "crude" coefficients are also of direct value, and I therefore record them in a later paragraph and draw inferences from them. This is supplementary to my work recorded in "Biometrika" some years ago.

three abilities are all correlated with one another, and the question at once suggests itself : how far is the correlation between any two of them, say Geometry and Algebra, due to the correlation of each with the third (Arithmetic), and how far is it independent of such correlation ?   The answer to the second half of this question is given by the partial correlation coefficient of Geometry and Algebra for a constant value of Arithmetic, and is calculated by means of the formula :

$$r_{12.3} = \frac{r_{12} - r_{13}r_{23}}{\sqrt{(1 - r_{13}^2)(1 - r_{23}^2)}}$$

where $r_{12.3}$ means the correlation between 1 and 2 for a constant value of 3.   To put the matter in a clearer light, and state accurately the reasoning at the base of this formula : suppose that out of our 83 boys there are, say, 25 of approximately equal ability in Arithmetic. Pick out these 25 boys and correlate their performances in Geometry and Algebra.   The result will be the partial correlation of Geometry and Algebra for a constant value of Arithmetic, and represents the extent to which geometrical and algebraical abilities are connected independently of their respective connection with arithmetical ability.   In our case the formula gives the following three partial correlation coefficients :*

Geom. Alg. 0.   Geom. Arith. 23 ±.07.

Alg. Arith. .75 ±.03.

Taking the *four* variables A, B, C, D, and applying a similar method, though a more complicated formula, I found that the partial correlation of C and D (i.e., for constant values of A and B)=.93.

---

* The correlations between Geometry, Algebra, and Arithmetic, uncorrected for " differences of form or class," are :

	Entire.	Partial.
Arith. Alg.	·79	·65
Geom. Alg.	·66	·39
Geom. Arith.	·58	·13

From the first result, I conclude that essential geometrical ability and essential algebraical ability are but slightly connected with one another; from the second that there is a very close relation indeed between memory of propositions in geometry and the power of recognizing general relations in a particular case in geometry.

Again, since CG and DG are both greater than IG, there is some justification for concluding, at least tentatively, that the ability to do percentage and proportion sums in arithmetic is more closely related to essential geometrical ability than to essential algebraical ability, and therefore that the geometrical method of teaching proportion is more " natural " and more likely to be effective than the algebraical or analytical method.

The slight connection between geometrical ability and algebraical ability would justify the view some mathematicians (e.g., Henri Poincaré) hold that mathematical reasoners fall into two distinct types, the geometrical or intuitional and the analytical or logical types.

One fact at least in the psychology of mathematics seems certain. Mere introspection will never give us the key to its secret. This can only be obtained by supplementing introspection by objective methods, and at the present time the objective method most appropriate would seem to be the statistical method of correlation.

The complete series of 36 correlation coefficients between the 9 part-abilities, A, B, C, . . . I, without correction for difference of form or class, were calculated, and it is interesting to observe how the coefficients are related to one another. Arranging them in order of the average correlation of each ability with all the rest, we have the table on p. 123 :—

In this table the coefficients *tend* to diminish in size from left to right and from above downwards, i.e., they

	C	H	E	I	G	A	F	D	B
C	×	·57	·47	·55	·59	·78	·51	·81	·60
H	·57	×	·69	·92	·53	·61	·55	·40	·26
E	·47	·69	×	·57	·76	·44	·82	·46	·23
I	·55	·92	·57	×	·49	·47	·49	·43	·22
G	·59	·53	·76	·49	×	·41	·64	·44	·26
A	·78	·61	·44	·47	·41	×	·46	·65	·49
F	·51	·55	·82	·49	·64	·46	×	·49	·28
D	·81	·40	·46	·43	·44	·65	·49	×	·37
B	·60	·26	·23	·22	·26	·49	·28	·37	×

tend to show a " hierarchical order." If this order is
" complete " (within the limits of probable error) we may
conclude, with C. Spearman, that all the correlations
may be explained in terms of two factors, viz., a general
factor, and specific factors different for each part-ability.
On the other hand, if the arrangement falls appreciably
short of complete hierarchy (although showing a tendency
towards it), " it is no longer possible to express each
activity completely by a general and a specific factor.
A third category of factors necessarily enters, composed
of Group Factors which are neither entirely specific
nor entirely general, factors which run through some,
though not through all of the tests. The Theory of Two
Factors must in this case be expanded into a Theory of
Three Factors, or better three *kinds* of factors, the three
which G. H. Thomson has called General, Group, and

Specific Factors. Each activity will then be determined by a number of factors, one the general factor, one the specific factor, and the others group factors." *

Spearman has shown that the degree of hierarchy can be tested by the equation

$$r_{13}\, r_{24} - r_{23}\, r_{14} = F.$$

F must be zero, within the limits of its probable error, if the hierarchy is to be regarded as perfect, i.e., if Spearman's Theory of Two Factors is to be confirmed.

Spearman and Holzinger have shown that, if the number of cases tested (N) and the r's are not small the probable error of F reduces to the quantity

$$\cdot 67449 \times 2r\, (1-r)\, \sqrt{N},$$

where r is the mean of r_1, r_2, r_3, r_4.

Testing the first four abilities in the table, viz., C, H, E, I, in this way, we find that

$$F = r_{CE}\, r_{HI} - r_{HE}\, r_{CI} = \cdot 053 \pm \cdot 03,$$

indicating a fairly complete hierarchical order. Again, testing the four geometrical abilities, A, B, C, D, we find that

$$F = r_{CD}\, r_{AB} - r_{AD}\, r_{CB} = \cdot 007 \pm \cdot 03,$$

which is evidence of very complete hierarchical order.

To test the entire table we should need to calculate 126 values of F, but sufficient has been done to indicate the general nature of the argument for General and Specific Factors or for General, Group, and Specific Factors. The results in Geometry can be explained entirely in terms of general and specific factors, but the whole series of 36 correlations probably needs the assumption of additional group factors (in Thomson's sense) for their explanation.

---

* Essentials of Mental Measurement, 3rd edition, 1925, p. 197.

PERSONALITY AND CHILD PSYCHOLOGY

(I)—MENTAL DEVELOPMENT IN CHILDHOOD
(CHAPTER X)

(II)—PROBLEMS OF ADOLESCENCE
(CHAPTER XI)

CHAPTER X

MENTAL DEVELOPMENT IN CHILDHOOD

ONE cannot think of personality and character in human terms independently of physical structure and physical function. It is important to realize that psychology as a science is in no sense a science of something independent of matter. The young child comes into the world as a physical organism; we believe also that it comes into the world with the beginnings of a soul; but we have overwhelming evidence that there is an extremely intimate relationship between the one and the other, so that in a sense we might say that the child as a physical organism is a representation to us physically of its soul, of its mind—its potentiality and already partial fulfilment.

In dealing with children it is very important to feel due reverence towards them. One should not regard them as mere objects of scientific study or of the application of theories and the testing of theories, but rather as growing organisms which will inevitably meet their own difficulties in the world, but which should not have too many difficulties placed in their way. Indeed, we should as far as possible remove unnecessary difficulties. In dealing with children we should respect their individuality and personality to the utmost; instead of forcing ourselves and our ideas upon them we should observe them in the spirit of sympathy, and endeavour, as far as possible, to understand them in the light of our own past experience and that of others around us, but least of all with the idea of verifying a theory or of formulating one.

The child comes into the world as a physical organism, pre-organized to a very great extent; definite organs are developed, including the nervous system, and the separate life of the child is a continuation of that development, particularly in the region of the nervous system. The organism itself, considered physiologically, is a system, an integration, the nervous system being, as it were, the G.H.Q. which keeps the rest of the body in due relationship. Besides the nervous system, there are the blood stream, the lymph stream, and other metabolic chemical changes going on with very great power of mutual adaptation. Therefore, when considering character we consider the human organism as a unit adapting itself to an environment. It is necessary to consider the internal adaptation of the organism as not merely a nervous one, but as also an adequate mixing of the " humours "—to use the phrase of the Middle Ages —which modern physiology shows to be of extreme importance.

We must bear in mind the very important function of the various glands of internal secretion (the endocrine glands) in adapting the child's organism to its ever-increasing needs and keeping the different parts of the body in functional relationship to one another. The functioning of the thyroid gland is that which is best known, so that we can definitely predict what symptoms will follow upon extirpation of that gland or disturbance in its development. We know that the pituitary, the adrenals, the sex glands and others, all act in a similar way, regulating the metabolism of the body; that they act in unison with one another, and that there is systematic relationship between all such endocrine glands. From the point of view of character formation it is to be noted that the function of these various glands plays a very important part in the consciousness of the individual. In hypothyroidism, for example, the individual loses the power of concentration and becomes dull and apathetic, whilst disturbance of the pituitary gland will produce a very pronounced effect upon character. If there is inadequate development of the anterior part of the pituitary, the child becomes unduly fat and sluggish, and sex development is delayed, whilst on the mental side the child is extremely backward. One of the modern theories of adolescent dementia is that the failure of psychological adaptation of the individual at the time of adolescence is due to degeneration of special parts of the sexual apparatus.

We cannot neglect this physiological basis of character formation, and in watching children—because it is in watching them that we can help them most—we should be on the look-out for any signs of failure of function of these glands and be ready to obtain the right advice and treatment. We should not fly to Couéism or other moral and mental methods of treatment, when the primary factor is obviously physical and could be explained by any physician who knows his work.

The theory of the influence of the glands upon personality has thrown such a flood of light upon the subject and has proved to be of such great value, that some people have gone to extremes and have rushed into print with highly-coloured accounts of how the endocrine glands determine the nature of personality. It is maintained that the different types of personality are determined by differences in the influence of the various endocrine glands.

9

It is quite sound to attach great importance to disturbing factors, but it is a different matter to say that the normal character as such is merely a chance mixture of various glandular influences from the body. That is to neglect the fundamental distinction between the pathological and the normal. So long as the argument remains on the scientific plane it is possible to consider the normal as one extreme in a whole graduated series leading to the more and more abnormal, and to say that there is no difference in kind between the two. But as soon as we pass beyond science, to consider from a more philosophical point of view what is the evidence, and what is our justification for believing, that we have truth, or degrees of truth in this matter, we find that we have to assume the *ideal* of truth and the ideal of complete normality; and similarly with beauty and goodness, we have to assume ideals which are never completely achieved. The normal is the ideal; it is a striving towards perfection; and the pathological is a falling away, owing to disturbance. Disease in general, whether physical or mental, is disorder which, originally functional, may become so pronounced as to cause structural change, which may be established in the course of successive generations.

It is most important to keep the normal distinct from the abnormal; to look towards children, so far as possible, from the normal point of view. We look out for deviations from the normal and deal with them, but with the feeling and conviction that as in every child there is a natural tendency towards health, so in the wider sense there are tendencies towards goodness, beauty and truth, which may be checked by various difficulties.

No individual, as such, is improved by a pathological disturbance of any of the endocrine glands, though one might qualify that statement in this way: It may happen that an individual who suffers from some particular disability may develop, in reaction to that disability, a greater degree of ability in some other direction than he would otherwise have done. Inferiority of function in some particular direction may call out an excessive manifestation of function in some other direction. This corresponds to Alfred Adler's doctrine of the "manly protest" as a reaction to "organ inferiority." The individual strives to be "a complete man." This is what is sometimes meant by the "inferiority complex," which is not a very good term for it. It means that the organism as a psychological and physiological unit attempts to retrieve a disturbed balance. If there is deficiency or weakness in one direction there is a tendency to react with excess in another direction. For instance, a child may not be able to see as well as others; perhaps refractive troubles so slight as to escape notice, may yet suffice to give the child a feeling of inferiority to which it may react in an abnormal way. A child may, because of its inadequate physique and its consequent failure at games, or through some other failure to achieve recognition from its fellows, take to crime.

In general, the inferiority complex may show itself in a disguised form. It may not be possible to understand exactly what is going on by direct observation of the child, without analysis. The child may be unduly diffident or unduly conceited and self-assertive. On analysis it may be found that the diffidence is due to a subconscious feeling of worth and subconscious ambition which the child's timidity prevents him from following up. Or the conceit of the child may be a screen for his more deep-seated humility and doubt of himself. Such a symptom as stammering frequently originates in that way. In brief, deficiency may be physical or mental, and in both cases there may be a mental result—an orientation of character in some specific direction.

The child brings into the world a pre-organization of the different parts of the body, including the nervous system. A further organization of nerve arcs and a corresponding co-ordination of those manifest activities collectively known as " instinctive " activity (which has been defined as " an untaught ability to perform actions ") follows. It is, however, a mistake to limit the word " instinct " to the muscular or the motor side of life ; it carries also a perceptive and an emotive side. The child instinctively tends to perceive or notice certain things and neglect others ; it also tends to feel in certain ways towards objects and events which impinge upon its life.

These instinctive-emotional dispositions become organized within sentiments, which are the lowest units of character formation. Sentiments in childhood are the various interests of the child. Interest in a particular thing involves the working of a whole number of instinctive dispositions. A good example of sentiment is friendship. It is possible to experience different emotions under different conditions with respect to one's friend owing to the previous formation of the sentiment of friendship. It is possible to consider a person's life as really made up of friendships. With friendliness towards individual objects, with interest in persons and things, the young child develops concrete sentiments, and in the further progress of intellectual development other sentiments are built up of an abstract kind—not only love of father and mother, and brothers and sisters, but love of country, love of music and of the other arts, of learning and, more abstract still, love of justice and duty. Sentiments are the normal reactions of the child which can be regarded as the means by which the world of values becomes revealed to him. One may regard the normal human mechanism, physical and psychological, as a mechanism of *revelation*. Just as in seeing and hearing the eye and the ear do not *produce* the visual and auditory sensations but only *reveal* visual and auditory objects, so following out the analogy, the various instinctive dispositions with which we are born and which later become organized in systems are the means whereby we have revealed to us the beauty and goodness of the world around us—the good and bad qualities of the people around us. Illness, disease, is a disturbance in the revelation ; it is always in the form of a falling away from it. With this conception, it is absurd to attempt to explain the normal in terms of the abnormal, e.g., to explain why a person is a great artist through so-called complexes or repressed tendencies. His art, so far as it is true art, is destined to live and is in harmony with the totality of things, is in harmony with the entire Universe. That is something that is revealed to him, and he has the power of appreciating it and so making it appreciable to others. He can create it so that others can see it.

It is only through a view such as this that one can allow any place whatever for truth, beauty and goodness. They are not explained in terms of chance reactions to environment. These values are eternal because they are out of time, although revealed in time. The purpose of life is to get in touch with them.

With regard to child psychology, this conception is very important and it corresponds with what has been said as to the need for not interfering with the child, which has its own life to live ; its own revelation will come gradually. Education should be a drawing out of the various powers of different children and giving them full opportunity, all the time avoiding the cramming, harassing, demeaning aspects of life for them.*

We cannot too early inculcate into the young child the conviction of the existence of God as a Loving Father, a Spirit of the Universe, with which we are all in contact, and from which we only separate ourselves through our own misdeeds or misuse of freedom, or through failure of our race and ancestors. The ideal is to retain a feeling of communion with the Spirit of the Universe throughout life. Never mind about doctrinal views. Religion as such is certainly truth and cannot be avoided. The child will spontaneously believe in a spirit of goodness, and that is sufficient until later in life. When its intellect is more developed it can grapple with those other problems. So often a child on coming to maturity has to jettison a great deal of what he thought was true, and with pain and grief finds himself out of harmony with those whom he has admired and trusted, but whose teaching on these subjects he is no longer able to accept.

---

* It is, for example, terrible to think how some mothers and nurses will allow their children to get jealous. Jealousy should be avoided. A child often has too much sense and good form to show it, but it is there; it is felt and crowded back and plays its part in the subconscious, so that when we doctors analyse our patients, we may find it coming up, as one of the causes of their symptoms. Again, the way in which nurses will allow fear to be instilled in the children in their charge is to me a terrible crime. Right from the beginning the child should be taught that there is nothing to fear, though there are certain things to be avoided, things that cause trouble, inconvenience and pain. The feeling of fear comes up as a danger signal. So far it serves a purpose, but beyond this it is merely in the way; it hampers and harasses, for besides the difficulties to which the child reacts in an abnormal way, he has the feeling of fear which he also has to deal with.

CHAPTER XI

CHARACTER may be defined as an organization of individual life. People differ in character to the extent to which the organization of their activities varies. The man of weak character is one whose activities are out of relation to his intellect, and are relatively disjointed and lack persistence. The man of strong character is one whose mental activities are well organized, that is, are in close relationship with one another, and have some persistent central theme around which the other more subsidiary activities are associated. The young child at birth has a character of his own, partly inherited from his ancestors, but already in process of formation by himself. He is not merely a creature of impulse. His various impulses have to do with the most primitive modes of reaction and modes of striving for personal survival. But he already has within him the elements of something higher, namely, the elements of will.

We may forthwith identify character with will. When we speak of will we do not mean some superior faculty added on to the other faculties of the mind, organizing them, leading them on to victory or defeat; we mean by will the totality of the mind in its organization, and in its task of facing reality with a united or relatively united front. It is clear that the youngest child has a certain amount of will in this sense. There is a problem of organization which has been handed on to him from his ancestors, which the child has to solve in the course of his own life, and although in one sense the will has to be trained by those around him—those older than himself can help him and give him hints in the conduct of his life—nevertheless, training alone will not suffice to give character; the child himself contributes the principal something to that task. I would say that the positive part of the training is in the main contributed by the child and the negative part is contributed by those around him. The family circle and those closely associated with the family circle should realize this, otherwise there is great danger of the so-called training of character being merely negative, merely repressive. The mother and father may be so zealous in their work of educating the new citizen to the duties of life, that they may overdo it. They may impress their own views too strongly upon him. The child has a unique outlook on life, not clear at first, but gradually becoming clear; his life is different from any other life. No child is meant to be a mere copy of anyone else, or a mere attempt to fill up an outline which has already been sketched. Something individual, something unique, is brought into the world with him. The task of the father, mother, nurse and others is to try to understand that unique something, to adapt themselves to it and to recognize that although there may be a certain amount of " original sin," a certain amount of crass impulse, there is much more that is genuinely good, genuinely useful, and a positive contribution to the reality of the world and to the value of existence. Parents should notice the various fundamental tendencies of the child and give them full play as far as possible. Encourage them, educate the child in the literal sense of the word, i.e., draw out from him all his potentialities. They should see that as far as possible fear and pain do not enter into his life. There is no reason why a child's life should be miserable. Let him be happy. Let him be encouraged in free self-expression, so long as this does not interfere with the claims of those around him.

One finds, then, that although there are those separate impulses to which we have referred in earlier chapters, the so-called instinctive dispositions of self-preservation, pugnacity, self-abasement, curiosity, the tendency to pursue the pleasant and avoid the painful course—apart from such primary dispositions there are interests which the child has, to which he may subordinate those impulses. The very fact that those impulses which move him may be in conflict with one another ensures that he does not become merely a creature of impulse. We cannot follow two conflicting impulses at the same moment. As a rule, e.g., we cannot satisfy the impulses of curiosity and fear at the same moment. If there is a conflict between the two, then that conflict produces something further, viz., the beginning of an organization of those impulses. There is, then, a preliminary organization already at birth, which the child has to continue with the help of those around him. Give him full scope, trusting to the good sense of his nature, the essential upward movement of his mind towards increased knowledge and power. Onward from the threshold of life conflict is the father of progress in character formation. Character is built upon conflict.

I have said that character and will are to a certain extent identical. They are the same looked at from different points of view. Character is an organization of impulsive tendencies. Will is that organization in action. The impulsive tendencies represent a fund or source of mental energy. Organization ensures adequate direction of such energy. This direction is carried out through the development of the intellectual side of the mind in relation to the emotional and instinctive side of the mind. In other words, increased knowledge on the part of the individual, knowledge of the results of his actions and activities, the results of trial and error on his own part, the results too which he has been taught by his elders to expect—all this contributes to the development of his character and to the education of his will. But we can conceive of two persons with the same knowledge and the same original impulsive tendencies and much the same experience, yet with different degrees of will. Here general physical health, such as the presence of enlarged tonsils and adenoids, or a disturbance of the glands of internal secretion, may help to explain the difference, but the chief deciding factor is the nature of the organization of cognitive and conative dispositions.

The growing child should be given plenty of scope in the practice of judgment and choice, and in the development of character along lines of his own. He should be encouraged to create and make use of opportunities and to develop increased power through his own exertions, and at the same time care should be taken to avoid any form of repression, irrational side-tracking, or cutting off of mental activity. The ideal of character development is unimpeded activity, free from irrational constriction. Since conflict is an essential element of all life, not only at the beginning but also as a factor in the later development of character, we must mean by repression something more than mere conflict. We mean by repression the irrational elimination, or attempt at elimination, of some particular impulse in favour of others. Repression represents an inadequate solution of a mental conflict—in this respect differing from restraint.

One psychological problem of great importance is that of the relation of the sex instinct to all other instinctive desires of the mind, and to the general organization of interests which we have called character. The child comes face to face with the great problem of sex at the time of adolescence, if not before, and needs some sort of help and preparation. The question is how best he may be helped, and this raises the general problem of sex education. Should the child be left to discover the facts of sex for himself—often through unpleasant and inaccurate information imparted to him by older children, servants, &c.—or should he be given formal instruction on the subject ? The universal opinion now is that a certain amount of instruction should be given, but still there is the question under what conditions it should be given. Information should be given in accordance with the requirements of the child. Children vary greatly in the rapidity of their development along these lines. Some children become curious about sex early in life. These children ask questions, which should be answered within the limits of the child's knowledge and powers of comprehension. The parents should tell the truth as far as it can be told. In other cases children may be so fully interested in work and play at school that sex matters do not trouble them. I know of one such child who reached college age before this question bothered him, and who suffered no ill-effects whatever from being allowed to remain in ignorance about it. On the other hand, such knowledge, although useful, may sometimes be dangerous, especially if forced upon a child, by unduly stimulating interest in the matter. In these and other matters the first principle is to take special care that no harm is done. Another point I would make in sex instruction is that it should be given before adolescence. Do not wait until the child is in the thick of his troubles of adolescence, because then the sex instinct may be further aroused by the instruction itself, and his temptations may be thus increased. I think instruction may sometimes be given, if needed, at as early an age as 9 or 10.

In some cases a very good time is when a boy leaves his preparatory school for a public school. Often the headmaster of the preparatory school is ideally suited for this task, if he is willing to undertake it. It is generally said that enlightenment comes best from the parents. That may be so in some cases, but I doubt if it is so in all. In some cases parents have their own sex difficulties and are therefore unsuitable persons for giving sex instruction. In other cases they feel exceptionally diffident about it. These might well depute the task to others. Those, however, who do feel sure of themselves should give their children information as it is required. In the elementary schools much may be done by means of special classes of instruction. Those deputed to give such instruction should be carefully selected. One great advantage of class instruction is that children are not so likely to feel embarrassed when taught in the mass as they would when spoken to individually. Lessons in biology may offer a good opportunity for imparting information without so much risk of shock. If shock occurs it may produce retardation of sex development and a set-back to the entire character.

Sex instruction then is necessary, but it is not sufficient. The child should be not only forewarned, but also fore-armed. When temptation comes what is the adolescent to do ? The temptation may be very severe and pressing. What has the individual to set against it ? There are two main paths of safety from that battle-ground of sex at the time of adolescence. One is the path of *substitution*, the other is the path of *sublimation*. By substitution I mean the deviation of mental energy from sex towards other fields of interest. If a child has plenty of other interests, then sex matters are neglected or ignored. Interest in sport and adventure, natural history, physical training, the work of Boy Scouts and

Girl Guides—all these make useful claims upon the general fund of vital energy in adolescence, and leave little or no energy over for sex interest. It is this method of substitution which has been assiduously followed in the English public school system. Although so successful it does not educate the child to deal with sex, but only relieves him from the immediate pressure of the sex impulse. In sublimation, however, the sex impulse is dealt with directly. The adolescent is encouraged to anticipate somewhat the best and greatest part of sex, passing beyond the mere desire for physical pleasure to the more spiritual side of it, to the high ideals of chivalry and parental love and self-discipline. Interest in art, in social problems, in philosophy and religion—all these interests are definite sublimations of the sex instinct. In regard to religion, however, great care should be exercised because there is danger of de-sublimation in the more emotional forms of religion. There is the danger of a person feeling the pressure of the sex temptation, and flying to religion as an escape from it, and thus gaining an inadequate or false idea of religion, and a religious aim infected with crude sex. Subsequently, a rapid de-sublimation may occur, with the reappearance of sex difficulties. In patients in mental hospitals sex and religion may sometimes seem to be closely related, but in such cases it is generally a matter of superstition rather than of true religion.

Sublimation then is an anticipation and an encouragement of the higher levels of sex feeling. It leads up to the ideal of social service, of a religion of humanity and—through humanity—of God. It is a very definite and direct way of combating those special diseases that continue to threaten social life. Such psychological prophylaxis may be expected to be of great effectiveness in stamping out these social evils.

One final point. It is held by many psycho-pathologists that psycho-neuroses may result from sex repression. Although this view is not untrue if the term " sex repression " be taken in the technical Freudian sense, we must emphasize the fact that suppression of ordinary or normal sex activity, i.e., ordinary continence, does not necessarily endanger nervous health. The only kind of neurosis that can sometimes arise from a checking of the normal sex tendencies is that which follows upon frustrated sex excitement. With strong sex instincts intensely aroused without satisfaction, there may follow a special kind of nervous disturbance known as anxiety-neurosis, characterized by a general feeling of irrational anxiety. But this danger can be easily avoided. It is no valid criticism of continence as such.

Individuals must recognize a law higher than themselves, the law of the family and of society in general. The individual is dependent on the family, and as a part of the family must recognize that he has received the benefits of family life and must on his side make his own contribution. To-day he must be ready to make a certain amount of sacrifice, if sacrifice be needed ; they may be real sacrifices in the case of a certain type of individual—for him the lesser good of the individual must give way to the greater good of the community. The individual has his general outlook coloured through and through by the family and the various other groups in which he lives, and the progress of human nature is undoubtedly bound up in the further development of these groups. These give the individual an opportunity of widening the scope of his life so that he lives not merely in his own circle of life, but lives in the group, country, and nation, and humanity in general. In that direction he passes along the road towards the highest and most perfect form of character, namely, the truly religious life, the life of communion with God.

PERSONALITY AND PSYCHO-PATHOLOGY

(I)—PSYCHOLOGY AND MEDICINE
(CHAPTER XII)

(II)—THE EARLY TREATMENT OF MENTAL DISEASE
(CHAPTER XIII)

(III)—SUGGESTION AND HYPNOSIS
(CHAPTER XIV)

(IV)—PSYCHO-ANALYSIS
(CHAPTER XV)

(V)—DISSOCIATION AND MENTAL UNITY
(CHAPTER XVI)

CHAPTER XII

PSYCHOLOGY shows its most direct bearing on the science and art of Medicine in the domain of nervous and mental diseases, and here at the very outset it is called upon to meet such criticism as J. S. Haldane has recently brought forward in his article on "Psychology and Biology,"* namely, that the real causes of illness in nervous disorders are physiological, and that these causes, when discovered, will give us an adequately satisfying theory of so-called functional nervous disorder. As far as I can make out, his view of psychology is this—that whereas all other sciences, even physics and chemistry, are abstract, psychology deals with actual experience—individual experience, and to that extent not only all formal investigators of mental processes, but also all good teachers and preachers, are psychologists. This view, however, really reduces us to philosophy rather than psychology, and no room is left for psychology as between the opposing claims of physiology and the other physical sciences on the one side, and philosophy on the other. Where I would specially deviate from his presentation of the situation, is in his remarks upon the nature of the psycho-neuroses, or so-called functional nervous disorders, because it is in dealing with functional nervous disorders that modern psychology claims, and I think rightly claims, to have made its greatest practical advances. Dr. Haldane seemed to imply that these functional nervous disorders only appear

---

* In *Psychology and the Sciences*, edited by William Brown. A. and C. Black, 1925.

of a different nature from the ordinarily recognized organic nervous disorders because a wrong, inadequate and too mechanical view of physiology, especially that of the nervous system, is held; and that we should make our physiological explanations more general, in terms of the entire organism, passing beyond the abstractions of the ordinary physiology of the reflex arc.   One gladly admits all that, and welcomes not only Haldane's own work in this direction, but also the work of those, like Sir Charles Sherrington and Henry Head, who have laboured especially on the physiology of the nervous system in recent years.   Henry Head, for example, in his recent exposition of his doctrine of Viligance,* has shown clearly how the functioning of the nervous system as a physical system can alter in many ways independently of any gross lesions, or structural alterations, in special parts of that nervous system.   Such a view, however, does not eliminate psychology; rather does it make psychology, if anything, more valuable in the full elucidation of nervous activity, because, although these discoveries are made without observing the consciousness (if any) of the individual (the experiments being carried out on animals) the interpretations of the experiments admit of amplification with reference to analogous situations in conscious human nerve function.

No doubt corresponding to every moment of conscious experience, there is some change going on somewhere or other in the nervous system.   Without that consciousness, however, we cannot get so adequate an understanding of these physiological processes as we can by making full use of the observation of that consciousness.   What psychology does in these cases is to get at the working of the nervous system from a new vantage-point.   Whereas

---

* Henry Head: " The Conception of Nervous and Mental Energy," *Brit. Journ. of Psychology*, vol. xiv., pp. 126–147, October, 1923.

the physiologist is investigating it from the physical side, observing physiological changes, the psychologist is investigating the same processes, or some of them, from the psychological side, and only with adequate psychological analysis can the physiological processes be fully explained.   Moreover, as regards the *treatment* of functional nervous disorder, physical and physiological methods of treatment have shown themselves thoroughly inadequate to cope with the situation.   Not that psychological methods of treatment invariably succeed, but one can say with absolute confidence, based upon the wide experience of a large number of enthusiastic workers, that the success in psychological treatment of functional nervous disorders transcends enormously the success arrived at by physical means alone, such as massage, electricity, baths, diet, drugs, and the various degrees of rest cure. What is of still greater scientific importance, psychological investigation in these cases of functional nervous disorder gives us an insight into their meaning which is a thousand times more satisfying than the very latest and completest knowledge that the leading neurologists and physiologists of the nervous system can give.   We are not claiming that these psychological processes which we discover by analysis in cases of functional nervous disorder occur independently of physiological processes.   What we claim is that our knowledge of these psychological processes is very much more complete than the knowledge of the corresponding neurological processes, and that, in all probability, even 50 or 100 years hence, physiology will not have succeeded in giving us a complete physiological account of the physical correlatives of these psychological processes.   Further, even if and when physiology does give a complete account of the physiological processes underlying these psychological processes, the explanation in psychological terms will be found to be the more completely satisfying of the two, because psychological explanation carries with it elements of *meaning* that can never be adequately explained in merely physiological terms. That merely means that psychological categories of explanations are more concrete than physiological categories. Although all the sciences deal with abstractions from actual experience, the abstractions that psychology makes use of are nearer to immediate experience, are less falsified by theory, than the abstractions of biological science or physical science.

Psychology can then at least help medicine by giving a detailed account of the psychological processes that accompany certain pathological changes in the organism. In its most scientific part, namely, in experimental psychology, we have instances of the great help that it gives to medicine in the study of abnormalities of sensation and perception, disturbances of recognition and disturbances of memory. Measurements of memory, immediate and remote, and of mental and physical efficiency and fatigue, can be accurately carried out only by the use of modern psychological technique. Further, in the general use of mental tests for classifying forms of mental backwardness and deficiency the work has all been done by psychologists, aided by the technique that they themselves have devised; namely, by methods that can eventually be traced back to the classical psycho-physical methods developed by Fechner, Delboeuf, G. E. Müller, and more modern psychologists.

Methods of exact psychological research have already been employed in the investigation of such functional nerve diseases as neurasthenia, hysteria, psychasthenia, and forms of insanity like dementia præcox. There is a well-known association test, first suggested by Sir Francis Galton and developed by C. G. Jung, in which words are called out to the patient, who is instructed to reply by the very first word that comes to his mind. The investigator measures the time taken by the first word to call up the second by means of a stop-watch. The associated word or response given by the patient is recorded. The experimenter notes the association time, and works through the list of words in that way, and finds variations in the association times and differences in the quality of the associated words which throw a flood of light upon the nature of the mental processes going on in the patient independently of his main personal consciousness. In one of the examples that I have myself investigated in that way, it was found that the word " death " called up after an interval of twenty seconds the response " geranium," without awareness on the patient's part of the connection between the two words. Further investigation of that peculiar result brought out a history of much mental and emotional disturbance in the patient's past life, a typical emotional triangle involving death and attempted suicide.* This word-association test of Jung can be supplemented by the measurement of what is called the psycho-galvanic reaction. If the patient is linked up by wires to a Wheatstone Bridge arrangement with a small battery in the circuit, with a galvanometer fixed up between the two pairs of arms of the bridge—that is, if the patient's resistance is balanced against the resistance of another arm of the Wheatstone Bridge so that the needle of the galvanometer registers zero—if now an emotion is aroused in the individual the galvanometer needle swings, showing that diminution of resistance in the patient has occurred. This diminution in resistance is most probably due to the occurrence of secretory processes in the sweat glands of the subject's skin.. The swing of the galvanometer

* *Suggestion and Mental Analysis,* University of London Press, 1923, p. 45.

apparently varies with the intensity of the emotion. But the galvanometer will also swing when the subject is not actually conscious of emotional change, although further analytic investigation may show that something analogous to that change has occurred in his sub-consciousness, that might be expected to arouse associational processes of a similar trend. Although the actual interpretation of the psycho-galvanic reaction still gives considerable difficulty, the apparatus does admit of fairly accurate records of measurement, and in nerve patients it helps to supplement results obtained by the word-association test.*

But the most useful psychological line of investigation and treatment in medical psychology is the general method of analysis independently of these aids from experimental psychology. It is found that such disorders as hysteria and psychasthenia have much deeper psychological significance than appears from their immediate symptoms. The subject may apparently suffer simply from loss of psycho-physical powers—loss of memory, loss of the power of speaking, of walking, of overcoming tremors or contractures ; but psychological analysis of these cases shows that very complex, in some cases extremely complex, mental processes have occurred to produce the symptoms. These processes have occurred on the margin of consciousness—it is even claimed in complete unconsciousness—so that the patient is unable to recognize that he ever had such experiences. But under analysis they come up into consciousness, and come up in such a form that they give meaning to the symptoms. What is more, the bringing of them up into consciousness gets rid of the symptoms.

To take one of the simplest examples of such hysteria cured by analysis. A war patient, an officer, suffered

---

* For a detailed discussion of the psycho-galvanic reaction, see W. Whately Smith, *The Measurement of Emotion*, Kegan Paul, 1923.

from contracture of the right arm after he had been blown up in the trenches ; he also suffered from loss of memory for all the incidents of the shock. The re-arousal of these memories, under light hypnosis, brought out the story that he had a close friend with him at the time, who had been smashed up by the shell, while he himself had been blown across his friend's body, falling upon his right arm. He had regained consciousness sufficiently to see what had happened to his friend, had immediately lost consciousness again, and was picked up in this state with a contracture of the arm. The contracture persisted from that moment until the moment that he came under treatment several months later. The detailed revival of the emotional experience brought about a relaxation of the arm, and cure of the patient, although a previous employment of physical means and ordinary persuasion had quite failed to produce any lasting benefit. The explanation that came out in the course of subsequent talks with the patient was that he was so horrified at the sight of his friend's mangled body that he wished to forget it. He felt that he could not face these memories, and so the memory traces remained there dissociated from his other memory traces, and inaccessible to his conscious mind. So long as they were thus dissociated, so long did the contracture of the arm persist. But, besides this, the contracture represented *symbolically* the individual's wish or desire not to remember. As soon as these painful memories had been forced into the patient's consciousness, this defence mechanism became no longer effective or necessary, and it disappeared. I should, however, add that some analysts would give a still more detailed explanation of a case like this. Some would attribute such shell-shock symptoms as this to reaction on the patient's part to a death wish. As far as I can make out, they would say, in a case like this, that the patient in some extraordinary way had wished for the death of the other man, and had reacted to it with intense grief, and at the same time with this amnesia and contracture. They would put the argument in the following form : When two people are together under intense shell fire and in great danger, the thought may pass through the one man's mind, who wishes to escape at all costs, " If any one is to be killed, let it be the other man rather than myself."* To my mind, there is not sufficient evidence for such an explanation. Yet some analysts will go so far as to explain grief that seems to be perfectly natural grief as a reaction to death wishes of the past. When an individual loses someone very dear to him, and feels intense grief afterwards, the grief may be a reaction to unconscious wishes of earlier years for that other person's death. Now that, of course, may seem at first sight to be an extraordinarily absurd theory, but it may well be that, in extreme cases of pathological grief, some mechanism of this sort is at work. That is, although there is such a mental state as normal grief which is perfectly normal and natural and carries with it its own explanation, there may be forms of grief that are pathological, that do not carry that explanation, where there is no adequate explanation on the fully conscious plane. It is quite true that on the loss of a beloved person thoughts may come up of how one had not always treated him as one should in the past, and one becomes abnormally conscious of one's shortcomings. Here a similar psychological mechanism may be at work.

I can now pass most naturally to forms of mental illness that seem to be psychologically explicable in these terms. In so-called compulsion neurosis or obsessional neurosis, where the patient is obsessed by a tendency to

---

* I have heard this explanation given by a leading psychoanalyst in the course of a scientific discussion.

carry out a certain ritual and obsessed by absurd fears
or by certain feelings of taboo, mental analysis sometimes
shows that these symptoms must have arisen as a reaction
to mental tendencies of a quite different nature in very
early years. For example, over-conscientiousness, or pathologically irrational and excessive anxiety about the welfare
of others, may sometimes be shown in the course of
analysis to be a reaction to an exceptionally strong
tendency towards cruelty in very early years. Freud
would explain such a case as a reaction to what he calls
sadism, or the tendency to be cruel to those we love.
But Freud would go further. He says, quite paren-
thetically at the end of one of his articles,† that, in the
same way, sympathy is a reaction to sadism. He would
explain normal sympathy as a reaction to an impulse to
hurt in earlier years, just as some analysts would explain
grief as a reaction to death wishes in the unconscious,
dating from earlier years. Such mechanisms, no doubt,
may explain pathologically intensified grief and sympathy,
but grief and sympathy are normal reactions of the
mind and should be themselves taken as explanatory
factors. It is in cases like this that the unsatisfactory
nature of much psycho-analytical work shows itself—
I mean the tendency to take results attained by investigation of pathological cases, and to use a theory based upon
those results as the ground of explanation of normal
mental processes.

One may see a further example of this in arguments
based on the facts of " projection." Certain patients
show in very pronounced form this phenomenon of
projection. They may, e.g., imagine that they are being
persecuted by others who are jealous of them and are
hindering them in their legitimate efforts to make a

† " Triebe und Triebschicksale," *Sammlung kleiner Schriften zur
Neurosenlehre.* Vierte Folge, 1918, S. 265.

career for themselves. Analysis shows that these feelings
and delusions are really to be explained as a defence
reaction to the same feelings that the individual himself
has had towards other people, often in much earlier years,
although feelings in later life may contribute their quota.
In some quarters* this pathological concept has been
used to explain ideals that are generally recognized as
perfectly normal activities of the mind. The most
general instance is the conception of a God. It has been
suggested that we form the conception of a God, project
him outwards, as it were, because we have need of certain
things ; we have certain desires—in general the desire
for a feeling of security, which we cannot attain by
reference to our ordinary experience of life. Not meeting
with direct palpable satisfaction of such desire, and
finding the lack of certainty intolerable, we project an
imaginary fulfilment of the desire into the outer objective
world in the form of a belief in God. In addition
to this factor of projection, another pathological factor
co-operates in creating the religious sentiment, the factor
of "regression." The individual feels desperate, feels
that the limit of his resources has been reached, and is
conscious of his own weakness and insecurity, and in the
face of the great mysteries of life and death he retires
baffled, regresses to the earlier type of mental activity
of childhood. The feelings he had towards mother and
father, as those who gave him security at that time, are
again projected outwards, and contribute to his conception
of God. Both projection and regression are factors that
can be verified as occurring in pathological cases, but
analysis of these cases, so far as it is successful, removes
both the projection and the regression and the patient
becomes more normal, with less regression and less

* *Cf.* J. Kinkel: "Zur Frage der psychologischen Grundlagen und des
Ursprungs der Religion," Imago, Bd. VIII., 1922.

projection. On the other hand, the religious feelings which the individual has are not diminished in their essence by the analysis; rather are they increased, although superstition and spurious religiosity do tend to disappear.

The general explanation of the psycho-neuroses, then, is in terms of mental conflict and repression, the repressed tendencies dating mainly from early years. In other forms of nerve trouble, such as intense depression, the conflict may be of more recent date, may be a conflict between the natural man and his ideals, his conscience. We find, for example, that in some forms of depression, where the patient seems to be continually upbraiding himself, depreciating himself, and complaining of himself rather than others, deeper analysis shows that the complaints and the hostility are directed against something or somebody else intimately related to his life. They are really directed towards somebody or something with which he has in a way identified himself in the past, and who or which has disappointed him. He may have had a close friend for whom his affections took the form of an unconscious identification. He found that he could, as it were, identify himself with the other individual, so that his affection for this individual was of the so-called identification or narcissistic type, the type of self-love. If, now, that individual disappoints him so completely that his emotional energy can no longer go out towards him, the energy is withdrawn into himself, becomes turned inwards upon himself, not in the form of love, but in the form of hate. He seems to hate himself, but that hate is so persistent because it is really directed against the image of the other individual who has disappointed him.

Such a description, as I give it, seems a very metaphorical way of explaining the symptoms, and I admit that it is difficult to choose words adequate to the situation. But the central fact stands fast, that if one analyses cases of depression, one frequently finds, not only that their hostility to themselves is really hostility to someone else, but also that when they realize the situation fully, the depression clears up. The therapeutic test is all-important in this domain. I do not mean that cure is overwhelming evidence of the truth of the theory. The situation is really this—that a negative result, where benefit does not occur, does not exclude the possibility of the truth of the theory ; on the other hand, actual recovery is not conclusive evidence in favour of the theory upon which the treatment may have been based. But where recovery occurs in whole classes of patients in the degree to which certain mechanisms are revealed in analysis, we may justly conclude that these mechanisms are of great importance in the causation of symptoms. And if we can, on the basis of the analysis of some cases, predict what will be found to be the cause in other cases, this will be still more convincing evidence. That is what is happening almost every day. A case is brought to one suffering from fear of infection or over-scrupulosity as regards dirt, etc., and one knows before one begins to analyse the patient that the result will show ultimately that the patient is suffering from revulsion of feeling in the first two or three years of life in regard to means of cleanliness, and to certain fundamental instinctive processes. The analysis is a long one ; the result is that if one succeeds in getting to those early memories the patient does improve and may recover.

It is sometimes objected that this general method of analysis is unconvincing because it allows so much scope to the imagination of the analyst and gives him much opportunity of unconsciously suggesting into the patient's mind his own ideas. That may occur in the case of

unskilled inexperienced analysts. But after some practice
one finds that there is very little danger of this, because
the whole process is so very detailed and extended over
so long a time that the patient is in quite a different state,
or should be, from that in which he is influenced by
suggestion. At times when he gives his " free associations,"
he is in an uncritical state of mind. At other times,
and this is the method I myself would advocate, at certain
stages in the analysis he is encouraged to be as critical
as he likes, and he is encouraged to argue the matter out,
and gradually he is driven to realize the situation for
himself ; he is driven partly by the physician and partly
by himself and he gets into a state where he must obtain
relief, and he can only obtain that relief by facing the
facts more and more honestly. This is especially the
case with obsessional neurosis. Fortunately for the
theory, unfortunately for the patient himself, these
obsessions give him little peace, and in the course of
analysis they may at first become much more intense
and he is driven on and on by the gadfly of this impulse
to discover the reason for it. You may try him with
suggestion treatment ; at first he benefits somewhat, but
he may find that the benefit does not last. It becomes
more and more clear to him that there is an underlying
cause which he must find out for himself, and that is
what carries him through the analysis.*

I have hitherto avoided mention of suggestion treatment, not because I think suggestion treatment is
unimportant or ineffective in psychotherapy—it may
often suffice to produce quick and permanent cure—but
on the theoretical side the further question always
remains : Why should this particular patient respond to
this particular suggestion ? Let us consider the simple

---

* A fundamentally important factor in all analysis is the factor of
" transference."

elementary explanation of functional nerve disorder :
the patient has become ill through bad auto-suggestion,
and therefore he will get well if given good counter-
suggestion. But the further question remains : Why did
he succumb to this particular bad or pathogenic suggestion
in the past ? His mind was open to all sorts of suggestions,
both good and bad, and the only way to answer this
question is to analyse the situation. To take one of the
simplest types of war neurosis : a soldier became functionally paralysed in his lower limbs because a shell
burst near him, and he became paralysed by fear. He
thought he was permanently paralysed (pathogenic auto-
suggestion) and remained so until he was treated by
therapeutic suggestion. Further analysis showed a strong
desire to get away from the firing line, to get a wound
which would enable him to leave the trench without
dishonour, and that, together with the emotion of fear
from which he suffered at the time, furnished a satisfying
explanation of his illness. That analysis confirmed his
cure and made it permanent.

It is no explanation to say that a patient got ill or
well by suggestion. This is a statement of the problem,
not its solution ; and far from the general question of
suggestion being a very simple one, which we can now
leave aside as settled and pass on to something else, it
still remains one of our most important problems in
psychotherapy. In the immediate future, I can safely
predict that we shall meet with many articles on
suggestion in scientific journals, and the reason why
suggestion is going to be so very important theoretically
is that analysis has advanced far enough to be able to
make its contribution to the explanation. Earlier forms
of analysis emphasized repressed tendencies and native
propensities that have been held in check in an irrational
way, and thus become causes of illness. Modern analysis

is moving rather on the lines of analysing also the repressing tendencies, considering what are the factors in the mind that produce the repression, what are the mental and neurological forces bringing about this partial or complete dissociation of the activity of one small part of the nervous system and mind from that of the whole system. If we face the problem from the point of view of repressed tendencies, we may find ourselves in the company of those who, for the most part, believe in rigid determinism, in mechanical determination of conduct. If we approach the same problems from the point of view of analysis of repressing tendencies,* our view may be very different. We may hold to some form of self-determinism, but we shall feel that further explanation is needed of the nature of personality, and of the nature of individual volition which may make it impossible for us to accept the current solutions of determinists like Freud and his school.

In conclusion, I would point out that though the work of psychology is of most value to medicine in the treatment of psychogenic nervous disease and earlier stages of insanity, it is also of considerable value in the treatment of the recognized organic diseases, especially of the " functional overlap " of early organic nervous disease. The state of the patient's mind, his mental attitude towards life, is of the utmost importance to his cure, and we may confidently expect the doctor of the future, who will receive training in psychology as well as in other biological sciences in his student days, to achieve still greater success from its practice than he achieves at present by his intuitional and common-sense methods. On the other hand, physical methods of treatment of mental illness should not be neglected, and

---

* Freud himself has dealt with this question in a recent publication, *Das Ich und das Es*. For a discussion of his views, see Chapter XV.

possible disturbance of functioning of the endocrine glands should be looked for, and, where found, corrected. In a fully adequate therapy the illness should be treated from both sides, mental and physical.

CHAPTER XIII

In considering the question of the early treatment of mental disease, we may start with the assertion, of the truth of which there is very little doubt, that all mental disease is also physical. In all mental disease there is physical disturbance, however slight, going on somewhere or other in the organism, and in the treatment of such disease it is obviously necessary as far as possible to deal with that physical disturbance directly. Experience shows that a great deal of mental disturbance which may become relatively permanent follows upon infections in different parts of the body, with toxic absorption and consequent deterioration of nervous activity through chemical injury. Again, that disturbance of the activity of the endocrine glands, such as the thyroid, etc., has a pronounced reaction on the functions of the nervous system, and so upon the mind. Indeed, these two general physical causes of mental illness or derangement are sometimes related, in that infection and toxic absorption seem sometimes to react primarily upon the thyroid gland, and through it to influence the nervous system, and so the mind. It is obvious, therefore, that in the treatment of mental disease due care should be taken to make an adequate physical examination and to deal with any physical infection there may be—from carious teeth, septic tonsils, chronic constipation, indigestion, sub-acute appendicitis, and other forms of physical illness—to look for evidence of endocrine disturbances, and to give appropriate treatment in the form of thyroid and other gland extracts, etc. Also, still considering the purely physical side of mental disease, we have to bear in mind the possibility of fatigue and physical exhaustion being factors in the mental trouble, and we should deal with them on the physical side by prescribing physical rest. We need not emphasize these factors, because the whole force of medical tradition is likely to ensure that they will not be overlooked. Even at the present day there is little danger of the physical factor in mental disease being underestimated. The danger is on the other side—that medical men may be too ready to trust entirely to physical methods of treatment and neglect another avenue of approach, namely, the psychological.

These physical causes, to which we have referred, produce mental disturbance in certain cases, partly directly through diminution of nervous activity, partly indirectly through the reaction of the mind to the illness. The patient is disturbed by his physical illness, and becomes mentally ill, with general symptoms such as diminution of powers of concentration, weakness of memory, a tendency to depression, and sleeplessness. These symptoms become more fixed and lead on to further mental symptoms.

But in many forms of mental disease the causal factor is more directly psychological. The individual has from the cradle onwards needed to adapt himself to the circumstances of his environment, physical, mental, or social, and at every stage in his career he is met with the possibility of failure. Adaptation to special periods in his life may be peculiarly difficult—the time of leaving the nursery for school, leaving a preparatory school for a public school, the time of passing on to college, or choosing a profession, the period of becoming engaged, getting married, providing adequately for his family, the prospect of old age and a general diminution of physical powers—at all these points in his life fresh adaptations have to be made. He may fail more or less in making adequate adaptation, with the result that his mental outlook is disturbed, and he may show symptoms of mental illness of one kind or another. The mental illness is a physical illness in that it is a disturbance of the working of the nervous system, through which disturbance of other parts of the body may be involved. By getting depressed, his physical functions may become more sluggish, with consequent toxic absorption which reacts on the nervous system, and a vicious circle is set up. The patient's condition may become still worse through feelings of maladaptation and insufficiency. So that in most cases there is an intricate combination of mental and physical factors interacting with one another and producing a complex result.

As regards early treatment of this mental disturbance it is obvious that we should learn as far as possible what the situation really is before we bring one or other of our methods to bear on the case. So far as physical factors can be demonstrated, they should be dealt with along appropriate physical lines. Septic teeth, chronic constipation, insufficient action of the endocrine glands, etc., should be dealt with in appropriate ways. On the mental side, so far as mental factors can be discovered, they should be directly dealt with on psychological lines.

This is where the real problem of the early treatment of mental disease comes in. As a rule, when the specialist sees such a patient, the disease has already progressed a certain way, and a definite mental disturbance of one kind or another has shown itself, but it is not easy at first glance to diagnose what kind of mental disturbance it is. The state of psychological medicine at the present day is still very unsatisfactory as regards diagnosis, or discrimination of different types of disease.

At the beginning one distinction is of fundamental importance, namely, that between so-called functional and so-called organic or structural nervous disease. Mental disturbance is a disturbance of the nervous system, and that may be due to (so-called) merely functional disturbance or to organic and structural change. When we say that a disease is functional we really mean that it shows itself only in the disturbance of function, that the correction of this disturbance of function can be brought about by psychological means, and that this will neutralize or cure the slight structural change that must be present. On the other hand, in so-called organic or structural nervous illness correction of function is inadequate to produce correction of structure.

It is usually said that mental disease often involves a *purely* functional disturbance of the nervous system, with the assumption that there is no structural change. The disease is a purely mental one, and because of that can be corrected by mental means. The difficulty of such a view is that it is impossible to conceive a disturbance of function without some disturbance or other of structure. But nevertheless there is a great difference, from the practical standpoint, between so-called functional and so-called organic or structural nervous diseases. One set is amenable to mental treatment, the other is not. The reason of this is that in so-called functional nervous disease the disturbance of function can be corrected by special means of a psychological nature, and this correction of function will bring about a correction of whatever slight structural defect was present. On the other hand, in organic or structural disease, correction of structure cannot be produced, because an attempt at correcting function has no influence on the structural alteration.

I myself think of it in the following way. In a so-called functional disease such as hysteria, which comes especially in this category, the structural change is a kind of reversible process, whereas the structural change in organic nervous disease is an irreversible physical, chemical and biological process. Hysterical patients have the defects of their qualities, and the qualities of their defects—they are open to good suggestion and to bad suggestion, to pathogenic and therapeutic suggestion. One means a disturbance of equilibrium in the direction of degeneration, the other a more or less adequate restoration of that equilibrium. There is, then, this great distinction of the functional and structural which is a helpful indication as to the kind of treatment to be used, if we can first decide whether the disease is predominantly functional. If so, it is specially amenable to psychological treatment, because psychological treatment has the effect of altering function and behaviour.

We can go still further in our diagnosis. It is at the present time fairly easy to discriminate hysteria from other forms of mental illness, and although different authorities hold slightly different opinions about it, they seem to agree in the practical discrimination of this disease from others. In hysteria the patient's state of mind is characterized by a pronounced suggestibility, a tendency to psychological automatism, crude mental dissociation and restriction of the field of consciousness. In other mental patients at an early stage we find the psychasthenic characteristic described by Pierre Janet as a general feeling of inadequacy or incompleteness, with phobias, impulsions, and other obsessions. We have again cases of intense mental exhaustion, depression, and lack of interest which need different treatment. Finally we find forms of mental illness which, if left to themselves or inadequately treated, or in spite of any and every form of treatment, eventually lead to melancholia, manic-depressive insanity, dementia præcox or other so-called psychoses. We must not be too ready to discriminate these psychoses or insanities from the psychoneuroses previously described, in their early stages. The truth is, it is only in later and more chronic stages that mental diseases show pronounced identifiable characteristics. We still lack sufficient knowledge of them in their earliest stages, of the nature of the mental factors at work in their inception, to be able to say that psychologically they are two entirely different categories of disease. Although we must admit that the hereditary factor appears to play a very much greater part in the psychoses than in the psychoneuroses, this difference may be illusory and due to a difference of complexity of the factors involved.

These different forms of mental illness have different mental causes, and call for different mental methods of treatment. In hysteria, suggestion treatment, either with or without hypnosis, may be a quick and satisfactory method of improving the patient's mental condition, and enabling him to achieve greater powers of mental synthesis for himself, and a higher level of general mental energy. In such pronounced forms as spontaneous or natural somnambulism, hysterical fits, and hysterical amnesias (losses of memory), the patient is invariably found to be easily hypnotizable, and under the skilful use of hypnotism (which is, of course, artificial somnambulism) the natural somnambulism is destroyed—rather unexpectedly perhaps. It might be expected that the production of somnambulism artificially would only intensify the somnambulistic tendency already present, but this is not necessarily so. The person who walks in his sleep is easily hypnotized, and under hypnosis one may put him through the experience again, and after appropriate suggestion he wakes up remembering the circumstances in which he walked in his sleep, with the result that the subsidiary tendency in his mind has become re-associated with his main consciousness, and falls under its sway once more. In such patients, after one or two treatments, the somnambulism may be completely cured. In hysterical fits the patient is readily hypnotized, and under hypnosis a fit can be artificially provoked, and the psychological concomitants of the fit can be discovered. It can be discovered what shock in his past life, or what set of incidents, has caused the fit, and been repeated in this automatic way again and again. The emotional tendency is worked off and re-associated with the main consciousness or the main personal self, and once again falls under its sway and the patient is cured. In amnesias, or loss of memory for definite stretches of past experience, containing incidents that had been disturbing to the patient, and had been out of harmony with his main personality, one may recall such memories under hypnosis, and re-associate the mind. The consequent re-integration of personality means a higher level of mental activity, and is a protection against further lapses of this nature. This method of hypnotic suggestion may thus be used not only to clear up the symptoms but to diminish the hysterical tendency which is at the base of the symptoms.

There are alternative methods of dealing with hysteria. One is to analyse the patient's mind in much greater detail, without the use of hypnotism or suggestion, and this is the better method. It may often be very lengthy, and in some cases it is. more convenient to combine the two methods—clearing up the symptoms by hypnotic suggestion, making certain discoveries of past events through hypnotic analysis, and by further general analysis working over the mind to diminish the patient's morbid susceptibilities and to re-integrate him and produce a more normal outlook and attitude toward life.

In the general case of psychasthenia, hypnotizability is conspicuous by its absence. These patients are not hypnotizable, in the sense of being capable of falling into the state of artificial somnambulism. They suffer from a general feeling of incompleteness which needs help on the conscious level by encouragement, mental training, and rest, both mental and physical, to enable them to increase their general fund of mental energy, and to raise the level of psychological tension. A general re-education may be needful, whereby they are dissuaded from continually butting their heads against a blank wall of impossibility as regards their obsession or compulsion.

But here again, the more thoroughgoing method is the method of analysis, to discover the past and present psychological causes of the patient's illness. This method of analysis is capable of different degrees of thoroughness. In its simplest form it is a general psychological investigation of his past life and present difficulties. The analysis is of the nature of arm-chair conversation, in which the patient talks out his life, and one intervenes from time to time with questions and suggestions to help his own interpretation of his past, and one guides him where he seems to fail to appreciate the real significance of some incident or other in his past, or the extent to which his own reaction at the time was inadequate and unsatisfactory. One also encourages him to scrutinize closely his present mental situation, his troubles and difficulties, his ambitions, hopes and fears, and to submit them to detailed analysis, and relate them to earlier memories and mental tendencies. Furthermore, one may help him to build up a general philosophy of life, in relation to his own individual case, using the Socratic method rather than that of dogmatic instruction. This general psychological analysis, which I have called *autognosis*, may not require many hours' treatment, but the patient gains immensely thereby. The symptoms become more intelligible to him, and it may then be found that the more automatic part of the symptoms may be diminished by formal suggestion treatment in the sub-waking state. The patient is asked to lie on a couch, with voluntary muscles relaxed,* and to concentrate on the idea of sleep, avoiding effort while doing so. The physician then makes suggestions in a firm tone of voice, suggestions of a general nature as regards the patient's health, and of a special nature as regards the various symptoms from which he is suffering, on the basis of what has been discovered in the preceding psychological analysis.

A more thoroughgoing form of analysis is the general method of psycho-analysis, in which the patient reclines on a couch and gets into a meditative state, where he waits for ideas and memories to come into his mind, and then describes them to the physician who is sitting near but out of his sight. The analysis is carried out for one hour at a time, daily, if possible, for many weeks and months. In working over his past life in this way and considering various aspects of his present difficulties and experiences, the patient comes up against " resistances " from time to time. He sometimes finds it difficult to impart to the physician what comes into his mind, and at other times discovers in himself a general emptiness of mind, but with perseverance thoughts and memories sooner or later do come up, which are often of an unpleasant nature, representing tendencies and experiences

---

* Muscular relaxation and freedom from emotional tension are more easily attained if the patient breathes slowly, regularly and deeply.

out of harmony with his general personality and outlook on life. By overcoming these resistances,* and imparting the information to the physician, he makes progress in the analysis and derives benefit from it. A good deal of emotion is shown, and the patient becomes aware of tendencies in his mind that have not shown themselves recently in clear consciousness, yet have been working in the background to influence consciousness. The greater the extent to which they are made conscious, the more completely they fall under the control of the main personality. Among these tendencies and incidents of the past may be discovered some which help to explain the conscious symptoms of the patient, and the bringing of such tendencies and memories into consciousness may be sufficient to diminish or destroy these symptoms. The ground is thus, as it were, cut from beneath the feet of the symptoms. The radical cure is always some form of analysis.

Psycho-analysis as a method is intimately associated with the theory of psycho-analysis developed by Sigmund Freud, according to which all these nervous symptoms are to be explained in terms of disturbance in the development and manifestation of the sex instinct, taken in the widest sense of the term. This theory we can leave aside for the present. We may not discover sufficient evidence to constrain us to accept the theory in its entirety. Although we do find in certain cases that sex factors of a more or less general nature play a pronounced part in the causation of mental illness, we must admit that in many cases the sex instinct may seem to be little, if at all, disturbed, and the patient's difficulties may arise

---

* This is helped by the " transference," i.e., the tendency to transfer emotional and affective attitudes of earlier years from their original objects to the physician. The transference itself may, later on, constitute one of the most serious of these resistances, and needs to be resolved by further analysis.

more directly from disturbance in other instinctive tendencies in the course of life, especially in the instinct of self-assertion, and the instinct of self-preservation and escape. These instinctive tendencies with their appropriate emotions may in various ways have given the patient great difficulty in the past, and the actual experience of the patient's life in relation to these instincts may involve maladaptation which the patient has subsequently attempted to correct by other reactions. So that we may find that what is apparent in the conscious mind of the patient is sometimes the exact opposite of what is discovered by deep analysis among the more primitive tendencies and earlier memories.

A method which I have myself found specially useful is to commence with ordinary psychological analysis, to work over the ground in that way, ready to discuss things with the patient face to face, and then, after ten or fifteen hours of work of this kind, if further treatment is needed, to turn to the more thorough-going method of psycho-analysis.

There are other general methods of treatment in the early stages of mental disease which should be mentioned. There is the method of isolation, whether partial or complete, the plan of segregation in a special hospital, or the mere separation from relatives for the purpose of diminishing the strain of social life upon the patient's mind. Social life involves its own special demand and strain upon mental activity. Adaptations to society are of great complexity, and seem to take up a great deal of mental energy, sometimes more mental energy than the patient can afford, and in this case it is important to diminish the expenditure of mental energy at once by removing him from his social *milieu* and giving him a rest. Treatment in mental hospitals has its advantages as well as its disadvantages. Its disadvantages are that it may unduly emphasize the patient's illness and give him as companions people themselves ill, and that through imitation of these others he may find it more difficult to get better. All these objections sound more serious in theory than they are found to be in practice. Among the advantages are the well-regulated life and the greatly reduced demands on the patient, so that he is enabled to store up reserves of mental energy in an atmosphere of cure, knowing that other patients have received great benefit. There is the possibility of dealing with any disturbance of physical function, and indeed with all the physical aspects of his illness, very conveniently, and, further, the possibility of systematic mental treatment. The one drawback is that owing to the expense of such a home for the patient, he may be unable to stay as long as might otherwise be necessary to get well, and owing to the difficulty of medical staff in the home, the individual patient may not get sufficient treatment of a directly psychological nature. It may be impossible to give thorough analytic treatment to many of the patients in mental hospitals. Personally, I find that there is a very large number of patients who are able to continue their work while receiving treatment, who do not need to go into hospital, to whom continuation of work is really a help, not only financially, but therapeutically, and who under these conditions are able to afford a much more lengthy course of treatment, and benefit accordingly. The ideal method is the deep analytic method, but unfortunately it is impossible in every case. A mental home is needed where the patient is too troublesome in his own home, and may be a danger to himself and others. In cases of excitability and of great depression a home is essential.

CHAPTER XIV

SUGGESTION AND HYPNOSIS

HISTORICALLY, the problem of suggestion has been approached along two distinct paths. Up to quite recent times our knowledge of it has been a secondary result of the study of hypnosis; during the last few years the line of investigation has been that of mental analysis. There can be no doubt that the latter form of enquiry is likely to be the more fruitful of the two.

The problem of the relationship of suggestion to hypnosis is brought to a point in two distinct classical definitions that we have of the hypnotic state. According to the Salpétrière School (Charcot, Janet, etc.), hypnosis is an artificial hysteria or mental dissociation. According to the Nancy School (Bernheim, Coué, Baudouin) hypnosis is a state of artificially-increased suggestibility. According to the former of these two definitions, we should expect suggestibility to be increased in hypnosis, because mental dissociation would tend to carry with it diminished self-knowledge and self-control, with the result that ideas elicited in the subject's mind would tend to realize themselves by their own momentum, as it were, unchecked by more far-reaching thoughts and higher forms of mental control. The difference between the two schools of thought would then seem to be this—that, whereas the Salpétrière school puts mental dissociation as a cause of any increased suggestibility that may occur, the Nancy school makes no definite statement as to the cause of this increased suggestibility.

The problem of deciding between the merits of

these two definitions can be dealt with by an appeal to experience. During the European War a great spontaneous natural experiment was carried out through the agency of the actual conditions of fighting. Soldiers suffered by the hundred from crude mental dissociation, showing itself by amnesia or loss of memory for definite terrifying events and experiences, together with loss of psycho-physical functions, such as the power of speaking, of hearing, of walking, the power of controlling tremors, etc. Investigation of these patients immediately after their injury showed that they were readily hypnotizable. Moreover, that the ease with which they could be hypnotized was in direct proportion to the degree of their mental dissociation. In other words, one discovered a definite correlation between degree of dissociation and ease of hypnotizability. Such a finding harmonizes with the Salpétrière definition of hypnosis, as an artificial dissociation. On the other hand, in these cases it was found that the suggestibility, though certainly increased in milder degrees of dissociation, was often conspicuous by its absence in more pronounced degrees of dissociation.

It is clear that we must here call to mind a fundamental distinction in the matter of suggestion. If we define suggestion, as, e.g., McDougall does, as the acceptance of an idea or proposition independently of logically adequate grounds for such acceptance, the further question arises—whence comes this idea that is accepted? If it is elicited by the patient's outer environment, the people around him, the general physical and mental situation, the process may be called that of hetero-suggestion. If, on the other hand, the idea arises spontaneously in the patient's own mind or is deliberately presented to him by himself, the process may be called that of auto-suggestion. In cases of deep hypnosis, such as we have just referred to, where a patient's suggestibility seems sometimes to be diminished rather than increased, it may well be that it is merely a diminution of hetero-suggestibility—auto-suggestibility may be intensified.

Before passing on to a more detailed consideration of the nature of suggestibility, we must emphasize the fact that on the one hand crude mental dissociation facilitates hypnotism, and on the other, that this mental dissociation, although sometimes caused by mental conflict and repression, may often be caused by pronounced physical means, such as physical shock to the brain, and in a small proportion of individuals appears to be an inborn characteristic. That is, in certain cases of physical shock to the nervous system, and in certain other cases, the state of hypnosis can be produced with exceptional ease, without any obvious psychological reasons.

If we remain in thought on the level of suggestion and suggestibility in our consideration of the causation and cure of psycho-neurotic symptoms, we have some such crude view as that of Babinski, who holds that hysterical symptoms are produced by suggestion, and therefore are curable by persuasion. In other words, the patient falls ill under the influence of pathogenic auto-suggestion, and recovers from his illness if these are neutralized by therapeutic suggestion, either given by a physician or others, i.e., hetero-suggestion, or by himself, i.e., auto-suggestion. So far as it goes, this explanation is not incorrect. In simple cases of hysteria, such as those seen almost in process of formation during the war, hysterical symptoms, such as loss of the power of walking, loss of voice, etc., were demonstrably the result of the patient's belief that he had become paralysed, or that he had lost his voice permanently; and the symptoms disappeared at once if the patient was informed that this was not the case, and was strongly assured that the power of walking, talking, etc., would forthwith return to him. But even in so simple a case as this, the further question arises—"Why was the patient so susceptible to the pathogenic auto-suggestion, the suggestion of illness ? " The answer can only be found in terms of desires in the patient's mind. Sometimes these desires are fully conscious, but, in the majority of cases, their true nature is not realized by the patient. In war neurosis, the desire for personal safety, to get away from the firing line, was a pronounced factor in the causation of these symptoms. The patient desired to get away *at all costs* from the firing line, and it was because he did not fully realize the nature and significance of this desire that he could become self-deceived and fall a victim to hysterical symptoms. He did, indeed, consciously desire to get away from the firing line, but with honour, without disgracing himself or betraying his comrades ; but at the back of his mind there was a more vigorous desire to get away *at all costs*. This desire welcomed the experience (say) of his being struck with fragments of earth thrown up by a bursting shell. The thought passed through his mind that he was paralysed, and this thought became a fixed idea because of the intense desire.

It is sometimes said, as, e.g., by Baudouin, that emotion is an auxiliary factor in suggestion ; in other words, that a patient succumbs more readily to suggestion when under the influence of some emotion or other. The truth is this : emotion is aroused in relation to the activity of some instinctive tendency, such as the instinct of escape, the gregarious instinct, the sex instinct, etc., and these are not so much auxiliary factors in suggestion, as the essential factors. Suggestion only works in relation to the activity of some instinct or other. When in full consciousness, instinctive processes are controlled or directed by reference to the entire conscious self, and in such cases suggestion has little or no scope. It is where, through conflict and repression, certain instinctive desires, associated often with definite sets of memories of the past, are dissociated from the main stream of consciousness, that they can realize suggestions which would be unacceptable to the fully conscious personality if their meanings were thoroughly understood.

One might provisionally harmonize the suggestion theory of causation and cure of symptoms and the analytic theory as follows: mental conflict and repression may produce hysterical symptoms as compromise formations which simultaneously satisfy repressed desires in the unconscious, and desires of another nature in the conscious mind, but the nature of the symptoms themselves is also partly determined by auto-suggestions arising as the result of diminished unity of the self—chance thoughts, they may be, which otherwise would have no influence over the patient's mental state, and to which he would not succumb. He is in a state of mind divided against itself; he is afraid for himself, afraid of ill-health, afraid that he may fall sick, and yet many desire sickness, for reasons that can be discovered by deeper analysis (e.g., as a self-punishment, or to tyrannize over relatives, etc.). So the idea gains a hold upon him. In this way the dissociation we have previously emphasized does favour the acceptance of auto-suggestion On the other hand, what particular auto-suggestions, from among all the different possible suggestions, are accepted, is determined by the wishes, desires, etc., of the patient's mind. In order, therefore, to understand fully the realization of suggestion, we must analyse the patient's mind and learn as much as we can about these mental factors.

One analytic view of the nature of suggestion and suggestibility is the well-known Freudian view that

12

suggestion is a form of transference, in which the patient reacts to the physician as he reacted in early life towards his own father, or towards others closely connected with him in childhood. In other words, the reaction is an erotic one, using the word " erotic " in the widest sense. At first sight such a theory as this seems to be extremely improbable, since, besides the sex instinct, there are many other instincts which may be plausibly appealed to for an explanation of suggestibility in special cases. The instinct of escape, with its emotion of fear ; the gregarious instinct, with its own peculiar emotion ; and the instinct of self-abasement, with its emotion of negative self-feeling, may be specially singled out in this connection. So much suggestibility seems, on the surface, to be the result of fear, or of a standing desire to be in harmony with one's fellows. We must, however, remember that Freud has a definite theory of group psychology and of the gregarious instinct in terms of libidinal relationship of the individuals of a crowd or other group towards the leader of that group—the leader corresponding to the father of the horde in more primitive times. Such a theory brings the concept once more within the circle of Freudian doctrine, and recently Freudians have explained auto-suggestion in terms of narcissism or libidinal self-love. Indeed, Ernest Jones explains all suggestion in terms of narcissism. He writes : " If the primary narcissism has been released and re-animated directly, by concentration upon the idea of self, the process may be termed ' auto-suggestion ' ; if it has been preceded by a stage in which the ego ideal is resolved into the earlier father ideal, the process may be termed ' hetero-suggestion.' "*

It is clear, then, that the problem of suggestion and

* " The Nature of Auto-suggestion," *Brit. Journ. of Med. Psychology*, 1923, vol. iii., p. 209.

suggestibility is far from being a question of the past, now superseded by analytical theory. It still remains one of the central problems of modern psychotherapy. Whether suggestion is always a libidinal relationship, is not entirely free from doubt. Instead of saying, with Freud, that all suggestion is transference, we are probably on safer ground in holding that the transference situation is, indeed, one of the conditions under which suggestion may occur, but that suggestion may also occur in psychological situations when there is no transference. But the question can only be finally decided by " deep " analysis.

In conclusion, a word may be said on the relation of suggestion and auto-suggestion to the will. It has been noted by many observers that over-anxiety counteracts the effects of therapeutic suggestion. If one feels anxious to get to sleep at night, one may become wider and wider awake. Similarly, in the attempt to recall a forgotten name, anxious effort to remember generally brings failure. Coué has summed up these and other similar observations in his so-called Law of Reversed Effort. " When the will and the imagination are in conflict, the imagination always wins." Such a formulation is only true of states of incomplete will, where fear of failure has prevented the full development of volition, and the word " will " should be replaced by " wish." The completed state of will or volition is incompatible with any such fear or doubt. One of the best definitions of volition† is that given by G. F. Stout : " Volition is a desire qualified and defined by the judgment, that, so far as in us lies, we shall bring about the desired end because we desire it." The " judgment " in this definition comprises, of course,

---

† W. McDougall defines volition as " the supporting or re-enforcing of a desire or conation by the co-operation of an impulse excited within the self-regarding sentiment." For general psychological purposes this is a still more satisfactory definition.

belief, and if completed, it is superior to " imagination " (suggestion) acting alone.

The advice given to patients to avoid effort in the practice of suggestion is a sound one, since effort tends to arouse the idea of possible failure and the fear of failure. If these do arise, they gain the mastery over the original suggestion. Most cases of successful auto-suggestion are characterized by avoidance of thoughts and fears of failure, and may, therefore, be considered as instances of supplementation and completion of the volitional process through adequate control of the imagination. To call the method one of auto-suggestion is really somewhat inappropriate and it might be more accurately described as a method of training the will. In practice the passivity of mere suggestion and auto-suggestion is quickly superseded by the activity of faith and calm determination to succeed.

What is acquired is a new mental attitude which protects the patient from suggestions of ill-health and incapacity. To make this protection complete, or as nearly complete as possible, the patient also requires a course of psycho-analysis or autognosis, to rid him of complexes and other dissociations and thus enable him to face the world with a unified personality.

CHAPTER XV

REFERENCE has already been made, in elementary terms, to the general method and theory of psycho-analysis, and, without any further consideration of Freud's views in detail, it will be convenient to restrict our present summary to a brief consideration of the general view as to the structure and functioning of the mind set out in his recent essay, *Das Ich und das Es*. Whereas, in the early stages of his theory there was a tendency to identify the unconscious proper, as distinct from the pre-conscious, with that which is repressed, his view now is that it also comprises a repressive factor.

The mind is in its essence unconscious.* Consciousness is an additional characteristic of certain moments of mental activity. Mental activity occurs primarily in an unconscious form, but may become conscious under special conditions, e.g., of distribution of attention. Consciousness is, as it were, "a sense organ for the perception of psychic qualities." † Besides the processes that occur consciously, there are processes that have previously occurred consciously, and have now fallen back into the unconscious in an undistorted form. These belong to the so-called pre-conscious ; they are unconscious mental activities and memories which can become conscious as soon as they attain a certain degree of

---

* "Everything conscious has its preliminary step in the unconscious, whereas the unconscious may stop with this step and still claim full value as a psychic activity. Properly speaking, the unconscious is the real psychic." (S. Freud : *Interpretation of Dreams*, p. 486.)

† *Interpretation of Dreams*, p. 488.

intensity, and thus attract sufficient attention to themselves. But besides the pre-conscious, there are mental processes that cannot appear in their true form consciously. They are kept from consciousness ; the path to consciousness is barred by a resistance. It was this resistance which Freud observed when he first began to analyse patients. He found that although they could recall a certain number of recent memories and even memories of remote times, they were not able to recall other memories and mental tendencies which were in disharmony with their general character ; their resistance to the recall of these memories could be overcome, if at all, only by urging or by circumvention through still more prolonged analysis. Repression is something not directly observed ; what is directly observed is resistance to the recall of certain memories.

Freud's theory, then, was that these mental processes had been held back from reaching full consciousness by a resistance which he called the censorship, and he divided the " descriptive " unconscious into the two divisions of the " systematic " unconscious and the preconscious. The systematic unconscious was the repressed unconscious, while the pre-conscious was the unrepressed unconscious. But now he admits that, within the circle of individual personality there are unconscious factors which cannot directly come into consciousness (i.e., which belong to the systematic unconscious), but cannot be classified under the heading of repressed. These factors are derived not from the libido, but from the ego. There are certain parts of the ego, as well as repressed libidinal tendencies, which are unconscious in the true systematic sense, not in the merely descriptive sense ; and in his recent essay he considers the nature of these unconscious repressive forces.

In the earlier accounts of Freud's views, it was often

assumed that the repressive force was the conscious personality, the developed moral personality. Certain tendencies or temptations were supposed to be held in check because they were out of harmony with the conscious personality, and so were prevented from passing from the unconscious into the pre-conscious. Freud now definitely states that the repressive forces are themselves in the unconscious mind ; they are part of the unconscious.*

In Freud's view, the unconscious is more powerful and more impersonal than the conscious and pre-conscious parts of the personality. The unconscious and the conscious (including the pre-conscious), although they are in the main continuous with one another, are cut off from one another in respect of actual repressed tendencies —tendencies that have been driven back into the unconscious after they have passed into the conscious. Each (viz., conscious and unconscious), occupies its own domain, but a sort of bridge may be built up spanning the two by means of verbal presentations and verbal images (*Wortvorstellungen*)—the process of expressing things in words is the bridge that may link up the unconscious with the conscious and pre-conscious. Whatever is unconscious is inexpressible in words, but verbal imagery can serve as a bridge from it to the pre-conscious and the conscious. In this process there is, however, no changing of the unconscious into the conscious, or conversely.

In spite of the metaphorical nature of this account of the situation, it does seem to correspond in some way to observed fact. Continued psycho-analysis brings about

---

* Even in the first edition of his *Interpretation of Dreams*, Freud described the censorship as " the resistance watching on the boundary between the unconscious and the pre-conscious " (p. 430), indicating that it was itself unconscious.

an increase of power of the conscious and pre-conscious —of the ego—over the repressed portion and over the unconscious generally. This seems to be essentially bound up with the process of talking things out. In the analysis, the patient talks about his past life and his present difficulties. He continues talking—he talks for an hour each day—and, quite apart from, and in addition to, the actual increase of intellectual insight into the nature of his mind, and into the way in which different motives work and conflict (autognosis), further changes occur. These further changes seem to be bound up with the actual process of talking out—of expressing himself in words to another individual. Words do seem, in some mysterious way, to serve as a bridge between the conscious and the unconscious, and thus to increase the power of the former over the latter.

Whence comes the repressive force (the censorship), and what is its nature ? In Freud's modern view, as we have seen, the repressive force belongs to the unconscious, and takes origin in the Œdipus complex,* so named after the myth of Œdipus, who unwittingly killed his own father Laius, and married his mother, Jocasta. Avoiding unduly crude and schematic formulations of this complex, one may describe the general psychological situation as follows. The young boy, in his earliest years, finds himself in relationship with two different kinds of people—one his mother or nurse, on whom he is dependent, from whom he receives help, and through whom his primitive needs are satisfied. He thus learns to love that person according to a special type of love—

---

* Freud writes : " This complex may be more or less strongly developed, or it may even become inverted, but it is a regular and very important factor in the mental life of a child ; we are more in danger of under-estimating than of over-estimating its influence, and that of the developments which may follow from it." (*Introductory Lectures on Psycho-analysis*, p. 175.)

the dependent type. But if there is a father, or someone occupying the place of a father, the relationship to that person is somewhat different. So far as he responds to the father with affection, that affection is predominantly of the identification type. The little boy, in loving and admiring his father, spontaneously identifies himself with his father. But, besides this, according to Freud's view, the dependent type of love for the mother calls out simultaneously a feeling of hostility to the father, a desire to have the mother all to himself, and not to share her with the father. So there arises a certain feeling of opposition to the father, a hostility which may not be very intense (although Freud seems prepared to regard it in its essence as very intense and even deadly in its aim). This comes into conflict with the boy's love, of the identification type, for his father. The little boy feels hostility towards his father, and at the same time feels what he imagines the father would feel in response to such hostility. He feels that the father would resent it and so he himself resents it and represses and checks these feelings of hostility in himself. In his earliest years the love for his father, of the identification type, means that he not only thinks of his father as resenting hostile feelings, but he himself resents those hostile feelings, and so his mind is divided against himself, and there is the beginning of conscience. There springs up in the boy's mind a rudiment of an ego-ideal, or what Freud now calls the " super-ego."†

---

† Freud's theory of the *Ueber-Ich* or super-ego is summed up in the following passage : " So kann man als allgemeinstes Ergebnis der vom Ödipuskomplex beherrschten Sexualphase einen Niederschlag im Ich annehmen, welcher in der Herstellung dieser beiden, irgendwie miteinander vereinbarten Identifizierungen besteht. Diese Ichveränderung behält ihre Sonderstellung, sie tritt dem anderen Inhalt des Ichs als Ichideal oder Über-Ich entgegen.

" Das Über-Ich ist aber nicht einfach ein Residuum der ersten Object-

It is this super-ego which is the repressing force, whose origin we have been seeking. Quite early in the child's life his libido, or sex energy, is directed towards his mother, but is repressed by his super-ego. And although these experiences may be in the earliest times conscious, later on they form part of the true unconscious, and that is how it is that the repressing factor, as well as the repressed factors, belongs to the unconscious, and not to the conscious (or pre-conscious).

Thus, Freud's general idea of personality is of a conscious ego between the upper and nether millstones of the super-ego and the repressed libido. The poor ego may find itself unable to hold its own against the claims of the repressed libido and the claims of the super-ego, and develop hysteria or obsessional neurosis or melancholia, according to its character and to the conditions of the case. The super-ego, developing directly out of the Œdipus situation, is the germ of conscience,* and in some cases of mental illness there may occur over-conscientiousness explicable in this way.

In some cases of analysis where, after a certain degree of progress, a stage is reached where things come to a dead stop and no further progress seems possible— although it used to be considered that such cases were due to excessive narcissism, excessive self-love, so that it was impossible to draw any more of the libido to the personality of the physician (i.e., to obtain further

---

wahlen des Es, sondern es hat auch die Bedeutung einer energischen Reaktionsbildung gegen dieselben. Seine Beziehung zum Ich erschöpft sich nicht in der Mahnung: So (wie der Vater) sollst du sein, sie umfasst auch das Verbot: So (wie der Vater) darfst du nicht sein d.h. nicht alles tun, was er tut; manches bleibt ihm vorbehalten." (*Das Ich und das Es*. Wien, 1923, S. 40.)

* Freud also brings in another psychological factor to explain this, viz., the *castration complex*, " the reaction to that intimidation in the field of sex, or to that restraint of early infantile sexual activity which is ascribed to the father." (*Introductory Lectures*, p. 175.)

" transference ")—in some such cases it may be (Freud now thinks) that the primitive conscience of the individual has been aroused and intensified. The patient feels that he does not deserve to get better, and it is this feeling which stands in the way of his recovery. Such a situation is extremely difficult to deal with analytically.

From the above account, it will be seen that Freud makes the Œdipus complex the kernel of personality. Within the unconscious the repressed libido is, to a great extent, the libido that is in earliest years directed towards the mother (or the father, in the case of the opposite sex); the beginning of the ideal of personality arises at the same period from the individual's idea of his father, from his identification with his father and love for his mother; and the beginning of psychical repression, the beginning of conscience, results from a conflict between the ego and the super-ego, the latter being that part of the individual's mind which is derived from the individual's idea of his father as a representative of the moral law. Thus, the beginnings of morality are to be found in the unconscious. Freud keeps to his view that consciousness itself does not matter, that the general relationship is one of determinism—a determinism which is practically mechanical.

In opposition to this, as an alternative view, I propound the following general theory: that the young child does model his character in relationship to the people about him, those for whom he feels affection, and that, as Freud says, this affection may be partly determined by dependence and partly by admiration. There is thus a tendency to love in these two ways, according to the principle of identification and according to the principle of dependence. But there need not necessarily be any strong feeling of jealousy, envy, hostility, or anything of that sort ever present in the young child's life. Under special conditions such feelings may arise. If they do, if a conflict of loyalties, as it may be called, occurs in very early years, that may serve as a beginning of a self-reproach within what later becomes the unconscious, and then that self-reproach may later on show itself in the form of irrational or unintelligible over-conscientiousness. But normal conscientiousness develops along different lines, namely, on the conscious level. Instead of looking for the beginnings of conscience in the unconscious, and explaining conscience and morality in terms of unconscious activity, I hold that, although forms of conscientiousness of a pathological nature may be explained in this way, through the conflict of loyalties that has not been adequately resolved in early years when character was still unformed, and so is left there as a problem—on the other hand, conscience is a definitely conscious product resulting from the ever deeper insight which the individual gains into his relationship to the social world around him—into the claims of society upon him, and his attitude towards it. Like volition, or will, so conscience is an essentially conscious thing. So far as the mind is free, it owes that freedom to its consciousness. Bergson considers that consciousness as such *is* freedom. The mere fact that an event is conscious means that it has a certain degree of spontaneity. But I have argued that the *organization* of conscious activity gives much more real freedom, working up that spontaneity into a form of self-determinism. Conscience is an important factor in self-determinism. It is the conscious feeling we have when we act, or contemplate acting, counter to the organization of our mind, when we surrender our freedom, or use it wrongly.

The view that identifications in early life are important for character formation is an extremely valuable one.

The individual in very early years does begin to develop an ideal of character, modelled upon those for whom he has great respect, admiration, and love. The further suggestion which is valuable in Freud is the conflict between the influence of the mother and of the father. One might put it in a different (and non-Freudian) way, avoiding the sexual emphasis. So far as the mother and father have different ideas about their children, so far as they have conflicting hopes and expectations for the child, and so far as the child is conscious of that, the child incorporates in itself the conflict, so that an outward conflict between the parents is incorporated in the child's mind. That is not at all the same theory as Freud's theory of the Œdipus complex. It is, nevertheless, doubtful whether anything so definite as the sexual factor in the Œdipus complex is supposed to be is invariably involved in early character formation.

As regards the sensory experiences of early childhood, it is important to note that, even within the first few months, incidents happen of importance to character. We find from the analysis of patients that it makes a great difference to the young child whether, e.g., it is brought up on the breast or on the bottle. Some analysts claim that they can tell beforehand whether their patients have been brought up in the one way or in the other. Anyhow, the explanation is that a child brought up on the bottle is denied a great deal of the sensory satisfaction, the feeling of contact with the mother's body, which seems to be important to it in its further development. This fondling by the mother, this contact with the mother in deriving nourishment in the earliest months, seems to be the natural means of drawing out what Freud calls the libido in its sensory form towards another person; and if the child is denied that and is brought up on the bottle, it tends to seek sensory satisfaction in its own person, whence arises the danger of auto-eroticism —getting sensory satisfaction from its own body. It is now urged that mothers who are unable to feed their children should, at any rate, nurse them ; that when the child is given the bottle, it should also have the sensory satisfaction of contact with the mother or the nurse. There seems some evidence that babies who are denied this, and, in a hard-hearted way, are left to themselves to get their nourishment from the bottle, are more likely to become self-centred, and run greater risks of developing certain bad habits later on, than the child brought up normally.

Another factor important in early life is the factor of fear.* It is quite obvious that causes of fear should be removed from the child's environment. Parents and others should never show fear in the presence of a young child. The latter cannot understand the cause of the fear, and responds to the fear all the more violently for that very reason. Tendencies towards irrational fear easily spring up under these conditions. Later on, when the child's intellect has developed sufficiently, it can be explained to him that certain acts and risks are dangerous and may do him harm. But even then it is doubtful whether it is wise to stimulate the fear instinct. This instinct is only too ready to be stimulated in any case, and as regards the development of character, probably the advice should always be in the other direction. One should always avoid giving occasion for the arousal of fear.

Then again, excessive stimulation of ambition, or of the self-assertive instinct, in early years is dangerous,

---

* The harmful possibilities inherent in the early stimulation of the instincts of self-preservation, self-assertion, and self-abasement have already been referred to in Chapter VI. Their importance is my excuse for re-stating them and enlarging upon them here.

because it may incorporate in the child's mind an ideal which he may find it too difficult to live up to, although such an ideal, if presented to him later on, at the age of, say, 12, 13 or 14, may be really helpful. It is helpful for a person to aim high, but if this ideal is presented to him and developed within his mind too early in his life, it forms part of his early unconscious tendencies, and from the cover of the unconscious may influence him in a compulsive and detrimental way. The evidence for this may be obtained from psycho-analysis. One finds in certain cases whom one has analysed that they have tried themselves too high without knowing it, and have become more and more discontented with themselves, and have criticized themselves ruthlessly in later life because of these early ambitions—ambitions which should not have belonged to them, but have come from their parents and others around them—e.g., from schoolmasters of private schools; not so much from masters at public schools, because a boy there is generally old enough to manage his own destiny; but if he has had constantly put before him in earlier years the possibility of very great achievements and of surpassing others, there is that at the back of his mind which produces excessive dissatisfaction when he is not succeeding.

Excessive stimulation of the instinct of self-abasement, or of self-depreciation, in early years is also detrimental, and may produce the so-called "inferiority complex." This may reveal itself later in the form of excessive and ill-judged self-assertiveness, alternating with moments of undue self-depreciation. But there are also many other ways in which this complex may reveal itself in conscious-ness. In the course of an analysis of one patient who suffered from bouts of depression, I found that she had shown excessive dependence upon her father in very early years, and had suffered from his excessive domination at that period of her life. He had hindered her from developing along the lines natural to her disposition, and had imposed upon her his own personality—which was over-cautious and over-critical—so that she had eventually lost all confidence in herself. After a prolonged course of analysis, combined with general encouragement to develop new interests and to get into practical touch with life once more, she made a complete recovery. She shed the false personality that had been imposed upon her by her father in those early years, with its false conscientiousness and excessive self-depreciation, and regained her own true personality. Indeed, one may look upon prolonged or " deep " analysis as a method of release, which liberates the personality from the distorting effects of some of its past experiences and allows it to appear in its true form, with a maximum degree of mental efficiency.

There seems to be plenty of evidence that repressive tendencies, springing up in early years, may lapse into unconsciousness, and yet, from the depths of the unconscious, may continue to exert influence upon the conscious personality. But so far as these repressive tendencies take the form of conscience, they are not true conscience. They belong to the pathological and not to the normal. One would refuse to explain the " categorical imperative " in terms of the Œdipus complex, as Freud does. The explanation of conscience which he gives us is an attempt to explain the science of ethics in terms of the science of psychology. As long as we keep the two sciences apart, we have in psychology ways of explaining how difficulties may arise in the fulfilment of the moral law, in the form both of excess of conscientiousness and of deficiency. But conscience and moral obligation cannot, as such, be explained in merely psychological terms.

Space allows only the briefest reference here to the views of two other outstanding scientists whose names are associated with the beginnings of the psycho-analytic movement.

" C. G. Jung and A. Adler have broken away from the direct Freudian line of thought, but any adequate description of their views is impossible in a short notice. Jung calls his method that of analytic psychology, and he emphasizes the special need of analysing the present situation of the patient, interpreting the past in the light of the present, quite as much as conversely. He does not accept the Freudian view of the sexual ætiology of the psycho-neuroses, and although he uses the word libido in his general theory, this means for him general psychic energy, not specifically sexual energy. His general theory is one of indeterminism in contrast with the rigid determinism of Freud.

" Alfred Adler emphasizes the important part played in the formation of nervous symptoms by the fundamental instinct of self-assertion—the will to power. In his view many neurotic symptoms are compensatory, representing the patient's (unsuccessful) striving ' to become a complete man '—that is the phrase he uses—and to hide his insufficiency from himself as well as from others. The patient constructs a safety net, as it were, around himself, so as to prevent his sensitive ego from being unduly pained by the consciousness of its inadequacy. Adler would explain many cases in which a sexual ætiology seems more obviously involved as really caused in this other way, through disturbance of the self-assertive instinct. The patient's self-assertive instinct cannot realize itself in ordinary ways, so it realizes itself in a roundabout way. All the time there is a tendency for the person to conceal from himself his own inadequacy, or to prevent himself from facing a situation where his

13

own inadequacy might become too obvious. He may become ill in order to escape having to face a task to which he knows he is inadequate. The feeling of inadequacy is translated into a feeling of illness. This inadequacy may show itself in the most various ways. Adler claims that the psychological essentials of a case may often be revealed in a single interview."*

---

* I quote from my article on " Psycho-therapy " in the Supplementary Volumes of the *Encyclopædia Britannica*, 13th Edition, 1926.

CHAPTER XVI

In the psycho-pathology of personality, a phenomenon which has always bulked large is the dissociation of personality. Pierre Janet's theory of dissociation is the obverse or complement of his theory that the normal personality is a unitary system of psycho-physical tendencies and powers, which may break up into its component parts under certain conditions. The type of mental dissociation which is most instructive is that found in hysteria.

" In extreme cases of hysteria, loss of memory and disintegration of personality may go so far as to produce either an alternation or a doubling of personality. Instances of this are a matter of common knowledge, and do not need detailed explanation and illustration here. Suffice it to say that they show all degrees of mental disaggregation, from mere alternation of mood and conflict of motive compatible with mental health to extreme cases where two souls seem to share the tenancy of one body. The best known recent example of the latter case is that of Miss Beauchamp, which Morton Prince has described with such a wealth of detail in his book *The Dissociation of a Personality*. This individual was at a certain stage of her life possessed of three distinct personalities or centres of consciousness. Two of these alternated with one another, each retaining her own series of memories, but amnesic for the experiences of the other, while the third, the now notorious ' Sally Beauchamp,' not only had a separate consciousness of her own, with a cheerful and irresponsible temperament quite alien to those of the others, but claimed that even when not alternating with them she had direct knowledge of the thoughts, feelings, and even the dreams of one of them. Morton Prince eventually cured Miss Beauchamp by hypnotism, suppressing ' Sally ' entirely, and re-synthesizing the other two personalities with their separate memories and experiences into a normal individual similar to the original personality as she had been before the emotional shock which was the cause of all the trouble.

" More recently Morton Prince has met with another case of dissociated personality quite as remarkable as that of Miss Beauchamp, and closely similar in several respects. He calls her B C A.* C is the normal personality as she was before and after her mental illness, and B and A are the two dissociated personalities into which she disintegrated as the eventual result of several years of severe nervous and emotional strain. B and A alternated with one another, but whereas A had no direct knowledge of B's existence, B was immediately aware of A's thoughts and memories even when herself in abeyance. B and C also shared each other's memories as well as those of A, but A was entirely shut up within her own circle of memories and experiences. Neither C nor A remembered her own dreams, but β, the hypnotic personality corresponding to B, was able to recall the dreams of both. A was neurasthenic and represented the ethical and religious aspects of the original personality. She lived in a continual mental atmosphere of gloomy and apprehensive conscientiousness, and was appalled by the freakish and irresponsible behaviour of B, who lived only for pleasure, was completely egoistic and ' emancipated,' and during her periods of alternation enjoyed

* See *Journal of Abnormal Psychology*, vcl. iii., 1908–09, *passim*.

the most robust health. B thus showed a close resemblance to ' Sally ' in the Beauchamp case, and the importance of this resemblance will perhaps be clearer when we consider it in the light of Freud's theory of hysteria. We may note that B was co-conscious with A, or existed simultaneously as a subconsciousness, in Janet's sense of that term. Morton Prince was able to prove this in various ways, apart from the statements of B herself and of her hypnotic personality β. One illustration will suffice. It was arranged with β (unknown to A) that she should add together certain figures while A was present, and should show that she really had carried out the operation co-consciously by giving the answer immediately upon A being changed to β. She, of course, was not told what actual figures would be given. A was then brought and was asked to write out some lines of poetry in the middle of a large sheet of paper ($8\frac{1}{2}'' \times 11''$), in the left-hand upper corner of which was written the number 53, and in the right-hand lower corner the number 61. A repeated aloud what she was writing and commented upon her mistakes of memory, showing that she was alert and not in a somnambulistic state. On being questioned afterwards she averred that she had noticed no other writing, such as numbers, on the paper. It had appeared quite blank. Even if she had noticed the numbers she would not have known what was to be done with them, since she is amnesic for B and β. A was changed to β. ' Immediately on appearing β exclaimed, almost shouted: " 114," which is correct.' More complicated arithmetical calculations were carried out under similar circumstances with equal success.

" Certain memories of the patient's earlier years, which were lost to all the personalities even in hypnosis, were recovered by automatic writing. In this way it was discovered that her irrational fear of cats took origin from an incident of her childhood, when she was intensely frightened by a white cat she was holding having a fit. Her dreams were frequently of cats, accompanied by a feeling of intense horror."*

In the earlier history of Freudian doctrine we find Freud explaining the dissociation of personality in terms of mental conflict and repression. Certain parts of the mind split off from the rest because of incompatibility with the main parts. In Freud's recent work, *Das Ich und das Es*, he makes the further suggestion that the foundation of dissociation of the personality may well be looked for in the early tendencies of individuals to identify themselves with different types of character. Such various identifications may not be in full harmony with one another, and so tend to fall apart. The individual may identify himself with Napoleon or the martyrs, or St. Francis, and he certainly has a strong tendency to identify himself with his father and mother. And in cases where these characters are different, especially where there is strife at home, the strife is internalized in him. He takes the family strife into the depths of his own character. There is a lack of at-one-ness which may not be apparent in earlier years, but which may show itself later when he has to choose a career and face the problems of adult life.

The general trend of all psychological discussions of personality is in terms of multiplicity—looking for unity as a result of interaction between the many, instead of regarding the unity as something ultimate. This theory is not a proved fact. We always have before us the opposite possibility that the mind may be a unity from the earliest times, but that under the influence of conflict and strife, and the conflicting claims of one's

---

* I have quoted these paragraphs from my book, *Psychology and Psychotherapy*. Edward Arnold and Co., 1921.

environment, lack of unity is introduced into the personality. The problem to decide in the end is as to which is the more ultimate, unity or multiplicity. The unity of the developed adult mind is to a great extent an acquired unity. But we have further to ask the question whether that acquired unity, the result of training, centres round an ultimate unity or an ultimate multiplicity. Undoubtedly we are multiple as well as unitary, but the feeling of unity is certainly there at every moment of consciousness. Although there is multiplicity there is also unity, and often a person who is alienated from himself and feels " beside himself," can only feel " beside himself " because he is a unity. If he were not a self he would be unable to feel alienated from himself. From day to day our mood changes, we pass through stages of unconsciousness, but we wake up to a feeling of some identity with our past. A materialist would say that this is a simple consequence of the identity of the body. Not so ; we pass in the argument to identity of the body from identity of the self.

We can say that nothing in psycho-pathology forces us to surrender a belief in the unity hypothesis. We cannot say that the unity is proved, but it remains not only a possibility but a probability. A mind is one from the start, but although its aspects then are fewer than they become in later life, and in old age they may seem to diminish, there is the possibility that the self is something beyond the phenomenal, owing its apparent multiplicity to the conditions of its physical existence, but able in its unity to survive bodily death. We simply do not know. If psychical research could prove the survival of character and personal identity it would greatly increase our belief in the unitary nature of the self. One often finds people saying that researches in personality prove that the mind is not a unity, but those who study these cases closely at first hand are the first to admit that the multiplicity is less fundamental than the unity. Although there may be a break in the memory, so that when the person is in one psychological state he has no access to memories to which in another state he has access, that is not derogatory to the reality of his unity. We observe the same in the most normal person, who finds from day to day the scope of his memory varying. On certain occasions he finds certain memories associated with certain interests very readily accessible to him, and others accessible with difficulty or not at all. The fact that we can say these interests are not in harmony with one another in ourselves shows that there is an underlying unity. If we set one desire, ambition, and mood against another, and realize their incompatibility, in that very process we are forming or rather emphasizing an underlying unity.

Theoretically, at any rate, all the probabilities are in favour of ultimate unity. We are told to watch a young child and see how slight a unity there is. The child's interest flits from one thing to another, he passes from laughter to tears, is ready to forget what has occurred a moment ago; but the fact that he can gradually synthesize these moods and hold in the unity of his consciousness a larger and larger field of psychological tendencies and make it into a system, shows that there is something there beyond and at the back of his experience. The experiences do not come together of their own accord and join up into a unity. One can observe plainly the work of association, but as one observes that, one is forced to contrast it with the deeper and more thorough-going forms of unification of the mind, and recognize in spite of our changes that there is and has always been a continuity. If we turn to the animal world we may prefer to say with William James that the only unity is the unity of the " passing thought " that connects what has gone before with what comes after. " Every thought is born an owner and dies owned," to quote James's phrase. That is not convincing. If we start from that we cannot understand the higher unities of the mind. And indeed it seems to me that the results of psycho-analysis itself show an underlying thorough-going unity. The patient's mental development has been distorted, twisted by different forces or conflicting influences, and under analysis he gets free from these influences, and yet there is something left behind—the more normal self. The person becomes more normal because there was a normal unitary self all through. Though there was a tendency to multiplicity, the analysis itself has diminished that. And we might go further and say that even the person who has to spend his last years of life in an asylum in a completely alienated state of mind may hope to regain his freedom and real self at death. Although psycho-analysis is not capable of undoing the facts of heredity, yet this twisting and strain is a matter of the mind and body rather than of the mind itself.

If the reader has followed what I have been trying to express, he will realize that this is certainly my own view. The perfectly normal mind is in direct relationship to the world about it ; its perceptions and its appreciations of value are direct revelations. It is through stress and strain in the physical organism that it gets a distorted view of things and is kept back from adequate apprecia-tion of beauty and truth. Although the body seems to serve as an instrument to bring the individual into relationship with those realities, it may be quite as much something that stands in his way. Difficulties are produced in the body. The body working at its best is an instrument which reveals to him a reality outside, and in doing so it does not make any contribution itself. The person whose brain is working quite normally is not conscious of the different organs of his body. It is often said that the *joie de vivre* of a perfectly healthy normal person is based on organic sensations from the smooth functioning of the body. This is a possibility but by no means a certainty. We are not forced to accept a view like that. The genuine pleasure of being really in touch with things may be a purely mental feeling.

Nothing that we can learn from physiology and biology prevents us from believing in mental entities in relation with physical structures. Take an extreme case. Take the case of the feeble-minded, of idiots. There the general doctrine is that it is a deficiency, a lack of certain parts of the brain, so that a person is unable to live a full and complete life. Certain ranges of existence are withheld from him. He is unable to pass beyond the most primitive level of morality or intelligence. But the same situation is explicable in terms of a faulty instrument. Through lack of some power of the instrument, other parts of the instrument are not able to function, and so the mind cannot get into adequate touch with the external world. Why a person should be abnormalized in that way is, of course, a serious problem.

While considering the pathological and the normal, we have borne in upon us the parallelism between pathological states and corresponding normal states. Take the higher and lower states of mysticism. There is a form of mystical experience which is pathological as well as one which is pre-eminently normal; such is the mystical experience of the hysterical, who sees pictures in the clouds, etc. The individual is not in direct communion with ultimate reality, but suffers from a disturbance of the instrument which should bring him into touch with reality. In all true religious experience it looks very much as if we come into touch with the spirit of the universe within ourselves rather than outside ourselves. Each one of us is in direct relationship through his own subconscious with the divine, and our view of religion is blurred and obscured by our complexes, the twists in our character, and the unfortunate experiences that disturb our belief. That is the reason why analysis and autognosis will increase a person's power of experiencing genuine religious feeling. A patient will tell one that after a time in the course of his psychotherapy he has re-acquired the power of prayer that he had lost.

Here, again, one is always confronted with the alternative possibility that religion is an infantile thing,—primitive, undeveloped,—and that in analysis a person is taken back to his childhood, to primitive credulity, to the trustfulness of the young child which is undeveloped and needs to be corrected by experience. Surely we can allow for that, and admit that there is infantilism in religion as experienced by the ordinary man which stands in the way of his clear religious vision, and yet hold that true religion itself dates back to the earliest years. It is the trustfulness and faith of the young child—call it primitive credulity if you like,—not merely ideomotor action but a direct awareness. The child is aware of something beyond itself even in its earliest years. That may later on through experience become suppressed, and with analysis may come back. I am strongly against any criticism of psychoanalysis from the point of view of the risk of its endangering religious belief. When carried out by inexperienced or otherwise unsuitable people there may be some danger ; but if carried out with due regard to the needs of the situation, there is none.

PERSONALITY AND ETHICS

(I)—PLATO AND ARISTOTLE

(CHAPTER XVII)

(II)—MORAL VALUES

(CHAPTER XVIII)

CHAPTER XVII

THE history of men's views on the nature of the emotions
or passions is part of the history of ethical speculation in
general, and as it is only within the last few decades
(with several prominent exceptions) that the psychological problem has been attacked for its own sake and
with a minimum of reference to its ethical aspect, so it
is only in the most recent years that moralists are finding
it necessary to set themselves once more the question,
What is the significance and importance of the emotions
in the formulation of the moral ideal ?

Practical needs must have instituted, and language
fixed, many distinctions in the conception of the life of
feeling in quite primitive times ; but if one turns to the
earliest known forms of philosophical speculation, the
ancient philosophies of India, one finds the emotions
and morality there related to one another in a merely
negative way. Individual life, the life of the emotions
and desires, is considered to be full of pain and misery,
of vice and worthlessness. The only right rule of conduct
is that which attempts the suppression of all desires, and
chiefly of the desire for life itself, from which all miseries
flow, so that the individual " Atman " may at length
escape the wheel of continual re-births and lose himself
in the universal passionless existence of Brahma, the
substance of the cosmos. In pre-Buddhistic times the
way of salvation advocated was asceticism or self-martyr-
dom of the most rigorous kind, an asceticism directed
not only against the body but also, and much more

especially, against the soul, in order to eradicate every desire or tendency to desire and so eventually to bring about its complete annihilation as an individual existence.

Gautama, the founder of Buddhism, changed, not the end of action, but the means to that end. Recognizing the futility of mere bodily asceticism and its impracticability as a universal course of conduct, he advocated greater attention to the suppression of desires at their source, within the mind itself, and preached the doctrine of humility and universal benevolence. In such wise, by more and more complete renunciation of the will to live, the soul at length entered Nirvana, a state marking the end of all its wearisome transmigrations.

In Greece, the earliest attempt to give a rational account of ethical laws and ethical practice is connected with the name of Socrates. Nevertheless, apart from the remarkable moral example set by his manner of life and death, the method of inductive enquiry which he inaugurated, and the profound impression made by both upon the mind of his brilliant pupil Plato, his positive doctrine that virtue is knowledge and that the good is the useful would set him but a little way ahead of the sophists of his time, among whom he was not altogether unjustly classed. Since complete knowledge carries with it *eo ipso* correct action, any scientific description and classification of the primitive impulses and passions are superfluous for his system. Ethically considered, they all fall into the same class as being naturally submissive to right reason.

Plato follows his master closely in the formal side of his ethical theory, and provides a metaphysical support for the identity of virtue and knowledge in his doctrine of ideas, in which the idea of the good is given the place of honour as the *fons et origo* of all the rest. On the material side, he has recourse to psychological analysis, and divides the human soul into three parts or faculties, viz. : (1) τὸ λογιστικόν, the rational part, (2) τὸ θυμοειδές, the spirited part, (3) τὸ ἐπιθυμητικόν, the appetitive part. He arrives at this classification on the principle that wherever there is *conflict* in the soul, the two elements at conflict are really distinct psychological elements. Thus, when the appetite of thirst is checked, that which checks it, *e.g.*, reason, is a different element from that which thirsts. Despite a superficial resemblance, there is really little analogy between this classification and the modern tripartite division of consciousness into cognition, conation, and feeling. The spirited principle and the appetitive principle each involve both conation and feeling, nor can they exist without cognition. Even to say that conation and feeling are respectively predominant in the mental processes corresponding to these two parts would not be entirely true.

Each of these parts of the soul has its own particular excellence or virtue ; that of the rational part is wisdom, φρόνησις or σοφία, that of the spirited part valour, ἀνδρεία, and that of the appetitive part temperance or moderation, σωφροσύνη. In the conflicts of the soul the spirited part, which is the basis of such affections as anger, sense of honour, etc., usually sides with reason against appetite, and indeed should be expected to do so. Its virtue, therefore, is higher than that of appetite, the latter consisting solely of submission to reason. Spirit (θυμός) is both subject and ally of reason ; appetite is subject only.

The union of these three virtues in correct proportions constitutes a fourth virtue of the soul, viz., justice, δικαιοσύνη. Since, however, man's chief good can only be attained within a state, Plato describes an ideal community where the three psychological elements of the individual man are represented, " on a larger scale," by three classes of citizens, the rulers and educators, the

14

warriors, and the craftsmen and agriculturists. Each class is to possess its own particular virtue—wisdom, courage, or temperance, as the case may be—and justice within the community implies each citizen and each class of citizens doing its own work and not meddling in that of others. It is to be noted that members of the third class, the craftsmen and agriculturists, are denied the virtues of wisdom and valour, and are supposed capable of temperance only. This pronounced sub-ordination of the individual moral end to the more universal end of the state, which is worked out in such detail in the *Republic*, is to a great extent abandoned in the *Laws*, where class distinctions are less emphasized and wisdom recedes somewhat in favour of moderation or temperance as the essence of moral activity.

The need and importance of the process of *habituation* in producing established virtue, although generally regarded as one of the advances made by Aristotle upon earlier views of morality, was thoroughly appreciated by Plato. Among several passages in which this view is explicitly stated, the following sentence from the *Republic* (444 c.) possesses a special interest as being expressed in almost the same words as those used by Aristotle, *Nic. Eth.*, Bk. II. It runs : Οὐκοῦν καὶ τὸ μὲν δίκαια πράττειν δικαιοσύνην ἐμποιεῖ, τὸ δ' ἄδικα ἀδικίαν; 'Ανάγκη. ["In the same way, does not the performance of just acts beget the virtue of justice, and the performance of unjust acts the vice of injustice ? Inevitably."] The distinction between " civic " and " philosophic " virtue also turns upon the fact that habituation is of itself sufficient to produce the former.

In the philosophy of Aristotle ethics is, to a very great extent, if not entirely, separated from metaphysics and based almost exclusively upon psychological data. The new concept of *will* is introduced and the importance of habituation or practice is emphasized. Adopting the Platonic distinction of the rational and irrational parts of the soul, Aristotle proceeds to give a greatly improved analysis of each of these elements. He calls them that which possesses reason (λόγον ἔχον) and that which partakes of reason (λόγου μετέχον), respectively. In the case of the latter he over-rides the distinction of θυμός and ἐπιθυμία and replaces it by a remarkably detailed and accurate analysis of the passions. This, the first scientific account of the passions to be found in literature, is given in the *Rhetoric*, Book II.* Passion is here defined as follows : " Passions are all emotions whatsoever on which pain and pleasure are consequent, by whose operation, undergoing a change, men differ in respect to their decisions : for instance, anger, pity, fear, and whatsoever other emotions are of such a nature, and those opposed to them." The complete list is : Anger, Placability ; Love and Friendliness, Enmity and Hatred ; Fear, Confidence (or Assurance) ; Shame, Impudence ; Benevolence (χάρις) ; Pity, Indignation ; Envy, Emulation. With the exception of χάρις, these passions exist in pairs of opposites.

Of each of them three things may be considered : (1) *How* men are affected, (2) *towards whom*, (3) *for what*.

Anger is a painful desire for revenge, arising from injury to oneself or one's friends. It is not entirely painful, however, since " there is a sort of pleasure consequent on all anger, arising out of the hope of avenging oneself." It is felt against individuals, not against the species.

Placability : " A subsiding and appeasement of anger," felt towards the repentant, the humble, the angry, those who are attentive to us, and those whom we fear. The

---

* The quotations that follow are taken from Buckley's translation (Bohn's Series).

last of these is emphasized by the statement that " it is impossible to feel anger and fear at the same time "—a view which is surely only correct, if at all, in cases of intense excitement of these passions.

Love or *Friendliness* is " the wishing a person what we think good, for his sake and not for our own, and, as far as is in our power, the exerting ourselves to procure it."

Hatred is the opposite of love, and is caused by anger, annoyance or vexatiousness, and calumny. It differs from anger in six respects : (1) anger is limited to injuries affecting oneself, directly or indirectly, hatred is not ; (2) anger is felt towards individuals only, hatred may be felt towards whole classes ; (3) time allays anger, but not hatred ; (4) anger merely desires to inflict pain, hatred to do deadly injury ; (5) anger is accompanied by pain, hatred is not ; (6) anger may eventually be followed by pity for the misfortunes of its object, hatred never. Hatred " desires the extinction of the object of hate."

Fear is " a sort of pain or agitation, arising out of an idea that an evil, capable either of destroying or giving pain, is impending on us." The objects which occasion it are danger, injustice, insulted virtue invested with power, *the fear of our enemies*, accomplices, the wronged, rivals, the mild and dissembling (which are more to be feared than the hasty).

Confidence or *Assurance* is the opposite of fear, and inspired by the opposite of what occasions fear.

Shame is " a kind of pain and agitation about evils present, past, or to come, which appear to tend to loss of reputation." The objects which occasion it are cowardice, intemperance, meanness, adulation, vanity.

Impudence is " a sort of callousness " about these things.

Benevolence (χάρις) is " that conformably to which he who has the power is said to confer a benefit on one who needs it, not in return for anything, nor in order that anything may accrue to him who so confers it, but that some benefit may arise to the object." This definition should be compared with that of love.

Pity is " a sort of pain occasioned by an evil capable of hurting or destroying, appearing to befal one who does not deserve it, which one may himself expect to endure, or that some one connected with him will; and this when it appears near." It must be distinguished from *horror*, which has a tendency to expel pity and produce a contrary effect.

This definition of pity is followed closely by Hobbes in the Leviathan, where he says : " Grief for the calamity of another is *pity*, and ariseth from the imagination that the like calamity may befal himself." Pity and fear are in fact excited by the same objects in relation to another and oneself respectively.

Indignation is opposed to pity. Whereas pity is felt towards the undeservedly unfortunate, indignation is aroused by undeserved good fortune.

Envy, which is also opposed to pity, differs from indignation in being aroused by the good fortune of the deserving. Persons likely to be envied are : equals, rivals, the successful, and those whose success is a tacit reproach to ourselves.

Emulation is " a sort of pain at the apparent presence of goods which are held in honour, and which admit of one's gaining them himself, in the case of those naturally our equals ; felt, not because they are present to *another*, but because they are *not likewise* present to oneself." Hence emulation is naturally or essentially a virtuous passion, whereas envy is essentially vicious.

(*a*) The persons likely to feel emulation are : the young and high-spirited, those enjoying the esteem of their fellows, those with worthy relatives or ancestors.

(*b*) The persons likely to be objects of emulation are : those whom one admires or desires to resemble.

(*c*) The things likely to be objects of emulation are : virtues, goods, wealth, etc.

Contempt is the opposite of emulation.

It may be observed that the detailed descriptions of the passions which he gives are all in terms of pain and pleasure,* supplemented by statements of occasions and causes which are not always strictly psychological in nature.

This view of the emotions, viz., that psychologically considered they consist merely of pleasures and pains, has persisted almost down to our own times.

Again, Aristotle nowhere says whether these passions are to be regarded as equally primitive and simple or subordinated one to another in complexity. On his theory of their psychological nature the question could not arise.

A slightly different list of the emotions or passions occurs in the *Nicomachean Ethics*, Bk. II., Ch. v., §2, where he says† " I mean by passions, desire, anger, fear, boldness, envy, joy, friendliness, hatred, longing, emulation, pity ; in short, everything that is accompanied by pleasure or pain." This is a loose enumeration given merely as an illustration of the meaning of πάθος. Desire and longing are obviously not co-ordinate with the others as states of consciousness.

In this same passage the important distinction is drawn between πάθος and δύναμις, a distinction which is almost identical with the modern one between " emotion " and " emotional disposition." Thus Aristotle writes : " I

---

* *Cf. Nicom. Eth.*, Bk. II., Ch. v., 2. λέγω δὲ πάθη . . . ὅλως οἷς ἕπεται ἡδονὴ ἢ λύπη.

† The following quotations are taken from the translations in the notes of Sir Alexander Grant's edition of the *Nicomachean Ethics*.

call those *faculties* (or dispositions, δυνάμεις) by reason of which we are said to be capable of feeling emotions, as, for instance, capable of being angry, of suffering pain, of feeling pity," and he proceeds to describe a third element or category of the mind, ἕξεις, (states or habits) " according to which we stand in a certain relation, good or bad, to the emotions ; as, for instance, with regard to anger, we are in a bad condition if our anger is too violent, or too slack, in a good one, if we hit the happy mean." Perhaps the difference between this and the preceding element might be stated in modern termino-logy as an antithesis between " acquired " and " innate " dispositions.‡ The parallels, however, in this and in the previous case are of doubtful applicability, since modern psychology has drawn its distinctions along slightly different lines.

With ἕξις we have reached the proper subject of moral judgments. 'Αρετή, virtue or excellence, is a ἕξις, a state or disposition of the mind, produced by habitua-tion through the activity of the will or deliberative choice (προαίρεσις §), in accordance with reason. The *material* of moral activity, then, is the whole gamut of the emotions or the emotional dispositions, and the moral activity or virtue is separate and distinct in each separate case—although Aristotle's superficial identification of emotions with pleasures and pains supplies him with a common denominator, as it were, in terms of which he might have built up a hedonistic system‖ which would have slurred over these distinctions, an error from which he is saved by a moral insight rising superior to his psychological theory.

‡ *Nicom. Eth.*, II., 5. δυνατοὶ μέν ἐσμεν φύσει.
§ προαίρεσις = βουλευτικὴ ὄρεξις τῶν ἐφ' ἡμῖν: deliberative appetition of things in our power.
‖ *Nicom. Eth.*, II., iii., 1. περὶ ἡδονὰς γὰρ καὶ λύπας ἐστὶν ἡ ἠθικὴ ἀρετή.

The *formal* characteristic which makes them all identical as virtue is given in his doctrine of the mean (μεσότης). The virtue corresponding to any particular emotion or emotional disposition is a mean state which avoids both excess and deficiency, both the too much and the too little ; not a mere objective quantitative mean, the arithmetic mean of two fixed upper and lower limits of intensity of the emotion, but a subjective qualitative mean relative to the character and circumstances of the agent. Thus the emotions of fear and daring, when occurring in excess, exhibit the vices of cowardice and rashness respectively, when in defect vices, anonymous in the first case and cowardice in the second, but when occurring with a medium intensity which avoids both of these extremes and is correctly adjusted to all the circumstances of the case, exhibit the virtue of courage. ὁ μὲν οὖν ἃ δεῖ καὶ οὗ ἕνεκα ὑπομένων καὶ φοβούμενος, καὶ ὡς δεῖ καὶ ὅτε, ὁμοίως δὲ καὶ θαρρῶν, ἀνδρεῖος· κατ' ἀξίαν γάρ, καὶ ὡς ἂν ὁ λόγος, πάσχει καὶ πράττει ὁ ἀνδρεῖος. *N.E.*, III., vii. 5.

Virtue is summarily defined in *N.E.*, II., vi. 15 as " that quality of the will which preserves the mean suitably to our nature, conformably to a reasonable definition, such as the man of insight would give."* It is reason, then, which fixes the mean, but this reason is practical, not theoretical ; it involves insight and judgment in the realm of particular facts, knowledge of the end to be aimed at in particular cases and also in conduct in general ; knowledge, too, of the means necessary to realize that end. Its excellence or virtue is φρόνησις, prudence or insight, an *intellectual* virtue, as contrasted with the *moral* virtues hitherto considered, embodied in

---

* Zeller's translation of the following passage : ἔστιν ἄρα ἡ ἀρετὴ ἕξις προαιρετική, ἐν μεσότητι οὖσα τῇ πρὸς ἡμᾶς, ὡρισμένῃ λόγῳ καὶ ὡς ἂν ὁ φρόνιμος ὁρίσειεν.

the φρόνιμος or man of insight. The φρόνιμος is the man who has acquired through moral experience a kind of moral " taste " (analogous to æsthetic taste), a sense of the moral fitness or unfitness of forms of conduct ; who is, as it were, the living criterion of moral activity. Although tradition, education, and training help to account for this virtue, they do not entirely explain it, and Aristotle has not quite escaped the charge of circular reasoning often levelled at him in regard to this view of φρόνησις and the φρόνιμος. Indeed, he may be not unjustly claimed as a supporter of *intuitionism*, since his description corresponds better to the purification, by experience, of a moral insight which had always been present as an essential potentiality of the human soul, than to a production of it from experiences and activities which do not themselves presuppose it.

Of the list of individual virtues which Aristotle draws up, the two at the head, courage and temperance, are based upon the animal nature of man as opposed to his social nature, δοκοῦσι γὰρ τῶν ἀλόγων μερῶν αὗται εἶναι αἱ ἀρεταί (III., x. 1). Courage is a μεσότης περὶ φόβους καὶ θάρρη, and is peculiarly related to the perils of war. It must include nobleness of purpose ; " to the brave man courage is something morally beautiful. Of this nature, then, must be the end of courage, for it is the end of a thing which in each case determines its character. Therefore the beautiful is the end for the sake of which the brave man endures and does whatever is brave."† In the course of the discussion on this virtue occurs the important passage, οὐ δὴ ἐν ἁπάσαις ταῖς ἀρεταῖς τὸ ἡδέως ἐνεργεῖν ὑπάρχει, πλὴν ἐφ' ὅσον τοῦ τέλους ἐφάπτεται (III., ix. 5): " it is not the case that in all the virtues virtuous action is accompanied by pleasure, save in so far as he attains the end." Aristotle in this case seems definitely to place

---

† *Nicom. Eth.*, III., vii., 6. Sir A. Grant's translation.

the idea of τοῦ καλοῦ ἕνεκα higher than the mere material
success, discounted by physical pain, etc., in his conception of the ἡδύ constituting the end of virtue.
In Bk. III., ch. viii. occurs an enumeration and description of five spurious forms of courage (ἕτεραι κατὰ πέντε
τρόπους), produced by (1) regard for reputation among
one's fellows, (2) knowledge and previous experience of
the particular danger, (3) anger, (4) light-hearted confidence, (5) ignorance of the danger.* Anger (θυμός) is
singled out as being most closely related to genuine
courage : φυσικωτάτη δ᾽ ἔοικεν ἡ διὰ τὸν θυμὸν εἶναι, καὶ
προσλαβοῦσα προαίρεσιν καὶ τὸ οὗ ἕνεκα ἀνδρεία εἶναι. Sir
A. Grant comments on this whole passage as follows :
" It is remarkable on what a high level Aristotle places
courage. It must be entirely, he says, prompted by a
desire for what is morally beautiful (οἱ μὲν οὖν ἀνδρεῖοι διὰ
τὸ καλὸν πράττουσιν) ; mere physical courage is only an
assistance in realising this (ὁ δὲ θυμὸς συνεργεῖ αὐτοῖς), and
the prompting of anger, etc., will make men pugnacious,
but not brave. . . . Perhaps Aristotle makes almost too
great a separation between true courage and this ' spirited
element,' which must be its physical basis. This is to
be attributed (1) to his high moral tone, (2) to his analytical mode of treatment." This contrast between the
lofty moral end of courage and the narrow restriction
of its sphere of application among the psychological
" springs of action " is very striking, and would be rather
surprising did we not bear in mind Aristotle's ground
principle of connecting particular virtues with particular
and mutually exclusive tendencies of the soul, and the
limitations imposed upon him by language and the
public opinion of his time and country. Here, as in so
many other cases, his desire to improve on Plato has led

* See Plato's *Protagoras* 351 A, for an anticipation of some of these
distinctions : ἀπὸ τέχνης . . . καὶ ἀπὸ θυμοῦ τε καὶ ἀπὸ μανίας.

him to prefer definiteness and precision of system to the attempt to do justice to a (then) so vague "promise and potency" of human nature which in later times developed into what is generally known as "moral" courage.

Temperance is the virtue which preserves the mean with regard to bodily as distinguished from mental pleasures, being restricted to the sphere of eating, drinking and sex. Although this conception of its nature and scope, which Aristotle sanctions in agreement with the spirit of his time, is based primarily upon the prudential considerations of health and self-control, Aristotle's account shows a clear recognition of the importance of subordinating lower to higher ends whenever conflict occurs. Its ultimate motive, as that in the case of all the other virtues, is the realization of human nature, and in this sense, as T. H. Green has shown, it is formally unimpeachable and points to as high an ideal as the moral sense and moral experience of the time admitted of being conceived.

The remaining virtues have more strict reference to the social environment of the individual. Briefly enumerated they are: liberty,[1] munificence,[2] highmindedness,[3] an unnamed virtue which is the mean state between ambition and lack of ambition, mildness,[4] truthfulness,[5] versatility,[6] friendliness,[7] modesty,[8] indignation,[9] and justice.[10] Of these, modesty and indignation (a mean between envy and malice) are not, strictly speaking, virtues at all. They are mean states of the passions— ἐν τοῖς πάθεσι καὶ ἐν τοῖς περὶ τὰ πάθη μεσότητες†—not of developed attitudes of mind or ἕξεις. The others, taken in order, are mean states in respect of spending or giving

---

[1] ἐλευθεριότης.   [2] μεγαλοπρέπεια.   [3] μεγαλοψυχία.   [4] πραότης.
[5] ἀλήθεια. [6] εὐτραπελία. [7] φιλία. [8] αἰδώς. [9] νέμεσις. [10] δικαιοσύνη.
† *Nicom. Eth.*, II., vii., 14.

money, on a small and large scale respectively (1 and 2),
self-respect, love of honour, temper (ὀργή), social deport-
ment (5, 6, and 7). Finally, justice occupies a place by
itself. Two forms of it are recognized, viz., " distri-
butive " justice and " corrective " (or adjustive) justice,
and the proportionate distribution of goods and penalties
is forced rather violently into the general scheme of
the mean.*

It was mentioned above (p. 216) that φρόνησις, one of
the so-called intellectual virtues, fixes the mean in each
case, and determines the steps to be taken in order to
attain it. This virtue gives unity to the plurality of the
individual moral virtues and guarantees the coherence
of the moral system. Aristotle will not, however, accept
without qualification the Socratic view that virtue is
knowledge. Knowledge is indispensable to complete
moral virtue, but virtue is dependent on more than
knowledge in the ordinary acceptation of the word.
This is shown by the phenomenon of ἀκρασία or incon-
tinence, where the agent knows the right and approves
of it as right, but does the wrong. " Video meliora
proboque, deteriora sequor." Aristotle's solution of this
problem, which is generally known as the *moral paradox*,
is based upon an appeal to the distinction between
actualized and latent knowledge. " The knowledge at
such moments is not really actualized in the mind ; it
is reduced by appetite or passion to a condition of
latency."†

Aristotle draws a clear distinction between the practical
and the theoretical life, between action and contempla-

---

* It is interesting to contrast the Greek conception of justice, which
has been summed up in the phrase " equals to the equal " (ἴσα τοῖς
ἴσοις), with that of a modern reformer : " To everyone according to his
need, from everyone according to his power."

† Henry Sidgwick : *History of Ethics*, 5th Edition, 1902, Macmillan
and Co., p. 70.

tion (θεωρία), as represented in the lives of the statesman and the philosopher. He decides unhesitatingly in favour of the latter, as the highest life that man can lead, and nearest to Godliness. Οὐ χρὴ δὲ κατὰ τοὺς παραινοῦντας ἀνθρώπινα φρονεῖν ἄνθρωπον ὄντα οὐδὲ θνητὰ τὸν θνητόν, ἀλλ᾿ ἐφ᾿ ὅσον ἐνδέχεται ἀθανατίζειν. *N.E.* X., vii. 8. We cannot entirely escape the " practical " life, but we should so organize it that we may achieve the fullest possible measure of " contemplation "—that we may " as far as possible live immortally." Immortality is not something to be awaited at the end of life, but can be achieved *now*, so far as we live the life of θεωρία.

CHAPTER XVIII

It might perhaps be expected that in passing from the psychological to the more strictly ethical aspects of personality we should devote special attention to a consideration of the origins of the so-called moral emotions. By these are generally meant the altruistic emotions, of which the typical instance is Benevolence. Some scientists even go so far as to state categorically that "Moral conduct is social conduct." This is a mere blunder. Morality is concerned with all forms of conduct and all forms of individual experience. The origin of some of these forms may be more apparent than that of others; although natural selection would seem capable of explaining altruistic tendencies, or tendencies subservient to the welfare of the tribe, clan, or species, quite as readily as those subserving the welfare of the individual. Our central problem, however, is to investigate the *value* of present-day human consciousness, and for this purpose the general theory of the sentiments together with an insight into the way in which these sentiments arise and form a complex conative and emotional system or developed character, are of more help than a knowledge of the origin of altruistic emotions, whether they have their source in the parental instinct or in the gregarious instinct or in some other primitive tendency. E. Westermarck, in his monumental work on *The Origin and Development of the Moral Ideas*, devotes many pages to a discussion of what he terms the "moral emotions." These emotions are, according to him, the emotions of moral approval and disapproval, which are respectively related to Anger and Revenge on the one side, and

Gratitude and other forms of Kindly Emotion on the other; and all of these states fall under the general heading, Retributive Emotions. According to Westermarck, all moral concepts and moral judgments are based upon these emotions. It is not my intention to discuss this theory. Whether correct or not, it envisages the problem of Emotions and Morals in a totally different form from that which I have set before me for consideration, and I explicitly mention it in order to avoid misunderstanding. Moral consciousness is co-terminous with emotional and volitional consciousness. Praise and blame are but incidents in the story.

The great objection to the " Moral Sense " school has always been that it seems to make " moral approval " simply an emotion among other competing emotions, and so to undermine the validity and authority of its judgments. Yet the alternative, and generally preferred, course of classifying all judgments of value under the heading " Reason " is a questionable one. Although we may agree with Henry Sidgwick, for instance, in holding that the principles of Prudence, Rational Benevolence and Equity are axiomatic for all Moral Philosophy, nevertheless, we find that, when we endeavour to bring them into relation with actual life and put them into practice, they involve us in interminable casuistry, and, when re-examined in the light of such detailed experience, appear reduced to mere tautology. The values are not here but in the concrete emotional life. Intellect is no doubt of great importance in the moral life, since by it alone can we trace the effects of conduct upon ourselves and upon the world at large, or—which comes to the same thing— obtain a full knowledge of what that conduct really is. This knowledge forms an integral part of the conduct as object for valuation. Valuation by whom or by what ? Not by some special faculty of the mind, whether reason, or moral sense, or conscience, but by the entire personality, in so far as it is developed and systematized.

The notion of value is of economic origin, and first occurs in explicit form in Adam Smith's *Wealth of Nations*, where it is identified with the satisfaction of man's needs and desires ; but only recently has it been made the subject of specialized study. The chief names deserving of mention in this regard, after Nietzsche, are those of Ehrenfels, Kreibig, Meinong, Eisler, Cohn and Witasek in Germany, Tarde and Ribot in France, and Münsterberg and Urban in America. Kreibig defines value as follows : " By value in general, I mean the importance that the content of a sensation or of a thought has for the subject, thanks to an actual feeling or to the state of tendency which is combined with this content either immediately or by association."

Witasek writes : " Value is always in intimate relation to desire," and again, " In morals, the essential is the value ; there, all value is feeling and inversely all feeling is value."

In the judgment of value it is probable that the feeling determines the judgment. Nevertheless, some psychologists and philosophers hold the contrary view. Meinong, for example, contends that the pleasure which constitutes a value, being only recognized as such by a judgment, is secondary to that judgment, which is the necessary condition of its existence. The inevitable biological view is represented by Eisler, who writes : " The true explanation is that which traces back the values to the generic functions of the vital activity, that is, to the constant mode of reaction of the ultimate elements, to the elementary processes ; which deduces them ultimately from the principle of organic conservation, understood not in the metaphysical sense, but in the empirical

sense of oscillation about a perfect state of equilibrium."
Ribot's contribution to the subject is an important book
on *The Logic of the Feelings*,* in which he describes forms
of "affective reasoning" consisting of a concatenation of
judgments of value all of which are directed towards,
and derive their value from, some particular end. A good
example is that of an individual inspired by some all-
absorbing passion.

This subject is intensely interesting and most important,
but I cannot linger over it. It is sufficient to have
emphasized the distinction between existential judgments
(ordinary judgments of objective fact) on the one hand,
and judgments of value on the other. These latter
judgments are an integral part of the subject-matter of
psychology. For an imaginary external observer, states
of consciousness are matter for existential judgments.
For the subject himself they are also matter for judgments
of value. This it is which makes psychology so peculiar
a science and so important as an introduction to ethics
and religious philosophy.

Since man is in course of development here below, both
individually and generically, his Chief Good or End is
but partly apparent. Hegel's doctrine of Personality or
Self-realization—"Be a person, and treat others as
persons"—would seem to be most in harmony with
psychological data, if we interpret personality in the
light of the partial results hitherto achieved. No system
of ethics can be entirely free from intuitionism, but an
economy in the number of intuitions appealed to might
be effected by summing up the principles of duty in the
words : "Seek always the Highest Good." Experience
teaches us that the richer and better organized is our
character the greater is our good, and that the helping

* *La Logique des Sentiments.* I have discussed the subject in an
article on "The Logic of the Emotions," in *The Quest*, vol. iii, July 1912.

15

of others to greater possibilities of personality still further enriches our own. Discipline, intellectual enlightenment, much renunciation and an ever-present readiness for it, are, of course, necessary for the individual and are proved to be so by the value-experiences of the race. Moreover, the maxim leads us to anything rather than to a comfortable egoistic doctrine of self-culture. The potentialities of the soul cannot be discovered except through experience, but we learn from experience that consciousness of a higher value results from self-denial and strenuous battle and even physical pain, in certain cases and in the long run, than from slothful passivity, timorous inaction, or careless enjoyment.

" . . . To be weak is miserable,
Doing or suffering."

Such estimates are no doubt subjective, as all strictly psychological facts must be. But are they *therefore* to be dismissed forthwith as arbitrary ? Reason, it is generally admitted, is the evidence both of itself and of the truth of its object, and needs no external criterion. May it not be so with the universe of values ? Moral insight does not, indeed, arise full-blown in the individual consciousness. As Hastings Rashdall has said : " Self-evident truths are not truths which are evident to everybody. There are degrees of moral illumination just as there are degrees of musical sensibility or of mathematical acuteness." There must, too, be fluctuation of preferences from individual to individual, corresponding to their varying powers of experiencing vivid emotion. But despite these differences, and the variations of character which arise out of them, there seems to exist a pronounced tendency towards fundamental agreement. Lord Balfour has remarked upon the curious combination of great divergence in the ways of thinking upon ethical problems with equally great agreement as regards the conclusions arrived at, which is shown in the writings of moralists. This fact seems to indicate that such theories should be classed as examples of the " logic of the feelings," whose nature has been described for us by Ribot.

Little has been said here about the intellectual side of ethics. It should, however, be distinctly understood that reason enters into our scheme of values. As is well known, Henry Sidgwick detected a fundamental tendency in the more developed forms of consciousness which he called " the desire to do what is right and reasonable as such." The satisfaction of this desire is a value, and it is one of the essential values of the higher life. Aristotle, after describing an ethical system for Greek gentlemen, in which the central idea was the moderating of the emotions, proceeded to sketch out a life of θεωρία or philosophic contemplation, which was alone worthy of the philosopher and his God. This tendency to give excessive value to intellectual activity has remained with us ever since. Nevertheless, while denying it a paramount importance, we can say that it is a *sine qua non* for morals. Virtue is at least knowledge. As some one has said : " There is no more appalling sight than ignorance in action."

The universe of values is not lawless or anarchic. It contains the evidence of its degrees of precedence in itself. The relative values of goods are intuitively discerned by the intellectually and morally trained individual. The only alternative is scepticism of the direst kind, emotional and intellectual alike—a tumultuous Nietzschean view which would indeed make of life
" a tale
Told by an idiot, full of sound and fury,
Signifying nothing."

MUSIC AND MORALS

It may be in place here to devote some remarks, however brief and inadequate, to the question of the psychology of Music. The close relation between music and morals has been the subject of remark from very early times. Plato desired to banish certain modes or scales of music from his ideal state, viz., the Ionian and Lydian, because they were too effeminate and " lax." On the other hand, he attached high moral value to the Dorian and Phrygian modes, since the one represented suitably " the tones and accents of a brave man engaged in a feat of arms, or in any violent operation, who, if he fails of success, or encounters wounds and death, or falls into any other calamity, in all such contingencies with unflinching endurance parries the blows of fortune " ; the other, again, expressed " the feelings of one who is engaged in an occupation not violent, but peaceful and unconstrained ; it may be, using persuasion and entreaty, addressing either a prayer to a god, or instruction and advice to a man ; or, on the other hand, lending himself to the prayers or advice or persuasion of another, and after this succeeding to his wish ; and not behaving arrogantly, but acting in all these circumstances with soberness and moderation, and in the same spirit acquiescing in every result."* That music, again, is *the art of expressing emotions by means of sounds* has been the unshaken belief of the majority of great musicians, and also of many philosophers, among whom Schopenhauer is the most prominent example. Music, like poetry, seems to have had its origin in dancing (especially the pantomime dance), which is probably the earliest of the arts and is to be regarded as a specialized form of that expenditure of superfluous energy known as Play.

* *Republic*, Book III, 399 b, c.

In its earliest forms it was a social activity, predominantly characterized by accuracy of rhythm, the social utility of which in pursuits involving concerted action is obvious. Indeed, among certain of the Kaffir tribes even of the present day a mistake in rhythm in their concerted songs and dances is said to be punishable with death (Wallaschek: *Primitive Music*). The social characteristic is also apparent not only in the use of incantations in primitive magic, and in the fact that upon the ancient monuments, musicians are never represented singly but always in a group assisting at some ceremony ; it is even prominent as late as the XVIII Century in the compositions of musicians like Bach and Handel, whose cantatas and oratorios were written for the use of the community, not for the satisfaction of art-critics.

The emotional theory of music is not without its rival, in the shape of a more " intellectualistic " view, supported by Kant, Herbart, Lotze, and even Rousseau, and expressed in its most concise and classical form by the Viennese critic, Hanslick, whose book, *Vom musikalisch-Schönen*, first appeared in 1854. According to Hanslick, music is concerned only with sounds, not with any subject, emotional or otherwise. In its essence, it consists of sound-forms in incessant movement, the auditory equivalent of *arabesques* in continuous kaleidoscopic change.

Hanslick does, indeed, admit that music may express the dynamic aspect of emotions, but not their contents. The theory is not unfitted to describe the achievements of mere technique and virtuosity, but as a general description of the art, the evidence against it is overwhelming. It is well known that Gluck, when composing the movement in " Iphigeneia in Aulide " expressing the anger of Achilles, behaved so strangely in the street that he barely escaped arrest. Gounod openly declared an implacable hatred of mere formalism, and regarded emotion as the essence and meaning of music. Wagner writes of the domain of sounds—which he compares to an unbounded ocean, with the science of harmony as its regulative law—" It is the material of which the innumerable nuances in pitch, timbre or intensity are the adequate and natural expression of the innumerable nuances which can be displayed by pure emotion, *emotion in itself*, independently of all the causes which explain it, of all the particular circumstances which characterize it."

Particular emotions cannot be adequately expressed by sounds, since they involve the idea of a particular object. Only generalized emotion can be so expressed, if indeed it is justifiable to use the distinction of particular and general in this sense at all. In opera the music is much more general than the words, and we are told that Wagner in many scenes of his operas composed the melody before the words. A certain amount of individuality is contributed by the different emotional characteristics of the different instruments of the orchestra, whereby the effect may be produced of emotional conflict between distinct individuals. The *Leitmotiv* is a device which, though partly conventional, completely fulfils its purpose of singling out a particular individual or a particular emotion. Those who go so far, however, as to assign to each key and scale its appropriate emotion, do so at their peril. Thus the key of E♭ minor, which for Schubert was the expression of the Trinity, in the view of Grétry indicated " an immanent catastrophe " !

Music has developed *pari passu* with verbal language, and it is not, strictly speaking, translatable in terms of the latter. It may, in literal truth, be named *the language of the soul*, in that it expresses directly, and not through the intermediation of abstract concepts or plastic images, the fundamental spiritual forces at work in Man and in Nature. In the combined action of rhythm and harmony within the melody we have a direct expression of the alternations of desire and fulfilment, estrangement and reconciliation,* pervading all Life.

" Well (and it was graceful of them), they'd break talk
    off and afford
—She, to bite her mask's black velvet, he, to finger on
    his sword,
While you sat and play'd Toccatas, stately at the
    clavicord ?

What ? Those lesser thirds so plaintive, sixths
    diminish'd, sigh on sigh,
Told them something ? Those suspensions, those
    solutions—' Must we die ? '
Those commiserating sevenths—' Life might last ! we
    can but try ! '

' Were you happy ? '—' Yes.'—' And are you still as
    happy ? '—' Yes, and you ? '
—Then, more kisses ! —' Did I stop them, when a
    million seem'd so few ? '
Hark ! the dominant's persistence, till it must be
    answer'd to !

So an octave struck the answer. O, they praised you,
    I dare say !
' Brave Galuppi ! that was music ! good alike at grave
    and gay !
I can always leave off talking, when I hear a master
    play.' "
             Robert Browning.—A Toccata of Galuppi's.

---

* " Entzweiung und Versöhnung," Schopenhauer, *Die Welt als Wille und Vorstellung*, Drittes Buch, Kap. 39. " Why rushed the discords in but that harmony should be prized ? " (Robert Browning).

CHAPTER XIX

THE most thorough-going attempt, in modern times, to produce a metaphysics of evolution is that of Henri Bergson ; and as his approach to the problem is psychological, we may obtain some light on the relation of evolution to personality from a detailed study of his philosophical system.

Like most philosophers, Bergson starts out from the individual consciousness. Here he finds that the most characteristic quality is change, continuous and progressive. No two moments of consciousness are ever exactly alike. So-called " states " of consciousness are hypostatized abstractions, resulting from the use of language to describe the workings of the mind. Consciousness is a stream, of which the successive pulses interpenetrate one another to a greater or less degree. We become aware of this interpenetration or continuity by an act of intuition in which the mind turns back upon itself, " does violence to itself," and in a fleeting moment transcends the subject-object distinction by being one with itself.

INTUITION AND INTELLECT

Within the individual mind itself there is, according to Bergson, a twofold tendency : one towards spirituality, in which the mutual interpenetration of mental processes would be complete ; the other towards materiality and spatiality, where the interpenetration is at a minimum and the states are really states external, or almost external, to one another. Mind is predominantly spiritual in an act of volition. It is itself moving towards spatiality and materiality in moments of passive reverie. In the

former case, the mind gathers itself together in its
entirety and propels itself forward into the future in a
free creative act. In the latter, it becomes materialized
in the form of extended externally-related images. The
antithesis is one between intensity or tension on the
one hand, and extensity on the other. Spirit is known
by intuition, matter is known by intellect. In most
cases both intuition and intellect are needed, since the
objects known are generally partly spiritual, partly
material. In fact, complete materiality or spatiality, in
which there would be mere quality-less points completely
external to one another, absolutely indifferent to one
another, is a limiting case never reached by actual matter.
The function of intellect is to know matter; it has
developed *pari passu* with the movement towards
materiality in order to know this movement, but for
unexplained reasons it has shot beyond its goal and
passed to the limiting stage of empty space. Geometry
expresses the properties of empty space, and intellect is
" ballasted with geometry." The method of the intellect
is essentially geometrical and mathematical. Its attempted
reduction of all quality to quantity, in the natural sciences,
is the logical outcome of its nature and functions.

Time and Free Will

The psychical " states," classified and described by the
empirical psychologist, are abstractions, moments of the
flux of consciousness torn from their context, instantaneous snapshots of the ever-changing mental life.
These states are then employed to reconstruct consciousness by being placed end-to-end, one after another, in a
homogeneous time which flows at a perfectly uniform
rate and exerts no sort of influence whatever upon them.
Such a picture may represent tolerably well for our
practical needs time that has elapsed. It is entirely

false as a representation of time and consciousness in the process of elapsing. The psychological present is not a mathematical point, but has a certain breadth in which the immediate past, the immediate future, and the experienced transition from one to the other, are present together. This " specious present " gives us real duration or real time. It is a continuous process, apprehended as continuous by intuition. It is to be carefully distinguished from the " elapsed " time just described. Elapsed time is a hybrid concept formed by the union of the concept of succession taken from the actual experience of duration and the concept of distinctness, given by experience of space. It is, in fact, " spatialized time."

The problem of the ireedom of the will has been made insoluble by a confusion of these two kinds of time. Determinists and libertarians alike replace duration or real time by spatialized time. Both loosen the solidarity of the past with the present ; both over-emphasize the distinction of the motive and the man himself, the will and the deed. Conduct, so far as spiritual, cannot be predicted, because it involves from moment to moment real creation. The knowledge of conditions necessary for any such prediction would have to be an inside knowledge, an actual living of a man's life, and this living would have to extend to the moment of consciousness of the act which was to have been predicted. Freedom of the will is a reality, since spirit is a reality. Indeed, freedom is spirit and spirit is freedom. Freedom is possible through memory, and we shall see presently that Bergson identifies memory with spirit.

Élan Vital

Turning from the individual consciousness to cosmic process in general, we find the evolutionary progress of the world most explicable in terms of an original *élan* *vital* or vital impulse, a creative principle which has deposited matter in the course of its progress and is now engaged in making this matter an instrument of freedom by organizing it. An unexplained interruption or inversion of the vital impulse at an unspecified moment of its history* originated a downward movement towards materiality and necessity, so that now the whole universe, like the individual mind, is a struggle between an upward expansive movement towards spirituality and freedom, and a downward movement towards materiality and a uniform diffusion which is space.

" Let us imagine a vessel full of steam at a high pressure, and here and there in its sides a crack through which the steam is escaping in a jet. The steam thrown into the air is nearly all condensed into little drops which fall back, and this condensation and this fall represent simply the loss of something, an interruption, a deficit. But a small part of the jet of steam persists, uncondensed, for some seconds ; it is making an effort to raise the drops which are falling ; it succeeds at most in retarding their fall. So, from an immense reservoir of life, jets must be gushing out unceasingly, of which each, falling back, is a world. The evolution of living species within this world represents what persists of the primitive direction of the original jet, and of an impulsion which continues itself in a direction the inverse of materiality. But let us not carry too far this comparison. It gives us but a feeble and even deceptive image of reality, for the crack, the jet of steam, the forming of the drops, are determined necessarily, whereas the creation of a world is a free act, and the life within the material world participates in this liberty. Let us think rather of an action like that of

---

* This introduces a very serious difficulty into Bergson's system— a difficulty which faces all those philosophers who believe in the ultimate reality of time.

raising the arm ; then let us suppose that the arm, left to itself, falls back, and yet that there persists in it, striving to raise it up again, something of the will that animates it. In this image of a *creative action which unmakes itself*, we have already a more exact representation of matter. In vital activity we see, then, that which persists of the direct movement in the inverted movement, *a reality which is making itself in a reality which is unmaking itself.*"†

Variation, struggle for existence, and survival of the fittest all find an explanation in terms of this metaphysical hypothesis. The different species and genera and orders are the outcome of the struggle of the vital impulse to overcome matter and convert necessity into freedom. Progress along certain lines of evolution has been more successful than along others. The greatest advance has been made in the cases of the Insects, headed by the Hymenoptera, and the Vertebrates, whose highest stage is Man. These two great divisions of the animal kingdom are diverging and complementary lines of evolution. In the one, instinct has developed at the expense of intelligence ; in the other, intelligence has developed at the expense of instinct. Instinct is to be regarded as a form of knowledge, and is identical with intuition. It may be unconscious knowledge, and is indeed a knowledge acted rather than felt. Intelligence, on the other hand, is a knowledge of relations. It is cinematographical in nature, that is, it breaks up the stream of Becoming into a series of instantaneous views, which it then puts in the place of reality and tries to explain in terms of their relations to one another. This form of apprehension has been developed for the purpose of knowing matter, mainly, if not entirely, with a view to acting upon matter. Its

---

† *Creative Evolution*, pp. 260, 261, Eng. Tr.

"instantaneous views" are things, states, and concepts, and its characteristic mode of procedure is to join like to like, because it is only through resemblances that the mind can predict material changes and practically interfere in their production. But, really, "there are no things, there are only actions." The intellect falsifies its data in order to get a practical knowledge of them, and needs to be supplemented by intuition. Now intuition, which is instinct, is not entirely absent in man. The compact and luminous nucleus of intellect is surrounded by a vague fringe of intuition, and philosophic as distinct from scientific thought consists in the use of this intuition to revivify knowledge and to put meaning into the laws and other products of intellectual activity. The value of the great philosophies of the past resides in their intuition. The play of dialectic, though useful and even necessary to test this intuition, is of subordinate value and importance. The one and only "method" of philosophy is the method of intuition. The philosopher is he who starts life with a special endowment of this faculty of insight and develops it still further by practice and attention to the facts of inner and outer experience. Intuition comes to one but seldom, and then only in brief flashes. The "practical" man ignores it even when it does come, and can find no use for it in his intellectual constructions and beliefs.

CREATIVE EVOLUTION

Mechanism and teleology are alike incapable of explaining the world-process. Both, alike, ignore the fact of continuous creation, and assume that "all is given." This is obvious in the case of mechanism, and a moment's thought will show that teleology is open to the same objection. According to teleology, the universe or the individual, or both, are in process of fulfilling a plan;

but, although the fulfilment is projected into the future, it exists, as a plan, *now*. The truth is that this distinction of form and matter is merely a distinction relative to our needs, a distinction made for this reason by our intellect. But knowledge is wider than intellect, just as reality is wider than matter. From the point of view of knowledge, there is an impassable gulf fixed between organized and unorganized matter. Intellect is capable of knowing the latter, being indeed in a sense identical with it and having a parallel evolutionary history. Not so, however, in the case of the former. The biological and psychological sciences make use of intellectual concepts, it is true, but they need the addition of intuition to grapple with the characteristics of reality which form the essence of their subject-matter.

The legitimacy of assuming a general vital impulse in the explanation of organic evolution is vindicated by its success. Random variations, be they continuous or discrete, finite or infinitesimal, will never explain how a complicated organ, such as the vertebrate eye, has become evolved. The eye is of such a delicate construction that variations of different kinds in different parts of it must be most accurately adjusted one to another, if they are not to interfere with the function of vision. The odds against this correlation happening by chance are too enormous to contemplate. Nor can individual variations be imagined as waiting for their complementary variations and being preserved in the meantime, since this is contrary to the Darwinian principle that useless variations are not preserved. The Lamarckian view of the inheritability of acquired characters does not help us here, apart from the great difficulty which biologists find in accepting it at all. But the complete inadequacy of the ordinary concepts of biological science becomes apparent when we find, as we do, similar structures appearing on divergent lines of evolution. The eye of a certain mollusc, the Pecten,* exhibits remarkably close analogies with the vertebrate eye. Yet by far the greater part of its evolution must have occurred after the divergence of the mollusc and vertebrate lines took place. The only mechanical explanation which can be suggested is that of Eimer, which would account for the similarity of structure by the identity of an external influence—in this case, light—to which the organs have been exposed. The two organs have been evolved in adaptation to a common influence. But adaptation may be either passive or active. It is passive adaptation alone which would be able to explain such a similarity of evolution as we have before us. Now, as a matter of fact, the adaptation of the eye to light does indeed start by being passive—the light causes the original pigment spot—but this form of adaptation quickly gives place to an active adaptation in which the organ and the organism make use of light for their own ends, and active adaptation no longer fits in with Eimer's theory. Consequently, we are driven back to the view of an original impulse pushing forward in different directions. The similarity of the eyes of the mollusc and the vertebrate is a consequence of the identity of impulse underlying their evolution. The materiality of an organ or organism " does not represent a sum of means employed [as in the case of an artificially constructed machine], but a sum of obstacles avoided ; it is a negative rather than a positive reality. . . . The vision of a living being is an *effective* vision, limited to objects on which the being can act ; it is a vision that is *canalized*, and the visual apparatus simply symbolizes the work of canalizing.

---

* Bergson's use of this illustration has been criticized by biologists, on the point of fact. But the criticism, although justified, does not destroy the main argument.

Therefore the creation of the visual apparatus is no more explained by the assembling of its anatomic elements than the digging of a canal could be explained by the heaping-up of the earth which might have formed its banks. A mechanistic theory would maintain that the earth had been brought cart-load by cart-load ; finalism would add that it had not been dumped down at random, that the carters had followed a plan. But both theories would be mistaken, for the canal has been made in another way."†

The unity of the function is the essential, the complexity of the structure is the relative view taken of it by the intellect ; although the mutual adjustment of parts is here again the expression of the singleness of function, and the necessary outcome of it.

Mind and Body

The general statement of Bergson's metaphysical position in the preceding paragraphs indicates his view as to the relation of spirit to matter, but a more detailed account is needed of the relation of the individual mind to the body with which it is found associated, on the one hand, and to the objects of its external environment which it knows and acts upon, on the other. This is given in *Matter and Memory*, the most psychological of Bergson's works. Indeed, it may almost be looked upon as a text-book of General Psychology, written from an original standpoint, and showing due regard to the intimate relation which exists between psychological analysis and explanation and philosophical first principles, and there is little doubt that it will exercise a considerable influence upon the nature of future textbooks on the subject. Bergson admits that he is a dualist, but claims that his view is neither realistic nor idealistic.

---

† *Creative Evolution*, p. 99.

" Matter, in our view, is an aggregate of 'images.' And by 'image' we mean a certain existence which is more than that which the idealist calls a *representation*, but less than that which the realist calls a *thing*—an existence placed half-way between the 'thing' and the 'representation.' This conception of matter is simply that of common sense. . . . For common sense, the object exists in itself, and, on the other hand, the object is, in itself, pictorial, as we perceive it : image it is, but a self-existing image."*

The individual body, its brain, and even its cerebral cortex, are images among, or by the side of, the other images which go to make up the universe. Realism and idealism stand alike condemned because they alike regard the individual brain, or a special portion of it, as the source, in one way or another, of our representation of the entire universe. They make the psycho-physical problem absolutely insoluble. Most psychologists are now willing to admit that this is the case with the realistic theory known as epiphenomenalism ; but the more popular theory of parallelism involves difficulties of the same philosophical order. That material changes in particular parts of the individual cerebral cortex, themselves parts of the whole material universe, should run parallel with, or be "the other side " of, consciousness of the entire universe, is an inconceivability if anything is inconceivable. The view is a philosophic generalization based on an incorrect interpretation of the facts of cerebral localization, which is in its turn determined by an incorrect estimate of the meaning and function of *perception*.

PERCEPTION

Perception is a form of *action* rather than a form of cognition. Its importance is *practical* rather than

---

* *Matter and Memory*, Introduction, pp. 7, 8, Eng. Tr.

speculative. Its distinction from memory is therefore a distinction of kind and not merely one of degree. Whereas memory has to do with the past, the interest in which is speculative only, perception involves an actual presence of external objects to the sense-organs, and is, in fact, the reflexion of the body's virtual or possible action upon these objects, or of the objects' possible action upon the body. An unbiased consideration of the structure and mode of working of the entire nervous system reveals this, although the truth is obscured for the psychologist by the admixture of affection and memory as factors in actual developed perception. The nervous system consists exclusively of nerve-fibres, each supplied with a nerve-cell, which run from the periphery (afferent) to the periphery (efferent) through more central junctions. These central junctions are in every case points of reflexion and redistribution of the nervous impulses. All agree that this is the case with the spinal and other subcortical centres of the nervous system. Anatomical evidence supports a similar view with regard to the functioning of the cortical centres. Here the incoming impulses find a large number of *alternative* paths open to them. The brain is so constructed that a number of incoming impulses can converge to bring about a single unit reaction, or, again, so that a single incoming impulse can dissipate itself along a multitude of efferent paths and so become sublimated†️ without producing any overt reaction. The brain, or rather the cerebral cortex, is thus a sort of telephone exchange and represents a certain amount of *indetermination* in the reactions. It is this indetermination which is the source of conscious perception. Mechanical reflex action is *necessarily determined* action and is therefore uncon-

---

† This use of the word " sublimation " is different from that found in the writings of Freud.

scious.   Perception is likewise action, a reaction to
a present stimulus, but it is not necessarily determined ;
its consciousness is a measure of its indetermination.

In the above account we have described perception
in its essence, as it is in theory rather than in fact.
Bergson calls this " pure " perception.   Ordinary perception as it actually occurs differs from this in containing
affection or " sensation," and the contributions of
memory.   The body, besides being exposed to a virtual
action of external objects, is subject to a *real* action.
It is this real action which constitutes affection.   Affection
is an (ineffectual) motor tendency in a sensory nerve.
It forms one of the subjective elements in perception.
The object of perception is perceived where it is, viz.,
outside the body ; the affection is likewise experienced
where *it* is, inside the body.   Again, perception is, in
fact, not absolutely instantaneous.   It occupies a certain
breadth of duration.   The successive moments of this
duration are strung together and condensed by memory,
and the *qualities* of sensation are due to such condensa-
tions.   We shall return to this point later.   Finally,
memories from the past mingle with perception of the
present and may even take its place.

" For if they have survived it, it is with a view to
utility ;   at every moment they complete our present
experience, enriching it with experience already acquired ;
and, as the latter is ever increasing, it must end by
covering up and submerging the former."*

Pure Memory and Rote Memory

" Pure " memory has no physiological correlate.   There
are no " centres " for memory.   The brain is merely a
motor organ.   Its structure is completely explicable in

---

* *Matter and Memory*, p. 70.

terms of useful reactions to environmental changes. It
conditions present perception directly, as we have seen,
but is related to memory only indirectly, viz., through
the motor reaction in perception. Successive perceptions
as they occur give rise to memories which are permanently
retained in all their particularity, but in an unconscious
form. These memories really make up what is known as
mind or spirit. In their pure unconscious form they are
unextended and in a state of complete interpenetration.
On the occasion of a later perception certain of them
may find the motor reaction or motor tendency congruent
with themselves and are then enabled to slip into the
perceptual process and identify themselves with its motor
prolongation. In this way they rise again in consciousness
as mental images. They thus become partly materialized,
as it were, and for the time being are no longer pure
memories.

One of Bergson's most valuable contributions to
scientific psychology is his distinction of pure memory
from rote memory, which he identifies with habit. In
learning a lesson by heart, we build up a motor mechanism
having all the marks of a habit.

" Like a habit, it is acquired by the repetition of the
same effort. Like a habit, it demands first a decom-
position and then a recomposition of the whole action.
Lastly, like every habitual bodily exercise, it is stored
up in a mechanism which is set in motion as a whole
by an initial impulse, in a closed system of automatic
movements which succeed each other in the same order
and, together, take the same length of time. The
memory of each several reading, on the contrary, the
second or the third, for instance, has *none* of the marks
of a habit. Its image was necessarily imprinted at once
on the memory, since the other readings form, by their
very definition, other recollections. It is like an event

in my life ; its essence is to bear a date, and consequently
to be unable to occur again."*

This distinction is similar to that drawn by some
psychologists between " personal " and " impersonal "
memories. It is absolutely essential for Bergson's theory
of memory. Corresponding to it he finds two distinct
kinds of recognition, one entirely mechanical based on
the working of pre-formed motor mechanisms, the other
starting from memories, among which the mind places
itself by an act *sui generis*, at a bound, and working back
to the perceptual and motor plane of the present. Cases
of " mental blindness," or loss of the power of recognition
whether visual or auditory, are not due to a real loss of
corresponding memories, but to injury or obstruction of
the motor mechanisms which give these memories the
opportunity of becoming realized as supplementary parts
of an actual perception. The facts of psycho-pathology,
especially those of *aphasia* in all its forms, decidedly
support this view. No memories are ever really lost.
We carry our entire past along with us,† but disturbance
of particular motor mechanisms in the brain may make
the recall of some portion of this past either temporarily
or permanently impossible. It is our entire past that
acts at every moment of conscious experience, but this
past is present at different degrees of *tension*, as it were,
on different occasions. Bergson represents it by a cone
standing upon its apex on a plane. The plane represents
the actual material world, which exists in a continuous
present, the apex of the cone corresponds to present
perception, the base to the manifold of our memories,
each with a date of its own and distinct from every other.
The memories are all represented in different horizontal

---

* *Matter and Memory*, pp. 89, 90.

† See *Psychology and Psychotherapy*, especially chaps. vii. and x.,
for evidence from hypnotic experiments in support of this view.

sections of the cone, but with a distinctness and at a tension varying with the area of the section. The nearer to the apex the section is taken, the greater the degree of coalescence and tension of the memories, the more impersonal and the more subordinated to action they are. The infinite number of sections which may be imagined correspond to an infinity of different planes of memory from which the past may be brought to bear upon the present. Mental activity is represented in the figure by movements up and down between the apex and the base. It corresponds to expansions and contractions of memory, having as object the discovery of just those memories which may best fit into the motor diagram of present perception. In this way the motor diagram itself may undergo extension, with the result that yet other memories may succeed in inserting themselves and thus come to overlie the percept. The power of the mind to produce contractions and expansions of itself in reference to present experience is, it seems, according to Bergson, a power *sui generis* and ultimate ; yet he nowhere clearly distinguishes it from the sum of memories themselves. Before bringing this very obvious criticism against him, however, we must remember that in *Matter and Memory* he definitely limits his consideration of memory and the nature of the mind to those aspects which are essential to his main problem—the relation of mind to matter. After saying that " with memory we are in very truth in the domain of spirit," he goes on to state that " it was not our task to explore this domain. Placed at the confluence of mind and matter, desirous chiefly of seeing the one flow into the other, we had only to retain, of the spontaneity of intellect, its place of conjunction with bodily mechanism."‡

Similarly, in his *Time and Free Will* Bergson does not

‡ *Matter and Memory*, pp. 320, 321.

undertake to give us a psychological theory of free will. He contents himself with merely showing that determinism and libertarianism are both impossible views, and that freedom is a psychological fact. Perhaps he will some day give us a book on the relation of memory and freedom to personality, and so complete his psychological system. If so, he will find plenty of material to his hand in the so-called New Psychology.

MATTER AND MIND

The ordinary views on the relation of mind to matter make the problem an insoluble one in three distinct particulars. They make the difference of matter and mind a contrast of (1) extension and intensity, (2) quantity and quality, (3) necessity and freedom. Taking these distinctions in a literal and extreme sense, they find the gulf in each case an impassable one. But the truth is that extensity is a characteristic of many, if not all, of the sensory contents of consciousness ; while, on the other side, matter is not completely extended. Space does not exist as something absolute in which material bodies are located.

" That which is given, that which is real, is something intermediate between divided extension and pure inextension. It is what we have termed the *extensive*. Extensity is the most salient quality of perception. It is in consolidating and in subdividing it by means of an abstract space, stretched by us beneath it for the needs of action, that we constitute the composite and infinitely divisible extension. It is, on the other hand, in subtilizing it, in making it, in turn, dissolve into affective sensations and evaporate into a counterfeit of pure ideas, that we obtain those inextensive sensations with which we afterwards vainly endeavour to reconstitute images."*

---

* *Matter and Memory*, pp. 326, 327.

This approximation of the two terms in the characteristic of extensity helps us to overcome the opposition between quality and quantity, between consciousness and movement. Although corpuscles (atoms, electrons) are at least as much figments of our imagination as the discontinuous and distinct external objects which our perception carves out in the continuous physical universe around us, yet the movements which these corpuscles are supposed to possess as attributes are themselves real. They show differences of rhythm or of vibration-frequency. The vibrations, by exhibiting a certain, though minimal, degree of interpenetration, constitute a real concrete duration. The sensations corresponding to them are in a sense identical with them, only in a condensed condition—an enormous number of them being summed up by the span of memory in one moment. " Between sensible qualities, as regarded in our representation of them, and these same qualities treated as calculable changes, there is therefore only a difference in rhythm of duration, a difference of internal tension."†

Finally, mind is essentially free since it has its roots in perception which, we have seen, is a measure of the indetermination of response to stimulation. As memory, it is free in a yet more concrete sense, bringing the past to bear upon the present decision, and also by virtue of its internal tension contracting an indefinite number of external moments in the duration of the present. Matter, on the other hand, is not entirely bound in the chains of necessity. " Absolute necessity would be represented by a perfect equivalence of the successive moments of duration, each to each."‡ Still, the contingency of nature must be extremely slight, and in Bergson's view even complete necessity in matter would be no bar to

† *Matter and Memory*, p. 330.
‡ Ibid., p. 330.

the interaction of mind with it. Matter is annulled, neutralized, or latent consciousness, and conscious perception is only related to it as the part to the whole. So freedom needs a basis of necessity and can only develop in close connection with necessity. The structure of the individual brain with its innumerable alternative pathways for the transference and discharge of nervous energy, making it a veritable " reservoir of indetermination," is something more than a mere symbol of this relation. It represents the intimate organization of freedom with necessity which is the essential characteristic of life and consciousness.

CRITICISM

Bergson's system of psychology stands or falls with his theory of " pure perception." It therefore behoves us to consider this theory still more closely, and to see what criticisms may be brought against it.

Perception, in Bergson's view, is essentially " discernment." The whole universe consists of images, of which our body is one, acting and reacting upon one another according to the laws of physical science. By virtue of the indetermination implied in the structure of the nervous system, the body isolates from among all the innumerable external influences streaming through it just those to which it can react with a greater or less freedom of choice. These isolated influences " become ' perception' by their very isolation." The relation between perception and external reality is thus simply that of part to whole ; " there is in matter something more than, but not something different from, that which is actually given."* Bergson denies that the nervous system or any part of it can add anything, in the way of new properties, to matter. " The nervous system,

---

* *Matter and Memory*, p. 78.

a material mass presenting certain qualities of colour, resistance, cohesion, etc., may well possess unperceived physical properties, but physical properties only. And hence it can have no other office than to receive, inhibit, or transmit movement."† Consciousness is not *produced* by interaction between the external environment and the individual brain. It already exists throughout the universe, though in an annulled or latent form. Each point potentially perceives every other point in the universe, since influences reach it from all these other points.

Perception and Thought

As regards the space problem in perception, Bergson is in complete harmony with the views of modern psychology in attributing extensity to sensations and in distinguishing perceptual from conceptual space. Sensations have not to be projected outwards in order to give the perception of an image or object in external space, for how should we know where to project them to ? Nevertheless, an immediate perception of the externality and extent of an image and an immediate perception of its exact position and size are two very different things. It is only with the former that we start ; the latter is in part a product of mental activity, and, as such, liable to error. We see a star above the horizon when it is really below the horizon. The refraction of the light rays, itself unperceived, has made us see the star in the wrong direction. Perception alone is incapable of correcting this error. Thought is needed, for it is through thought or intellect that *relations* are conceived. It is questionable whether we can ever with legitimacy speak of *perceiving* relations, on the Bergsonian view of perception which makes it identical with " discernment." Bergson

---

† *Matter and Memory*, p. 79.

himself regards the function of intelligence to be the knowledge of relations. It seems to me that such knowledge cannot be lightly brushed aside by saying that its *raison d'être* is simply utility. It is genuine knowledge, of speculative as distinct from, or in addition to, utilitarian value, and a kind of knowledge that cannot, on any hypothesis, be given by perception. Intellect certainly enables us to fill in, hypothetically, gaps in our perceptions, but it does much more than this. It gives us a deeper insight into the meaning of perceptions, and furnishes us with the real freedom of deliberation and choice, not that aimless freedom of spontaneous activity and pure duration which is all that Bergson can offer us.

The time and space relations of perception which interest Bergson himself are, as might be expected, those which concern reaction to stimulation, or utility, rather than those bound up with the difficulties of speculation. He writes of an animal at the perceptive stage of consciousness : " By sight, by hearing, it enters into relation with an ever greater number of things, and is subject to more and more distant influences ; and, whether these objects promise an advantage or threaten a danger, both promises and threats defer the date of their fulfilment. The degree of independence of which a living being is master, or, as we shall say, the zone of indetermination which surrounds its activity, allows, then, of an a priori estimate of the number and the distance of the things with which it is in relation. Whatever this relation may be, whatever be the inner nature of perception, we can affirm that its amplitude gives the exact measure of the indetermination of the act which is to follow. So that we can formulate this law : *Perception is master of space in the exact measure in which action is master of time.*"*

---

* *Matter and Memory*, p. 23.

The Meaning of "Image."

Bergson's theory of pure perception only escapes the accusation of being mechanical, even mechanistic, by the element of consciousness which is smuggled in by way of the blessed word, " image." If the Bergsonian reminds us that the emergence of explicit consciousness is explained by the " zones of indetermination " which individuals possessed of a set of cortical centres enjoy, we may reply that this conception of indetermination is either altogether vague or else refers to a form of mechanism which might work just as satisfactorily without explicit consciousness. When memory is introduced the matter assumes, it is true, a different aspect, but even here intellectual activity to the extent of, at least, comparison and abstraction, seems also to require to be assumed in order to make the indetermination a genuinely psychical one.

There is again the secondary question as to whether external " images " are to be regarded as *possessing* consciousness or as *being* conscious (potentially). Bergson writes : " That every reality has a kinship, an analogy, in short a relation with consciousness—this is what we concede to idealism by the very fact that we term things ' images.' No philosophical doctrine, moreover, provided that it is consistent with itself, can escape from this conclusion. But if we could assemble all the states of consciousness, past, present, and possible, of all conscious beings, we should still have only gathered a very small part of material reality, because images outrun perception on every side."* We may, therefore, assume that Bergson considers that images *are* consciousness (annulled or latent). But to this it may be objected that these images,

---

* *Matter and Memory*, p. 305.

when they are brought into explicit consciousness through the process of perception, fall on the *object* side of the subject-object relation. On the subjective side we have the *élan vital* itself, in an individualized form constituting the personality.

PERSONALITY AND RELIGION

(I)—PSYCHOLOGICAL METHODS IN
    THE STUDY OF RELIGION
             (CHAPTER XX)

(II)—SUGGESTION AND FAITH
             (CHAPTER XXI)

(III)—MYSTICISM
             (CHAPTER XXII)

CHAPTER XX

In considering how far psychology can throw light upon religion, it is desirable to set out from some general conception of what Religion is. Religion itself is a state of mind, a mental attitude towards the universe; it is an attitude which we take up towards the totality of existence. Now there are many different attitudes with which we may face existence. We may meet it with a question, as we do in asking what it is, what is the universe, and what are we as parts of the universe. We may endeavour to get to know the universe, and in some mysterious way we do succeed to some extent in understanding it, as a general system of physical and mental forces. Or again, we may enjoy the universe as a work of art or a collection of works of art. We may appreciate the beauty of the scenery and other things about us. We may deplore ugliness which we find intermingled with that beauty. Thirdly, we may face existence from the point of view of duty, of what should be done, or more adequately, in the light of the idea of the Good. There are, then, these three general all-inclusive attitudes towards the universe : (1) A cognitive attitude, based upon the desire to know ; (2) an æsthetic attitude, based upon the desire to appreciate, to do full justice to the beauty of existence, and perhaps to play some little part in adding to that beauty, if the individual is an artist ; (3) an ethical attitude, based upon the desire to achieve the highest good possible in individual conduct.

Is there a further general attitude remaining over after these three attitudes have, I won't say received adequate satisfaction, but at any rate have discovered their appropriate fields of activity ? There seems to be such a field in the experience of personal relationship towards the universe as that upon which we completely depend. That is, there is an attitude of complete dependence upon the universe which is distinct from the cognitive, æsthetical, and ethical attitudes. This attitude was first singled out by Schleiermacher as the essential element in the religious consciousness. But if we analyse the situation psychologically, we find that there are other forms of experience in this attitude besides the experience of complete dependence, and these additional forms of experience have been well analysed and described by Rudolf Otto in his recent book, *The Idea of the Holy* (*Das Heilige*). He shows very clearly that the feeling of dependence which is characteristic of the religious attitude is not one of merely causal dependence, not the experience of being a link in a series of causal processes, just a link in the chain of causation, but something still more thorough-going, the experience of what he calls creature-hood, that " It is God that hath made us and not we ourselves." We have been made by Him and so we are completely dependent upon Him in that sense, made by Him and therefore entirely in His power. And then there are the further feelings called out in our mind by that idea, the feeling of His infinite power, the feeling of the tremendous, of complete otherness, something entirely different from ourselves, the feeling of mysteriousness, of majesty, and of fascination in which fear and attraction are blended.

I am taking this particular line of approach to the problem, because it seems to me that in this way one can avoid so much of the arguing in a circle that is to be found in the historical approach, which is the usual so-called scientific approach to the question of the religious sentiment. Usually, we find introductory chapters on lower forms of religious observance, and we have explained to us how, in the course of evolution, there must have been a pre-religious state in which magic figured largely. In magic the individual attempted to get his own way with the powers around him by spells and incantations, and then later, as a result of failure, relative or absolute, of these spells, the individual turned from the attitude of magic to the attitude of prayer or supplication, and at the same time passed from polytheism to a form of monotheism. Along this line of thought, according to this natural history of religion, one is given the impression that the higher forms of religious feeling and religious insight are simply products of lower forms of mental activity ; religion has grown out of forms of consciousness that could not themselves be called religious. In a similar way, attempts have been made to explain knowledge as a development out of mental processes that are not themselves knowledge, the sense of duty as a development out of simpler mental processes not themselves involving the feeling of obligation, the appreciation of beauty as a development out of forms of mental experience not themselves involving beauty, but merely sensations of pleasure and displeasure. Such an approach to the problem of religion is inadequate, if not positively misleading. In considering the subject, we need to take a broader view. At the commencement, at any rate, we must start from a philosophical outlook rather than a merely psychological one. What is first in philosophy is last in science.

For the merely psychologically minded, progress in the science of knowledge, and in the other mental sciences too, might be presumed to mean a greater and greater restriction of the field of religion, and to some minds, at any rate, an ultimate explaining away of religious experience. It was fear that in the beginning of things created the gods, and through knowledge the scope of that fear has been ever more and more reduced. But what has really happened is rather this. Starting with a general attitude towards life, in which these various values of experience were not distinct from one another, where science and religion, ethics and æsthetics, were all mingled together, the development of knowledge and civilization has brought about a gradual separating out of these attitudes—each attitude, as I said at the beginning, has achieved its own general sphere of reference and of fact—and yet we find, after the claims of what may be called the profane sciences have been met, that there is something left over—namely, the distinctively religious experience itself.

It is true that this religious experience has been specially closely associated with ethical experience in the course of mental development in the individual as well as in the race ; forms of worship and religious appreciation have been linked up more and more closely with moral valuations, so that in the higher religions it is impossible to think away moral predicates from the conception of the Divine. Yet there remain non-rational in addition to these rational moral predicates, characteristics of the Divine which we can merely indicate in words—non-rational types of feeling, such as the feeling of dependence, of otherness, of the mysterious, the tremendous, etc., already referred to. These have their lower as well as their higher forms. In lower forms they appear in various species of superstition, fear of ghosts, the feeling of uncanniness, the otherness of the miraculous or the supernatural. These feelings gradually alter under the influence of increased knowledge, but do not disappear entirely. They are purified and pass from a lower to a higher form, and so in spite of all the progress of scientific thought there remains this particular mental attitude which has been called by Rudolf Otto the " numinous " (from the Latin word *numen*, divinity), and he claims, and I think rightly, that in this attitude we have a definite form of experience and a definite way of experiencing reality; not just a feeling that may vary from one person to another, that may come and go and perhaps disappear entirely with further mental development, but a way of experiencing reality on the same level with the cognitive attitude—the attitude of knowing reality—and the other attitudes which I have enumerated. The task of Psychology is partly to do full justice to this mental attitude by analysing it in as detailed a way as possible, partly to link it up with other forms of experience not generally recognised as religious.

A great deal of work has been done by the method of the questionnaire, in which the investigator sends out a series of questions about their religious feelings to a large number of people. One of the first to adopt this course was Starbuck in America, and in the first great book on the psychology of religion, by William James, Starbuck's results were largely used. James here marshals the evidence, and sums up the characteristics of the religious life (independently of the discrepancies of creed) as including the following beliefs : " (1) That the visible world is part of a more spiritual universe from which it draws its chief significance ; (2) That unison or harmonious relation with that higher universe is our true end ; (3) That prayer or inner communion with the spirit thereof —be that spirit ' God ' or ' law '—is a process wherein work is really done, and spiritual energy flows in and produces effects, psychological or material, within the phenomenal world " (*Varieties of Religious Experience,* p. 485).

It also becomes clear from the evidence that the phenomenon of *conversion* is a fundamental process in the religious life. Conversion may be defined as a change of general mental attitude from the merely naturalistic attitude towards life to a definitely spiritual attitude. The individual finds the world so full of strange and wonderful things that his mind is at first mainly occupied with getting to understand and appreciate it in a profane way, but he discovers that this is not sufficient to give him true happiness. In spite of his most earnest endeavours to adjust himself to his physical and social environment and to be true to an ethical ideal, a feeling of insufficiency weighs upon his mind, and produces depression from which he struggles to free himself. Peace may come in one way or another, and the process of passing from such a state of conflict and strain to a state of harmony and peace is the process of conversion. Among certain religious sects conversion is striven after along definite lines. The sense of insufficiency and sin is emphasized in the prospective convert. He is encouraged to struggle hard against his difficulties, to face them, and to realize them as fully as possible. He passes through a state of intense mental anguish, and then suddenly reaches a state of calm and peace. But in another class of individuals who take religious life just as seriously, such sudden conversion may not occur. Yet I do not think that we can say that conversion as such is absent, and I am inclined to believe that conversion in its general sense of turning from the merely naturalistic attitude towards life to a more spiritual attitude occurs in every case, but in many cases it may occur slowly and gradually, as a process of healthy growth. Cases of sudden conversion are often to some extent patho-logical. I do not mean that the conversion itself is pathological, but that the conditions and consequences may be in part pathological. The strain and stress of mental conflict may produce temporary disturbance of functioning of the nervous system, and in that way give rise to experiences that are not in every respect normal religious experiences ; depression, hallucinations, and even temporary delusions that show very close resemblance to the depression, hallucinations, and delusions met with in mental patients quite independently of their religious life.

The feeling of peace and relief may be partly explained on the psychological side as a transition from a state of division of the self, where one part of the self is fighting against another, to a state of unification and harmony. In this transition from division to unification a certain amount of energy is liberated which as a surplus allows all mental processes to occur more readily and freely, producing a feeling of happiness. This is an extremely crude theory, in terms of physiology and psychology, and certainly cannot be accepted as a fully adequate account of the process. The truth is that, so long as we speak merely as psychologists, we are tending to leave out the truly religious attitude altogether. Again, I can only illustrate by the analogy of knowledge. So far as we treat knowledge psychologically, we describe what goes on in the individual mind as a sequence of individual processes which, if taken by itself, would actually explain away knowledge. It would leave us without that conviction of the *validity* of our knowledge which is such an essential part of it. And so it is with religious experience. Psychologically, in the very effort that we make to describe religious experience as a sequence of mental processes in the individual's mind, we are invalidating that experience. We might, indeed, say that we are making an experiment, that we are seeing how far we *can* explain the religious experience of the individual in terms of that individual's own antecedent experience without reference to anything beyond, that we are for the time being putting aside transcendence, because directly we assume that the individual is in touch with an existence outside him, we are passing beyond psychology. All that psychology does is to describe as accurately and fully as possible what goes on in his mind.

Moreover, psychology, like other sciences, is committed to the principle of parsimony, the principle of " Occam's razor," to use as few hypotheses as possible and to explain experience as fully as possible in terms of the most general hypotheses ; and this brings me to the use made of the doctrine of the subconscious or subliminal self, and in more recent years to the doctrine of the unconscious, to explain or explain away religious experience. Following up the hints of resemblance of certain startling religious experiences to certain pathological experiences, the attempt was made by James to fill up the gap, or to soften down the suddenness of the transition in the individual mind from the state of depression and sinfulness to a state of redemption, by an appeal to processes assumed to go on below the threshold of consciousness, in the subliminal. In the case of sudden conversion, for example, the theory was that the individual's consciousness seemed to remain on a merely naturalistic plane of existence, with a naturalistic outlook on life ; in the depths of his mind, however, a change was going on, other considerations were being weighed, other motives were getting their way, a subsidiary self was being developed, a set of mental tendencies which gained in strength and at last broke through into consciousness, and just before breaking through produced a feeling of intense strain and depression. When, however, it had broken through, it was able to combine with what it found there, modifying it, transforming it entirely so that the individual felt a new man, as if he were born again. James himself goes further, and suggests that it may well be that the individual conscious mind comes into relation with the Deity through the intermediation of the subconscious mind. The changes in the conscious mind, in the direction of a more satisfactory religious attitude, may be produced through the intermediation of the subconscious, and in this way prayer may receive its answer. Influences may reach us through the dreamy subliminal which in the hubbub of waking life might pass us by.

From the scientific point of view, one would criticize such a theory as this, because it is not thoroughgoing enough. If you bring in the conception of the subliminal, and use it as an hypothesis, it is your duty as scientists to press that hypothesis to the utmost. Although James did not do this, it has been done by later writers, and in modern times we find a number of enthusiastic psychologists who look to the unconscious for an explanation of all these phenomena, but who, one cannot help feeling, have at the back of their minds the idea that they can only truly rely upon religious experience if it proves recalcitrant to this method. On the one hand, they will reject the supernatural, in the sense of the belief in a spiritual universe as distinct from the ordinary universe in space and time, because all the possibilities of explanation in terms of what goes on in the individual mind have not been exhausted, and yet, on the other hand, they are quite certain that these possibilities of explanation will never be exhausted. To all intents and purposes they are sceptics with regard to the validity of religious experience. The present situation of the psychology of religion is very similar to the situation as regards knowledge at the time when Locke, Berkeley, and Hume were writing. They were endeavouring to get to know what knowledge meant, their aim was to understand knowledge, to know about human understanding, but they used a predominantly psychological method, and although that psychological method increased their knowledge of psychology, it only made the central problem of knowledge more apparent, and it remained for Kant to show how completely they had failed to do justice to the science of knowledge. In the same way, at the present day and during the last twenty years, psychologists have approached the question of the validity of religious experience along psychological lines, not always realizing that, by the very method they have adopted, they are challenging or denying that validity. In other words, just as psychology as such cannot do justice to the validity of knowledge, psychology cannot do justice to the validity of religion. Of course, it is open to every one to pass beyond the psychological to the philosophical line of explanation, and it is just as essential to do that in the problem of religion as it is in the problems of ethics, æsthetics, and epistemology.

Having emphasized this side of the question, we can with a clearer conscience proceed to apply psychological methods and observations to religious experience, although at every step in our argument we shall find it necessary to supplement psychology with philosophy. I am thinking at the moment of the attempts made by certain members of the psycho-analytic school to explain away the main facts of the Christian religion in terms of concepts borrowed from pathological psychology. One continental writer, who does not himself belong to the Christian faith, explains the central or main tenets of the Christian doctrine in terms of " projection " and " regression." He contends that the Christian attitude towards life is an infantile attitude that arises as a result of the individual's complete failure to grapple with the mystery of existence. The individual tries to face the facts of reality, fails, and regresses towards more infantile modes of adaptation. Not being able to see adequate security among the forces of nature around him, he steps back to the mental attitude he had when a young child, of implicit faith in the power and goodness of his parents, in the modified form of a belief in a beneficent Deity. His belief in the Divine is simply this infantile feeling, which may surge up even in spite of himself. Again, his intense desire to conserve or preserve his values, logical, ethical, and æsthetical,—all those things that make life for him worth living,—may be so strong that it produces a sort of hallucinatory fulfilment. It produces a feeling in him that it is fulfilled, that everything is all right, that we are safe in God's hands. Just to illustrate the kind of explanation proffered nowadays, we may mention that another psycho-analyst undertakes to explain the feeling of original sin in terms of the Œdipus complex. The individual has a bad conscience because in his childhood he felt a strong affection for one of his parents, and hatred and jealousy towards the other, which he repressed, and, as a result of repression, there arose feelings of sympathy and bad conscience. These were projected outwards and formed the basis of the systematic doctrines of the Fatherhood of God, the Atonement, etc.*

We can meet these arguments in two ways : one theoretical and the other practical. Theoretically, we can say that they are guilty of what Aristotle called a μετάβασις εἰς ἄλλο γένος — the fallacy of explaining the facts of one science in terms of the concepts of another—of explaining the normal mind in terms of

---

* Although psychological factors of this kind, among others, may contribute their share to crude religious emotion, to use them to explain away the essential characteristics of religious experience would be to " pour away the baby with the bath-water."

the abnormal, without first giving an adequate theory of the distinction between normal and abnormal. An analogous situation exists in the neighbouring science of physiology. No one would explain physiological change in terms of pathology. Physiology benefits by knowledge gained from pathology. Pathology also clearly gains enormously from the knowledge of physiology. But the two sciences are quite distinct. Clearly pathology is in the main subsidiary to physiology. The second line of attack is the more satisfactory one of actual experience. According to one's experiences of the pathological processes of projection and regression and the influence of the Œdipus complex in a patient, these are usually diminished or eliminated by a course of psycho-analysis. If, therefore, the typical religious attitude towards life is explicable in these terms, the religious consciousness would be altered by analysis in the direction of elimination. One would expect, according to this theory, that deep analysis would leave the patient less religious than he was before. My own experience has been the exact opposite of this. After an analysis (for scientific purposes) by a leading psycho-analyst extending over ninety-two hours, my religious convictions were stronger than before, not weaker. The analysis had indeed a purifying effect upon my religious feelings, freeing them from much that was merely infantile and supported by sentimental associations or historical accidents. But the ultimate result has been that I have become more convinced than ever that religion is the most important thing in life and that it is essential to mental health. The need of forms and ceremonies is another matter, far less fundamental. In many patients whom I have myself analysed I have found a similar result. Although mere emotionalism and religiosity is diminished, the essentially religious outlook on life remains unimpaired.

CHAPTER XXI

WE may now consider in more detail the psychological factors at work in bringing us into relationship with the Divine, and there occurs at once to the therapeutic mind the problem of the general nature of faith, and its relation to suggestion. The modern psychotherapeutic doctrine of suggestion was a direct development from the rather extreme views of Christian Scientists of fifty years ago.* So-called faith cures were produced by Mrs. Eddy and her followers, supported by the enthusiasm they had for this line of thought, and many medical and other psychologists who investigated the matter came to the conclusion that, for the most part, the cures could be explained in terms of suggestion. It therefore behoves us to understand as clearly as possible what is meant by suggestion and the theory and practice of suggestion-treatment, and the bearing it has upon faith and other forms of religious experience. Suggestion may be defined as the acceptance of an idea by the mind, especially by the so-called subconscious mind, independently of adequate logical grounds for such acceptance. It is an instance of ideo-motor action. The idea is placed before the mind, or rather, aroused vividly in the mind, when the mind is in a state where opposing and conflicting ideas have no chance of making themselves felt ; whereupon this implanted or elicited idea tends

---

* I discuss this movement in an article on " Religion and Health," appearing in *An Outline of Christianity*, by various authors. The Waverley Book Company, Ltd., 1926.

to realize itself. It takes a certain time in doing so, known as the "latent period." In a simple case of suggestion, then, the mind of the individual is in a passive state, free from contradictory or conflicting ideas, receptive, ready to allow the suggested idea or ideas to be aroused in full force. The idea has a tendency to pass over into action, to bring about its own realization, in so far as it is not interfered with by conflicting ideas. Favouring factors in suggestion are a state of general passivity, muscular as well as sensory, combined with concentration upon some neutral idea. We find in psychotherapeutic practice, when we wish to produce benefit by suggestion, that our best results are obtained if we get the patient into a passive state, when the muscles are relaxed, a state not so much of attention as what is called by Baudouin *contention*—a state of con-centration without effort. We eliminate effort by requesting the patient to relax his muscles, and we encourage concentration by giving him something to concentrate upon. The mind, although passive, is not in a state of distraction. It is narrowed down upon some very general idea, preferably upon the idea of sleep, and if in that state an idea is aroused in the mind, an idea of some change in the patient's bodily and mental condition, that idea tends to realize itself to its utmost possible extent. A convenient time for giving suggestion is before rest at night. At that time the patient has relinquished all his interests in matters of the day, he is more able to get really peaceful and relaxed, and the background of his mind, the so-called subconscious mind, is more accessible to outside influences. In referring to the subconscious in this way, one seems to be speaking rather metaphorically, as if the subconscious were a sort of occult force. It is not exactly that, but rather a class concept, including mental tendencies which are not clearly present in consciousness. Indeed, it is those tendencies not clearly present in consciousness that are most important in suggestion treatment, because those which are clearly conscious have appropriate ideas linking them up with other conscious tendencies. The mind, so far as it is conscious, is alert and acts therefore according to more or less rational motives. Suggestion to the conscious mind has usually little effect—it is transitory if it takes effect at all. Persuasion, which uses rational arguments, is the more appropriate and effective influence in this sphere. Suggestion is a kind of affirmation, it is rightly addressed to the subconscious, to the fundamental tendencies of the mind that are not directly represented in consciousness.

The question then arises—What is the relation between suggestion, as we have thus explained it, and faith ? The following example may throw some preliminary light upon this problem. A few years ago I was treating a boy of thirteen for some disturbing nervous symptoms which interfered with his life at school, and which he was most anxious to get rid of, by means of suggestion (after a preliminary analysis of the conditions in which the illness began). The first two or three hours of suggestion treatment, during each of which he lay passive on a couch, receiving suggestions from me every five minutes or so, seemed to produce very little, if any, effect, till about the fourth treatment, when he suddenly burst into tears, and said in a voice charged with emotion, " Now I really do believe that it is going to be all right ; I feel absolutely certain about it." From that moment his symptom (enuresis) disappeared, and he became permanently well. In this case we have an interesting illustration of a transition from suggestion to a state of faith. In suggestion the mind is stimulated to produce an idea, and then this idea in its turn realizes

itself, because it has no competitors, it works auto-
matically, by its own momentum, as it were. In faith,
on the other hand, one finds a state of mind which is
essentially active ; as William James said, there is a will
to believe, it is a definite assertion or affirmation of an
active mind. The whole mind is active and the experience is accompanied by an emotion which is something
of the nature of volition, a determination to give oneself
up completely to the idea for some reason or other. It
may be just in order to get rid of a symptom, or for the
sake of higher development of the mind—with belief in
the possibility of such higher development.

Intermediate between suggestion and faith is auto-
suggestion, where the individual gives suggestions to
himself. In auto-suggestion he is passive, he thinks of
sleep, he gets for a moment or two into a comatose state,
almost free from all activity and yet in a state of concentration, and then, in some wonderful way, he is able
to present to himself the idea, or bring up before himself
the idea, of what he wants, the change he wishes to bring
about in his mind or body. He, as we say, affirms this
idea to himself, that, e.g., at night he will sleep well, and
wake up feeling much better and free from the stammer,
or nervousness, or difficulty of concentration, or whatever it may be—that he will be able to concentrate well,
to remember well, to feel cheerful and happy ; and
experience shows us that beneficial results definitely
follow. By perseverance in the use of this method the
patient can often transform his whole outlook upon life.
I look upon auto-suggestion as a bad term. It is really
something more akin to faith than to suggestion. It is
the cultivation of a special active attitude of mind, an
assertion of health and of faith in its possibility—a
particular kind of healthy-mindedness. If you treat
yourself by auto-suggestion, you get benefit so far as you

can make it depend upon the extent to which you can really believe and affirm to yourself the gospel of health, that health is more real than disease ; that so far as the will of God goes, He wills health rather than disease. With such a crude belief results actually do follow.

In dealing with these problems, which are, of course, really extremely difficult, it is necessary to take facts first and look for theories afterwards. We can say as a fact that suggestion produces results, that auto-suggestion produces still more permanent results, and that, if genuine faith is aroused, the most astounding results of a permanent nature may be produced. In this sequence, looked at psychologically, we see that the transition is from passivity to activity, that faith as such is a form of volition, and that auto-suggestion as such is not in conflict with volition, as M. Coué and his followers have wrongly contended ; it is simply a completion of volition. The so-called law of reversed effort, which Coué and his followers have made famous, may be expressed in this form : " When the will and the imagination are in conflict, the imagination always wins." The conclusion would seem to be that imagination is stronger than will ; but in the French the word *vouloir*, though sometimes meaning will, often means wish, and, so far as one can make out in Coué's own brief writings, he is thinking really of wish rather than of will. If there is a wish on the one hand and imagination on the other, the imagination-result is more likely to occur than the wish-result ; indeed, the situation is one of frustrated will. The process of wishing is on the road towards volition or will, but it has not yet reached the final stage of volition. In that transition from wishing to willing or volition, the imagination, lighted up and intensified by fear or some other disturbing emotion, slips in, as it were, gets the lead, and prevents the wish becoming the will.

18

Imagination then wins because the will has not been completed. On the other hand, that which has been called auto-suggestion, and which I think is a definite attitude of mind akin to faith, is a process of complete volition, turning mere wish into will by adequate control of the imagination.

This will become clear if we take an example. A patient suffering from a fear of open spaces, called technically agoraphobia, may be unable to walk a hundred yards down a wide street by himself or to cross it. As soon as he attempts to start on his journey his heart palpitates, he becomes breathless, tends to hug the wall, becomes less and less able to move, is glued to the spot, and has to give up and return home. Such a patient may be encouraged by his relatives and friends to pull himself together and to make a real effort, and may be told that if he makes an adequate effort he will succeed in getting over this difficulty. But he finds, on the contrary, that the greater the effort the worse the situation becomes, the harder he tries the less he succeeds. This seems to be a situation akin to that summed up in Coué's law of reversed effort : on the one side, the will to walk alone ; on the other side, the imagination, the fear, that he will not succeed ; and in this conflict imagination wins. But, on looking more closely into the situation, one realizes that there is no complete volition here. The patient is ill, his mental processes do not enable him to will completely in this particular situation. Why, is a matter to be discovered in other ways, through deep analysis—deep analysis will show why he is unable to will to cross the street. In his attempt to will to walk alone or to cross the street, the feeling of effort becomes more vivid and more intense, but it remains a mere wish or suggestion. Opposed to this effortful wish to cross the street, one finds the idea or suggestion of failure accompanied by the fear of failure. In this conflict the suggestion of failure accompanied by the emotion of fear obviously will win, as against the suggestion, unaccompanied by any strong emotion, that he will cross the street. This so-called law of reversed effort is thus merely a simple illustration of conflict between one suggestion and another, or between one " imagination " and another. If this is so, what do we mean by will ? We mean a wish or desire, accompanied by the judgment, affirmation, or belief that we shall fulfil the desire from our own resources, so far as in us lies—that we shall realize the desire because we desire it. In cases like that of agoraphobia* the object of the psychotherapist is to train the patient's will, so that one disagrees with Coué, and, instead of saying that a re-education of the will is useless, one rather points out that the patient has not achieved complete volition in this situation, and that he has to learn to will, after first discovering the cause of his incomplete volition by self-analysis or (much more effectively) by deep analysis carried out by the physician. In these cases mere suggestion as an automatic thing is rather ineffective. One may produce temporary alleviation by calming the patient's mind, and discouraging spasmodic effort and diminishing the tendency to intensify the symptoms by effort ; but the patient quickly falls back to the original state, because the cause is still there. The truth is, he has no faith in that particular treatment, nor in his power to cross the street, and there is reason for this lack of faith. In some cases one finds deep down in the mind a fear of fainting ; he has fainted on some previous occasion, and so he has lost confidence in himself ; he feels he will be right away from all aid, so the mere sight

---

* So far as the agoraphobia is a manifestation of " anxiety neurosis " it is physically caused, and is to be treated by advice on sex-hygiene.

of an open space arouses this subconscious idea, his heart beats rapidly, and the initial stages of a fainting attack set in with this feeling of anxiety, a feeling that he is " glued to the spot."

If, then, suggestion and faith are distinct, in what way can we indicate their relationship more clearly than we have already done ? From the theoretical point of view, I think we can say that suggestion is ultimately always dependent upon some form or other of faith, and not conversely. The patient may not be conscious of faith, he may respond to suggestion, and suggestion may be given in a mechanical repetitive way. He may have no conscious faith in the method, but he finds that the method benefits him. If one analyses him, however, one discovers that in his subconscious mind there is faith. The relationship between suggestion and such a general (often subconscious) background of faith is similar to that between the empirical investigation of nature by scientists, and the general metaphysical principle of the uniformity of nature, within the domain of knowledge. A scientist would not be able to make a single step forward in his investigations or theories about the universe unless he had that belief in the uniformity of nature—that A remains A unless and until it is altered by some other factor, that if A becomes B there is some reason for it in the intrusion of further factors. Unless he holds this metaphysical belief in the uniformity of nature, he is unable to form hypotheses, and by their means advance in scientific knowledge. His individual generalizations from facts of experience are based upon this belief. Similarly an individual benefits by suggestion treatment along special lines because of his more general belief or faith in the universe. The individual may not consciously hold such a faith, but somewhere in his mind there is that faith, the belief in a friendliness somewhere, and if he is completely lacking in it, then he will be completely inaccessible to therapeutic suggestion. Actually, in the case of everyone, there is the tendency, the readiness to believe in friendliness outside—based upon early childhood experiences and inherited tendencies. This again brings us back from the point of view of suggestion and faith to the more fundamental problem of " deep " analysis.

Some psycho-analysts consider that the facts of suggestion, of faith-healing, etc., are explicable in terms of early experiences within the bosom of the family, in terms of the Œdipus complex and psychological reactions thereto. The theory is a very complicated one and cannot be dealt with in detail here.* One may, however, consider it in its most formal aspect, and point out that the whole question of faith in terms of infantile experience is based upon an original postulate. It is not necessarily based upon facts at all ; facts may later on be discovered to support the special details of the theory, but the general theory has its real basis elsewhere, in the *postulate* that whatever is in the mind can be explained in terms of previous experience. It is the postulate of determinism. Some psychologists may think that determinism is on the road to being proved through the further development of psychology. That, of course, is reasoning in a circle, because what we do in psychology is to look for causes of the various effects that we see, on the basis of the postulate of determinism. In philosophy there is the fundamental principle of sufficient reason (Leibniz), the principle that there is always a sufficient reason why anything should happen rather than not happen. Determinism looks for the sufficient reason in any particular case always in what has already occurred.

* See especially S. Freud : *Totem and Tabu, Group Psychology and the Analysis of the Ego,* and *Das Ich und das Es.*

We therefore know beforehand, however rapidly deep analysis may develop—and it is developing rapidly every year now—we know beforehand that it will seem to restrict ever more and more the doctrine of the freedom of the will. The further psychology advances, the less will the idea of freedom, or of spontaneity of the mind, be apparent. But the very fact that we can predict this shows that it is not the result of psychological advance. Psychology cannot either prove or disprove determinism.

More cautious psychologists adopt the doctrine of self-determinism. They must adopt some form of determinism if they are to be psychologists at all, in order to link up and co-ordinate mental events within a wider system. But they take as their system not the antecedent processes of the mind only, but the entire mind right up to the present moment. The test of a determinist doctrine is the power of prediction, and, in the case of mental process, prediction is impossible unless we know every moment of the person's life right up to the moment when the action which we are supposed to be predicting occurs. The act is then completely determined because it is determined by his entire self. This is a doctrine of self-determinism, rather than determinism, because it is determinism within a self which is growing, and which acts as a whole. What we mean by freedom is the power of the mind of the individual acting as a whole. A person is free and is acting freely when he is most himself in carrying out an action. The kind of action that to us seems impulsive action, where we feel out of ourselves, out of our mind, and we wonder later on however we could have done such a thing, such action is not free. So far as conduct is the outcome of the whole mind working in its unity, so far it is self-determined, and free in the only sense in which we can understand freedom.

Although one may seem to have deviated along another line of thought, and to have left the question of faith, it is of significance for the problem of faith, because faith is such an affirmation of the entire mind. Someone has defined faith as a readiness to trust and to follow the noblest hypothesis ; it is an act of self-assertion, one decides to be on the side of the angels, takes one's side in the battle of existence, for battle it is. Ideally at least it should represent an attitude of the entire mind, but it may often be not so complete. It may often be rather a momentary mood, and so far as it is that, it may be followed by a relapse. Here the vexed question of spiritual healing arises. The process of spiritual healing is a process of arousing faith, the faith state, and that faith state may have different degrees of rationality, which is the same thing as saying that it may extend over a smaller or larger area of the self, and if it is limited to a small part of the self, it may mislead the individual instead of helping him. One reason why many of us are very doubtful of the wisdom of spiritual-healing services is that, for many who attend such services, it is an appeal to superficial emotion and to primitive credulity. There is the tendency to intensify that hysterical condition of mind from which many of the patients are already suffering. In some cases there may be a disappearance of hysterical symptoms and apparent cure, but only at the expense of replacement by another symptom—namely, reliance upon a quasi-miraculous possibility, the expectation of getting something for nothing, as it were, of getting direct gifts without full appreciation of corresponding demands upon personality. Mass-suggestion may produce startling results of a temporary and superficial kind, but individual treatment is more likely to produce deep and lasting benefit.

The whole question of spiritual healing is one of

extreme difficulty, and awaits further medical and psychological investigation. But among its more obvious dangers we cannot overlook the danger of intensifying the hysterical or the infantile attitude towards life that many neurotic patients have, and the danger of disappointment and of a set-back to their faith in the case of those who receive no benefit.

CHAPTER XXII

WE now come to a consideration of what is probably the most important form of religious experience—namely mystical experience—to which all other religious feelings seem to lead up. The mystical experience is an experience of apparently direct union with the Divine. It is a form of meditation which leads the soul up to divinity. In this mental state the person may lose the feeling of individuality, and may seem to pass beyond the limitations of space and time. When he endeavours to describe his experience he can only express it in negatives. He can say what the experience is not, but he is quite unable to say what it is. One of the greatest authorities on mysticism is Saint Teresa, and her own experience and general theory are summed up in that important book, *The Interior Castle**, in which she describes various stages of union with the Divine. In almost every form of religion in the world we find similar experiences described, although there are individual differences. Leaving aside these differences, we find quite enough identity to convince us that, just as religious feeling itself is a special mental attitude towards life and a sort of knowledge of reality, so here in mysticism we have its central core, the most characteristic way in which our religious knowledge comes to us. If only it were universal, there would be no further trouble about the matter. Unfortunately,

---

* *The Interior Castle, or The Mansions*, by Saint Teresa of Jesus (written 1577). Translated by the Benedictines of Stanbrook; revised with Introduction and Additional Notes by the Very Reverend Benedict Zimmerman, O.C.D. Second Edition, Thomas Baker, London, 1912.

so many people protest that they are unable to verify the occurrence of mystical experience in themselves; this is a serious difficulty in the way of its significance or validity, though not destroying its interest for psychology.

Before considering this matter further, it would be well to mention certain types of experience that are analogous to the mystical experience, but that otherwise are not regarded as of special religious value or importance. In the first place, there is the peculiar feeling of joy, exultation, or rapture that may accompany certain sensory experiences. Certain bars of music and phrases of poetry seem to have a quite irrational appeal that cannot be explained in terms of the actual associations of the sounds or meaning of the words, but apparently touch some hidden chord in the mind, and thereby stir the soul deeply. Muscular and kinæsthetic sensations sometimes arouse a similar feeling. Well-ordered muscular activity may often induce a feeling of unity with nature. On a beautiful spring morning, when away from one's fellow men in the fields, one may be suddenly overtaken with a feeling of the direct continuity of one's own life with the life of nature. One looks with different eyes upon the scenery and welcomes it as a part of one's self, or rather, as something infinitely greater than one's self in which one is merged. This feeling may be intensified in special circumstances, as, e.g., when riding, in which no doubt sympathy with the horse as well as the muscular exercise play their part. We might perhaps explain these, often extremely pleasant, experiences as a sort of reversion to an earlier and more primitive form of consciousness, when we were less aware of our own individuality and its problems: when we were more in touch with the animals and plants around us, and felt our kinship with them more vividly. Since it is not an experience constantly present, when it does come it comes with a special vividness, as intensified pleasure, which is not surprising; it is normal and healthy, not pathological. Communion is in general a healthy form of experience. It is the feeling of isolation from nature, animate and inanimate, which is the terrible thing, and which we find in such pronounced form among some of our mentally deranged patients.

Secondly, there are the mental states sometimes produced by anæsthetics—the so-called " anæsthetic revelation." Under the influence of alcohol, ether, chloroform, and especially of nitrous oxide gas, many people get extraordinary feelings of deepened insight into the meaning of things. They may come out of the anæsthetic with the conviction that they have solved the riddle of the universe, and suffer great disappointment because all they can find in their minds at the moment of awakening are some doggerel rhymes that have no significance whatever. Then again, a similar mystical experience can come over one in conditions of self-hypnosis. If one lies passive on a couch with the eyes closed and all voluntary muscles relaxed, and breathes slowly and deeply in order to increase that relaxation, one may feel oneself slipping away from the world of clear consciousness, losing the feeling of orientation and of sensitivity in the limbs. The body seems to be floating in the air, and later on one may feel that one does not possess a body at all. In this state, one seems to become de-personalized, as it were, absorbed in the " all," into the soul of the universe. One attains to what has been called cosmic consciousness.

Now can we find any identical factor in these various experiences ? In all except those accompanying muscular exercise, in the anæsthetic revelation, auto- and hetero-hypnosis, etc., one characteristic seems to be the abolition of the motor tendency. In a normal man who goes about his affairs with eyes wide open and mind alert, there is a definite adjustment of muscular activity to the needs of the situation. His muscles are tense and always ready to come into action, and his experience is essentially sensori-motor. It is probably this motor aspect of experience which intensifies the feeling of personality, and if it is brought into abeyance with anæsthetics or special artificial modes of relaxation, the sense of personality disappears with it. The individual is less conscious of the dividing lines between himself and the rest of the universe.

It is clear that, in mystical experiences proper, we ought to allow for the possible admixture of such experiences as these and discount them; although it is more than doubtful whether we can say that all religious mystic experience should be explained in terms of such cruder experiences. Some scientists tend to criticize all these experiences as abnormal, because they involve a disturbance of the sensori-motor attitude towards life. But this would be to make a very great assumption, an assumption analogous to the one we have already discussed in connection with determinism. Such scientists map out a general system of explanation, and everything they find in that system they call scientific. Everything not explained in terms of that system they attempt to explain as pathological, and in calling it pathological they deny the validity or importance of it.

An alternative explanation would be the following: It is very obvious that experience, as we know it, occurs and comes to us under the forms of space and time, because we are embodied minds, because we are limited, finite parts of the universe, and yet we have in us powers that can in some way lift us beyond these limits. It seems quite clear that one such power is that of thought; another is the direct insight of æsthetic appreciation;

and religious experience in its mystical form may prove
the greatest power of all in this direction. When, in the
mystical experience, we have the feeling of timelessness,
it is quite conceivable that we *are* passing beyond the
limits of time, and proving, to ourselves at any rate,
that time is appearance and not reality, and that
immortality is not something we have to wait for at the end
of this life, but something we can and do achieve in
varying degrees while still living this life. That has
been the view of leading philosophers throughout the
ages. We find Aristotle urging his readers, ἐφ' ὅσον ἐνδέχεται
ἀθανατίζειν, to be immortal as far as possible, even in
this life.

Thus we come to the tremendous metaphysical
problem of the reality of time, which is, perhaps, the
greatest metaphysical problem of the present day, and
especially important to our point of view of personality.
So long as we consider time as one of the conditions of
individual experience, we are tied down to a certain
theory of personality, which may easily be the wrong
one. All psychological theories of personality, of course,
are of this nature, and, to a great extent, they are for
that reason rather depressing, because they emphasize
the limits that we are all aware of. But in emphasizing
these limits they tend to make them much more complete
and ultimate than they really are for us. Again, if we
take physiological modes of thought in considering
psychological problems, we are impressed by rates or
rhythms of physiological processes. As physiological
psychologists we may be impressed by experiments which
show that estimation of time is most accurate with
a certain rhythm and less accurate with shorter or longer
rhythms, or again, that experience of succession has a
lower limit of causation. In the background there may
be the unspoken but fallacious assumption that the

experience of succession is the same as, or at least runs parallel with, a succession of experiences; and again the further assumption that a succession of experiences runs parallel with a succession of physiological changes somewhere or other in the organism. It is easy to show by metaphysical argument that the conception of time as something ultimately real leads us to definite antinomies or contradictions, from which we cannot escape unless we agree to regard time as appearance and not reality. But we still find it extremely difficult to understand most aspects of experience, unless we do regard time as real. If we consider experience in detail, we see how much time contributes to the quality of that experience. So impressed was Bergson by this fact that he has taken time as the very stuff of which reality is made. He speaks of *durée réelle* as something which is ultimate, although he regards the time of mathematical physics and the other physical sciences as spatialized time. Of course, many of the goods and pleasures of life seem to be bound up with the time function. Time is essential even to such a good as the ethical good, the good will. A good action is one which is definitely and deliberately intended and carried out, and can only be carried out in the course of time. If one imagines time transcended, it is difficult to imagine any strictly moral action, or indeed any action at all. It is difficult to attribute the characteristics of morality, which is one of our three general values, to a timeless experience. In transcending time, one seems to transcend morality as such. In æsthetic experience timelessness seems to be more possible. When we enjoy a picture, for the time being we feel ourselves out of time; its artistic meaning is timeless. But then when we turn to music, another form of art, time appears to be of its essence, though even here we should not be too certain of this. We know there is an anecdote about Mozart, who, in speaking of one of his compositions, explains how he first had it in his head before he wrote it down. He heard all the notes together —*zusammen*. That was a wonderful experience, he said, the like of which he never heard again. In music there is a degree of transcendence of time ; chords occur one after another, yet they have to combine in some way to give a feeling of harmony and melody, and one is conscious of what has gone before and what is about to come. One sees more meaning in the production the second time than the first, because one knows what is coming. So that one might say, with regard to music, that although the possibility of musical experience, and of the training of the ear, is bound up with the conditions of temporal sequence, yet the ultimate outcome when the trained ear appreciates the true inward meaning of music is something that is already on the way towards transcendence of time. As regards truth, it is quite clear that time is transcended—once true, always true. Although the proving to a class of schoolboys that the three angles of a triangle are equal to two right angles takes time, and individual boys take varying lengths of time in gaining an adequate insight into that geometrical truth, once they have acquired the truth the insight is beyond time. Moreover, it was true before they began to consider it, and it will remain true after they have ceased to think of it. Truth, as truth, is certainly beyond time.

Finally, as regards religious experience, one feels that it is essential to this experience, if to any, that it should be beyond time. Although it may be conditioned by time, in that one gains a deeper and deeper insight into its truths through an experience that comes to one in the course of days, yet the experience itself takes us out of time and enables us to attain to a mystic attitude towards the universe, beyond any opportunism that acceptance of the reality of time can give. If we assume that time is completely real for us, that we are bound down in a time process, and that we do not transcend it at all, then our ultimate outlook upon reality is very depressing and unmeaning. Despite temporary improvements in the conditions of human life and the advance of physical science, this earth will eventually become uninhabitable, degeneration will come sooner or later to the race, to the physical side of things, so that in terms of matter and material change and temporal process there seems little room for ultimate hope*. The life of the human race would really be " a tale told by an idiot, full of sound and fury, signifying nothing." But all the meaning we find in life is on the way towards a transcending of time. When we look towards a future life, we look not so much towards a life at some future time that some enthusiasts would like to prove and even describe for us, but to a life eternal, in which we pass beyond the conditions of the merely material, which, of course, is the temporal and spatial. We mean by matter something such that two portions of it cannot be in the same place at the same time—that is probably the best definition of matter which we can give. We can only think of matter in terms of space and time.

It is very significant that these various experiences that appear to transcend time, and also perhaps space, accompanied by disorientation in space and time, bring with them a diminution of feeling of individuality, so that at the end it looks as if we shall have to dismiss individuality with other aspects of existence as appearance and not reality. It is very doubtful whether we shall be able to preserve individuality as an ultimate value

* The further advance of science and of its power over nature may, of course, falsify this prophecy.

in the scheme of things ; it is a stepping-stone, no doubt,
and, as far as we can see of existence in this life, there
is a parallel process of individuation and inter-relation
going on, so that really great individuals, great personalities, are those who have individualized their lives so
that they are in closer communion with their fellows,
rather than in isolation from them. In a way this is
an absorption. The great statesman, the great man of
action, the great scientist, is the person who is able
to suppress his mere individuality in order that he may
gain a wider personality of the group or nation to which
he belongs. The great statesman speaks for an entire
nation because he is able to understand the various
needs of the individuals in it. He does not lose his
personality thereby, he does not efface it, he makes it
all the more real. On the other hand, the self-centred
paranoiac who has to be shut up in an asylum is convinced
of his own greatness, believes himself to be a reincarnation
of Napoleon or of the Messiah, or even God Himself,
and, corresponding to his intense feeling of individuality
and difference from others, we find a depressing bank-
ruptcy in his mental make-up. The great scientist is
he who keeps clear of fanaticism and crankiness by
continuous moral effort, by effacing his own peculiarities,
wishes, desires, and interests in the matter, in order to
get as unbiased a view as possible of the facts. He has
the greater task of effacing, not only the individuality
of nationality, but of humanity itself, and yet in that
process we cannot say that he is losing personality in
the true sense of the word. Personality, then, ought
to be distinguished from individuality. Individuality is
a mere difference from others. Personality is a process
of development, in which we have parallel processes of
individuation and assimilation. The man of personality
gives out to the world around him and also absorbs it

19

in himself, identifying himself as far as possible with others and sympathizing with their aims. Yet, however far developed, finite personality must be appearance and not complete reality, because in the universe there is no room for merely separate persons. Ultimately there can only be one complete person, he who is completely self-sufficing, and he can only be completely self-sufficing if he has complete knowledge and power over his environment, and therefore he must extend throughout that environment, and must be the totality of Reality itself. The only complete person is the Absolute or God, and progress towards personality in individuals seems to be partly intellectual, along the path of reason, and partly intuitional. One can see it as a union, ever closer and deeper, with the spirit of the universe, as an identification to a greater and greater extent with all that is highest in the universe, and that is the intellectual and intuitional counterpart of what we mean by the mystical experience.

One might perhaps do more justice to this problem of the mystical by admitting that there is a lower and a higher form of mysticism. The lower form is on the plane of immediate feeling, unmediated by thought. Such is the experience of the athlete, the drug-addict, the devotee of self-hypnosis, the primitive artist in man. Here is an experience of direct union on a lower plane of feeling. Then thought discriminates, distinguishes subject from object, objects from one another, holds the mind apart from its object, and yet, in that process, links it up more and more closely with its object until, when its work is done as far as it can be done, again there arises a communion, a feeling that the subject-object relationship is being transcended, and this is the true, the higher mystical experience. It will include various types of experience. We will not identify it with religious mystical experience because we have

already marked and separated that off from our other
general attitudes towards the totality of things—the
intellectual, the æsthetic, and the moral attitudes, and
in each of these attitudes we find the higher form of
mysticism.   There remains the mysticism which may
truly be called religious.   But even that does not completely satisfy us, since we are left with four distinct
things which we feel must in some way be unified.
Actually, of course, they are unified in an all-inclusive
experience, which is the real higher mystical experience,
the mediation by thought of all the other attitudes,
including the religious, so that just as the race began
life in a primitive religious way, likewise at the end,
after science and philosophy have done all that they
can, the fundamental attitude is once more a religious
attitude.   An individual who is unable to get that attitude
at all is to that extent incomplete.   We sometimes find
that such an individual is mentally sick, suffering from
repressions which cut him off from it.   With the removal
of these repressions by analysis the experience may
become once more possible to him.

It is only fair to mention here that one school of
thought explains all these mystical experiences in terms
of what is called Narcissism.   In such experience there
is a turning inwards of the mind upon itself, a drawing
in of libido, a concentration of libido upon the self.
An increase of Narcissism under certain conditions may
bring with it a feeling of intense pleasure and of liberation, transcending time and space, although it is really
a set-back, a regression, to an infantility of an extreme
type.   The actual evidence in support of so extreme
a theory is quite inadequate, and against it may be set
the general arguments of pp. 267, 268 above.   But we
should not overlook the rôle played by Narcissism in
some forms of religious experience.

CHAPTER XXIII

ANY theory of personality is faced with a special problem in determining the position of values—goodness, truth, beauty—and of religion within the circle of individual experience. We can only deal with it in its most general aspect here.

There is nothing very much to be said from a formal point of view with regard to ethics. On this side the real problem is that of obligation, and however much we may accumulate empirical knowledge on the subject of human conduct we do not thereby get any deeper insight into the nature of obligation than we should by considering ordinary cases of everyday life. Empirical considerations—considerations of the experience of different races at different periods of history—show that duties change and vary with circumstances. What is the right thing to do at one period of time, within one circle of culture, and at one epoch of history, may be different from what should be done at some other period of time. But in both cases there is a feeling of obligation involved, and something which is more than a mere psychological feeling, something which seems to go deeper than a mere human feeling, something which seems absolute—namely, obligation. " I have to do this ; this is my duty." And if you ask why, all you can say is, " because it is my duty." You cannot give a reason for it. In the end you give an approximate reason for doing some particular thing, and having given that reason you ask why you should act with reference to that reason, and the only reply is : Because I am bound to act so, it is obligatory on me to act as I do, e.g., to treat everybody as an end and not merely as a means, to avoid giving objectless pain to others, to promote the happiness of the world in general. If you ask the reasons why you should do it, you find none apart from this, which is more than a mere momentary feeling, which is a conviction. Thus duties change, but duty remains the same. Obligations change and vary with circumstances, but obligation as such is there, and cannot be evaded. We can ignore it, but we suffer by ignoring it and find ourselves falling to a lower level of spiritual development.

The situation is similar to that with regard to knowledge itself. You cannot explain knowledge as such. Truth itself cannot be explained. You can indicate the way in which truth arises—the way in which an individual may approximate more and more to truth through observation, and through the adequate and harmonious working of association. You can understand how error arises through false associations and how delusions may arise, but truth itself cannot be explained. It is an ideal which we feel is a reality, but a reality which is never completely reached by us. It is there. So far as we trouble to think at all, it is implied. So with the appreciation of beauty, or æsthetic experience, we can describe the conditions under which the individual becomes more and more expert in the appreciation of beauty of different kinds like music and the plastic arts, but in itself we cannot understand it. We can describe the concomitants specially involved in the contemplation of different works of art, the pleasure of a peculiar nature which we say is æsthetic, but that is not the æsthetic experience itself. In a similar way with morality, we can indicate how an individual becomes more and more moral by learning to be more and more disinterested in his outlook on life, but why he should be disinterested we cannot say. That is simply borne in upon us. We do judge others in that way at any rate. We put other people in the rank of moral excellence to the extent to which they fight for the good of the community and the whole of existence rather than for themselves alone.

How it is possible to pursue the ethical ideal is again really a mystery. We feel that true freedom is involved in this. It is true that the great ethical writer, Henry Sidgwick, used to protest that the general problem of freedom was of little importance to ethical theory, but others would not agree with him. I certainly should not. It seems to me that the truly ethical outlook on life is bound up with belief in self-determination, in the power of the mind to act from itself, from within itself. It must be active rather than merely passive. Instead of being merely moved from outside by various physically external or psychologically external motives, it must be able to take a definite stand, it must be able to identify itself with the moral law. That seems to me to mean freedom. In conventional morality you identify yourself with a code of conduct because you wish to do as others do, but such conduct is only by accident moral, if moral at all. In truly moral action you realize its rationality, but more than that and beyond that you realize its value, and you have in you some direct power of realizing its value. This is called conscience. Unfortunately the word conscience is rather spoiled for our purpose, because it is so often identified with accidental feelings that vary from time to time, and with individual experience that can be disturbed in disease.* A person can be over-conscientious, and it is interesting to notice

---

* It is here that Freud's doctrine of the " ego-ideal " or " super-ego " as set out, e.g., in his essay, *Das Ich und das Es,* is in place. But such a theory is quite inadequate to explain conscience and obligation as such. No merely psychological explanation could suffice.

in these disease cases that over-conscientiousness goes with a deficiency and not with an excess of morality. Patients suffering from over-conscientiousness are over-conscientious about less important things and not over the really fundamental things. One's attention is drawn from time to time to an announcement in the newspaper that someone has made an anonymous payment to the Chancellor of the Exchequer for income tax, and it is called conscience money. That conscience money is always a very small amount. The last amount I saw was £1 5s. You may be sure that if that person had been really guilty of defrauding the income tax collectors, and had taken the trouble afterwards to make restitution, the amount would be much greater than £1 5s. I look on cases like that as pathological disturbances of conscience, but conscience in a psychological sense and not in a truly ethical sense. One feels one needs another word. It is a direct feeling of obligation, just as much a rational thing as an emotional thing. The most moral people are not the most emotional people about conduct. So in matters of the intellect ; a person who is sound in his work as a scientist or a philosopher is generally not so emotional as one less sound. The same rule applies to æsthetic appreciation, e.g., in appreciation of music, in the course of the necessary training of the musical sense, one must learn to get away from crude emotion. That crude emotion is a temporary thing, showing that the mind is caught up and stimulated and is reacting, but the emotion is too individual, and one has to appreciate the general, the universal, in all these things. In the plastic arts, one has to appreciate, as Plato and Schopenhauer said, the *idea*. One has a direct vision of the idea, or of the relationship between ideas. And emotions stand in one's way. It is true that there is a peculiar feeling in æsthetic and intellectual and moral appreciation—e.g. in appreciation of duty done for its own sake, quite apart from, and in addition to, circumstances being considered, and the consequences. I am inclined to think that here one has the soul, the ego, reacting in its essence.

I have tried to avoid this, but I am brought now to the consideration of a view which by most people would not be regarded as sound. The self, the mind that psychology deals with, is not the same as the soul. Psychology is not the science of the soul; psychology is the science of the mind, of mental process in time, but corresponding with that mental process in time, and as a complement of it, you have the experiencing ego, and that ego has its own reality and its own unity. This is the idea of the pure or transcendental ego, as distinct from the empirical ego. Psychology deals with the empirical ego, shows how it develops in course of time, how the young child starts life with the empirical ego partially organized, to a certain extent inherited. The child inherits aptitudes and interests from ancestors, just as it inherits the organization of its physical body. Talent is inherited, but genius is not inherited. Talent is characteristic of the empirical ego, the inter-relation of the pure ego with the material environment. Genius is characteristic of the pure ego, which is out of time, although it reveals itself in time. The explanation of genius does not come from heredity anyway. If you consider Beethoven, you do not find any evidence—and if you are going to be scientific, you must judge by evidence—of that power of giving meaning to musical sounds and creating artistic form, in his ancestors or in the history of the race. Genius can show itself not only in art, but in philosophy and morals. Socrates and Jesus were moral geniuses. You are dealing all the time with a different level of reality.

A dualism like this is not, in the end, intellectually satisfying, for the reason that the intellect is a unifying thing, that what we mean by thinking is unifying, systematizing, fitting things within a system. When we form a hypothesis, what we do is to observe a number of facts, and see their implications and inter-relationships with one another, and so far as we find they form a unity, we consider that we are getting better insight. This unifying principle is an urge that forces us along. No dualism can be ultimately satisfactory. In our philosophy we must try to synthesize knowledge of the empirical ego and knowledge of the pure ego. That cannot yet be done. We do not know enough about it. It is better, however, to draw distinctions, so long as they are really the right distinctions, than to synthesize too hurriedly and mix things up. It is most important to distinguish this value-experience from the empirical experience. The distinction which emphasizes the essential importance of value over against chance experiences that occur to us from moment to moment and from day to day, is extremely important for our theory of personality, because it puts the centre of the gravity of the personality in the right place.

The value-experiences of the good, the beautiful and the true, are not identical with religious experience, although they are related to it. Religious experience is not exactly on all fours with them ; it is not on the same level, but is on a higher level still. Religious experience arises so far as the individual is facing the totality of existence. The feeling thus aroused, so far as the personality takes up a mental attitude towards the whole universe, is religious experience. Within it the value-attitudes are of the utmost importance, and we tend nowadays to emphasize the ethical attitude, the appreciation of goodness, duty, obligation, in relation to religion. But if we study it psychologically, we see that there is not always a point to point correspondence between genuine feelings of religion and genuine feelings of morality. A person may have strong religious feelings, which are not merely emotion but a genuine awareness of mystery, of the totality of things—of a great mystery with its own peculiar feeling of communion and satisfaction in communion—in relative independence of the extent to which he fulfils the moral law, or the extent to which his conscience is sensitive, or the extent to which he is aware of his duty—what he should do and his obligation to do it. And conversely we may find another person who reaches a very high degree of ethical excellence, who is very strict in doing his duty in life for its own sake, in the right way, not in the pathological way, and yet with no very intense feeling or conviction as regards his attitude towards the totality of things. We must separate the two. I do not mean that either of them can be completely absent. It would be going too far to say that anyone exists who is entirely deficient in the ethical or religious attitude, but because they do not tend to run parallel they must be distinguished on the psychological level. But the level to which they really belong is not the psychological level. It is a higher level and the level of religion is higher even than that of value. There is the level of value, but the level of religion is higher than the level of value in the sense that it is more all-inclusive and more face to face with totality and the innermost mystery of existence. Thus there are aspects, ethical, æsthetic and logical, which are all aspects of reality, but religion itself is an attitude to reality in its concreteness. The values are important, and it is difficult to conceive religion apart from them. We should probably be right in saying that normal human nature has a religious sense, not in the out-of-

date sense of faculty psychology, but in the form of a
primitive tendency towards the religious attitude—to
feel the mystery, the beneficence, and perhaps the stern-
ness of the spirit of the universe. This is gradually
revised in the course of the individual's life, it is freed
more and more from irrelevant experiences, just as the
appreciation of music or other forms of art is gradually
freed from irrelevant experiences.

With regard to this religious attitude, we must recognize how it varies in emphasis from person to person, and
we must be ready to attach importance to what we find
in the experience of those who are most taken up with it.
The saints and the martyrs, by living the religious life,
have shown the earnestness and the reality of it. There
is always the question of pathological emphasis that
runs through all this subject. As we see in the case of
conscience, a direct feeling may be emphasized pathologically, and our criterion there would no doubt be the
criterion of balance. We find that where the conscience
is pathologically over-emphasized it is out of proportion.
In a similar way some people are over-religious in a
pathological sense, they are unbalanced and their
religion carries with it a lot of crude emotion that does
not belong to religion at all. It is sometimes called
hysteria, or by some other name derived from psycho-
pathology. Even in the lives of great saints and martyrs
one finds distinguishing aspects and characteristics that
are pathological, especially in the conversion experience
which some of them have passed through. Yet by
taking them not individually but in relation one to
another, and comparing their inner experience with
their outward conduct, one gains a fairly satisfactory
impression of what in them was true religion and what
was spurious emotion due to a slight over-balancing of
the mind when face to face with this stupendous mystery.

Just as they themselves in examining their own lives gradually learn and advance in religious insight—learn to throw aside certain experiences or turn aside from them—so the observer, the psychologist or the philosopher, or the student of the philosophy of religion, comparing these individual experiences, can in that way learn what religion means in the lives of others. That is the empirical side. You cannot say *a priori* what religion should be, just as you cannot say *a priori* what beauty or morality or truth will be. That form of the *a priori* has been abandoned by everyone. When we say that these values are beyond the merely empirical, we do not mean to say that they are *a priori*. We learn them through experience, but in the course of experience we separate them out, we sift ourselves by self-discipline, and by observing others disciplining themselves we see how they get more and more direct insight into reality.

Let me try to make this argument more concrete in regard to æsthetic experience. Suppose we take architecture. A Greek column is æsthetically pleasing. Consider by the side of that Greek column the picture of Atlas holding up the world. You contemplate that and feel uncomfortable, you feel that it is something incongruous, not æsthetically pleasing. On the other hand, contemplate the structure of an ordinary wall. That is not in itself æsthetically pleasing—the Greek column is. What is the difference ? Schopenhauer's theory is that, in each of these instances, there are two ideas in relation to one another—the idea of weight and the idea of support. In the case of the wall the support is too great for the weight, and the two " ideas," support and weight, are not clearly distinguished. In the case of Atlas the weight is too great for the support. In the case of the Greek column weight and support, entablature and shaft, are adequately adjusted to each other.

It gives a feeling and an awareness of harmonious relationship. And the æsthetic reality with which one is in contact when appreciating the Greek column is not essentially one of pleasure in harmony, but a direct awareness of harmony in those two ideas—the aspects of weight and support. Two people may be able to appreciate the Greek column as a work of art to the same extent, but the one person may feel strong emotion about it and the other may not. One person may feel great pleasure, and the other not so pronounced physical pleasure. The æsthetic experience is not the same thing as physical pleasure. It is an experience of harmony. In the personality that experience comes from the soul itself, it is its inmost characteristic.

If a person asks himself what he really is, he finds himself faced with the need of analysis. A good way to carry it out is to get analysed over a long period, in which one works over all one's past, and in that way discards a lot of accidental accretions and hysterical and sentimental associations, looking upon the process as a sort of long death-bed repentance or μετάνοια (change of mind), facing one's past as something not entirely past and done with, asking oneself what it all amounts to, what one expected and expects of the world, what one really values in life and in others. One finds that it is not accidental or mere physical pleasure or any immediate and momentary sequence of experience. The temporal aspect as such falls away. One finds oneself seeing life more from the point of view of the eternal. Even temporal experience itself can be eternal. There are two general forms of temporal experience. There is the mere sequence of one's life from moment to moment— it is that form of the temporal that is appearance and not reality. That in itself is of no value. But we succeed more or less in transcending it the whole time, at one

time more than at another. In one sense the temporal
is a mere nothing. In another sense it is important,
because it is woven into our experience, inasmuch as it
is a condition of our appreciating, especially, e.g., the
sequence of notes in music. And yet in that sequence
of notes one realizes that true musical appreciation has
already transcended the sequence. One would be at the
animal level if it were not so. The work of art so far as
it is a work of art is beyond the temporal.

In ethics, an analogous relationship holds good. Moral
conduct is a sequence of cause and effect. In the circumstances that make the hero ready to risk his life for others,
there is a temporal sequence, but of course the heroism
is out of time. The general act of heroism is above mere
time, though it has to occur in time. Each one of us
has to think all this out for himself, he cannot learn it
from books. He must discipline himself and purify his
powers of appreciation. That is what I mean when
I say that we should examine ourselves as fully as we
can if we are to get an adequate view of what is meant
by personality.

My readers may object that I have never told them what
personality is, and have made my discussion very unin-
teresting by leaving out just the sort of things that the
world calls personality, viz., the individualism of people
who get their photographs in the paper and in other like
ways make themselves prominent. To my mind that is
not personality at all—that is a movement in the opposite
direction. Personality is within these values which we
have been describing, and passes through them to enrich
the higher or the more profound religious attitude. It
takes one beyond time and beyond the limits of the
individual, and that is what is meant in saying that
personality is in the end transcended in the Absolute or
God, and that there is only one complete personality.

We partake of these values ; they are revealed to us gradually. We learn to get into relationship with them. We find that the more sincere we are the more able we are to get into relationship with them. We find that what is meant by faith is conviction of our personal participation in these values, and what prevents us from having faith is ourselves. A person has no faith in himself because he knows that he is not sincere. To the extent to which we are not sincere we lack faith, and our sight is blinded, and we move away from the vision of true reality. So far as we are vouchsafed that vision of ultimate reality, we can only get it as parts of one another and of the totality of things. In the end it is the totality of things that is real, and not ourselves. We have reality only so far as we are parts of the totality.*

This is all so very obvious that it is difficult to understand why anyone should object to this theory of the absolute, of God the be-all and the in-all. We are members of one family, families are parts of one another, we are all brothers and sisters, we feel certain that unity of action for the sake of the totality of humanity must be the right action, not merely in the ethical sense, but in the true metaphysical sense, bringing us nearer to the ultimate meaning of things. Looked at from that point of view, pathology takes a wider scope. We are all of us pathological, not only in the sense of showing tendencies to psycho-neurosis or psychosis, but in the more general sense of being blinded in our insight, being cut

---

* " All we have willed or hoped or dreamed of good shall exist ;
   Not its semblance, but itself ; no beauty, nor good, nor power
   Whose voice has gone forth, but each survives for the melodist
   When eternity affirms the conception of an hour.
   The high that proved too high, the heroic for earth too hard,
   The passion that left the ground to lose itself in the sky,
   Are music sent up to God by the lover and the bard ;
   Enough that he heard it once : we shall hear it by-and-by."

off, being obsessed by our individuality, not going out sufficiently smoothly into touch with the totality of existence round us. That going out is not a vague mystic thing, but something definite. We have relationships to those nearest to us ; our family is relatively more important to us because we know more of it, and our knowledge helps us to act more effectively and truthfully, and our action must shade off as it covers a larger and larger radius, but we cannot put the circumference anywhere. We must take as our ideal, and stretch out our lives to include, the totality of existence. This does not mean absorbing totality into ourselves, but getting absorbed into it—not a form of disintegration, a sinking into the Nirvana of nothingness, but living the life of the universe so far as we can throughout our lives. From that point of view, as Nettleship said, " death does not count." It is a physical experience, generally involving a certain amount of pain and anguish, but as a reality we can pass beyond it ; before we face it we can see it as something that is just incidental, and when it does come it only affects the lowest level of our nature. We are people living on a different plane altogether from the plane of mere physical life and death. And so far as we get that totality, and sustain it to any length of time, we feel the question of individual survival after death is wrongly stated. We are already, in this life, in relation to eternal existence. We can partake of that eternal existence. We may, and probably all do, think that immortality or continued existence of some sort is probable, but whatever reasons we have for thinking that are derived from the eternal characteristics of experience, not from the temporal characteristics of experience. So long as we think of existence temporally in terms of sensation and association, we are bounded by mortality. When we die our

20

sense organs and our brains disintegrate. It is not that
kind of existence which is immortal. Memory may be
a different matter. This is a difficult problem—the
question of how far memories are associated with and
dependent on our brains and disappear when our brains
disappear. It may be that brain activity is responsible
for the recall of memories, but not for their retention,
and that so-called loss of memory is only a failure in the
power of recall.

The poets are nearer the truth than any prose writer,
and when Browning says, " The soul, doubtless, is
immortal—where a soul can be discern'd," he really
gives us the truth. We shall survive so far as we deserve
to survive, to the extent to which we are capable of
transcending the conditions of merely temporal physical
existence. Although much of the work of the Psychical
Research Society, the Spiritualists, etc., is important in
the effort to obtain empirical evidence of survival, one
cannot say that the results hitherto reached are particularly impressive or cheering, because in their triviality
they seem to tie one down too much to a merely temporal
sequence. The evidence such as it is may be valid, but
it is not inspiring. The loss of loved ones and the
longing for reunion with them is a legitimate and
powerful motive for our quest. Many have taken " the
Golden Road to Samarkand," only to return disillusioned
and disappointed. But apart from this, why think too
much about another life ? We have our reality here.
Let us realize the scale of values, seek always the highest
good, strive for that, and the rest is in the hands of the
Absolute. It seems to me that this is the best temper
of mind in which to lead one's life. Live immortally as
far as possible now, as Aristotle said so long ago—live
the immortal life at every moment. See things from
that angle, and live one's experience from that angle.

It is to the extent to which we do that that we are persons.

Yet personality itself is appearance rather than complete reality. In this view I am following F. H. Bradley. However much he has been criticized, that central position of his seems to me to be literally unassailable. Intellectually we are forced to think in terms of one—intellect means that; and spiritually we are forced to think in terms of one—spirit means that. Spirit means unity with something that is all-inclusive and is perfect, so far as we can appreciate perfection at all. Our imperfections of all kinds come from separates, from being separated off from one another. We have to be separated from one another, because each has to do his own work, and no two persons have the same work to do, but this separation is according to an all-inclusive law, joining persons up, so that the separation is only justified so far as it is an aspect of union. And that brings one to a form of mysticism; but it is not the mysticism of the spiritual sybarite who seeks pleasant feelings as such, but the satisfaction of the most central and also most all-inclusive characteristics of one's mind. And that is what the higher mysticism is. In the higher mysticism, which may be more pronounced in some conditions of mind than in others, the experience itself is other than mere emotion. It is a feeling of peace, of complete safety and satisfaction—a conviction that perfection, *i.e.*, God, exists, and that we may in however humble a way participate in that perfection and thus, and only thus, achieve realization of our inmost personality.

CHAPTER XXIV

As regards the possibility of personal survival of bodily death, the evidence of Psychical Research is clearly of scientific importance. All relevant facts should be considered and investigated with scientific precision. Any scientific statements should be based upon knowledge and not upon ignorance. Nevertheless, our belief in survival is but little influenced by the findings of Psychical Research. Evidence from that source falls far short of convincing proof. Alternative hypotheses are possible, and in the end the conclusion must remain within the realm of hypothesis, whereas the arguments in favour of survival which are really impressive are on a different footing, and have to do with a different level of our mind—the level that comprises the general scheme of values. We have already seen on more occasions than one that value-experiences are only indirectly the subject-matter of psychology, and yet are the most important parts of our mental life. Hence a theory of values is needed, which is to be not a merely psychological theory. Considerations of a psychological nature are relevant, but do not constitute the foundations of such a theory. The theory of values belongs primarily to metaphysics, not to psychology.

This question is intimately bound up with the theory of values. Is the life we live on this earth worth while? If we believe that it is, what are our reasons for such belief? We may find that the answer to this gives an answer to the further question : Are we likely to survive? We are likely to survive so far as we can continue a realization of values which we are in process of realizing

here.   This is probably the most decisive criterion.
We cannot get certainty.   Scientifically we do not get
certainty.   It has often been remarked that in psychical
research we have frequently seemed to be on the verge
of obtaining some conclusive evidence to settle the
question in a positive way, and through carelessness in
the reports of observers or through peculiar circumstances apparently accidental, this evidence has broken
down, producing the impression that we are possibly not
meant to know.   Possibly it is good for us not to be
scientifically certain about a future life, for reasons that
will at once suggest themselves.   One such reason is that
if the future life is happier than this life there would be
a greater temptation to leave this life when faced with
specially difficult circumstances, and so to lose the
discipline which this life has for character, and to miss
some of the factors of character-training.   If, as Keats
said long ago, this world is "the vale of soul making,"
it is fairly clear that many of the difficulties which we
would otherwise wish to avoid, and do attempt to avoid,
are of real benefit to us.

Secondly, if we were scientifically sure of a future
existence, we should lose whatever moral advantage
attaches to uncertainty.   The uncertainty is itself a
testing circumstance for character.   Different people
re-act to that uncertainty in different ways.   Some say :
" Let us eat, drink, and be merry, for to-morrow we
die."   Others says : " We have this life, let us make the
best of it and develop its possibilities to the utmost,
help one another while we are here, sink our merely
individual differences as far as possible, pursue the values
we clearly see without enquiring too much about the
more ultimate values of existence at present hidden
from us."   These are the two extremes.   On the one
hand we may find people giving up the pursuit of ideals,

adopting an Epicurean attitude towards life, regarding
the senses and direct physical pleasure as the most obvious
and the most important things in this life, and living
for them. On the other hand, we may find people
recognizing the value of evolution, approving of the good,
emphasizing it, and fighting for it without thought of
anything beyond—following virtue for its own sake
without thought of reward. Perseverance in that
attitude of mind is itself a training of character, and most
likely to develop to the utmost the potentialities of
character. A conviction, grounded in scientific knowledge,
that there is a future life, would not necessarily interfere
with such training ; but in the previously mentioned
type of person it might encourage a different order of
" goodness "—it might encourage such persons to look
at spiritual things as means to an end instead of as ends
in themselves. Probably, if men were certain of another
life, the actual differences between individuals would
remain much as they are now.

If we believe in super-personal values, which are, as
it were, caught up in, or participated in by, the individual
personality—if we believe that the individual achieves
personality partly through submission, living for values,
striving to purify his power of appreciation of those
values, and partly through affirmation of them, we pass
beyond individuality towards a more general outlook on
life, a super-individual outlook, in that way lessening
individuality but gaining rather than losing in personality.
As the individual disciplines his mind to an appreciation
of this hierarchy of values, he gains another attitude
which is also a personal attitude, the attitude of religion,
in which he faces reality not in its abstract aspects of
truth, goodness, and beauty, but in its concrete character
as the spirit or soul of the universe, which includes these
values in itself, and realizes them in its own life. The

individual in losing his individuality, gains it again as part of this all-conclusive spiritual unity. And if we take the individual personality as a very faint reflection of what we may believe the Universal Mind to be, we may feel that its development and realization is cut short in this life. However long we may live, fulfilment is denied us in every case, more in some cases than in others, and the adequate fulfilment from the point of view of the imperfect human mind can only be achieved by continued existence in later lives. This would appear to be a much more powerful argument for belief in a future existence.

Another argument for survival is that from the absolute value of love and affection. Many people who would claim to have no particular wish or desire for personal immortality, yet have a feeling that the ending of all friendships in this life would be so pronounced a violation of any principle of conservation of value as to be profoundly irrational. Most men think more of the immortality of those dear to them than of their own immortality. What appears much more of a waste than that of merely individual excellences and achievements, is that of the bonds of affection that spring up between individuals and raise them to a higher unity. It is, indeed, in such a higher unity in this life between individuals who are unselfishly fond of one another that we may see an analogy of what may be eventually the communion of saints or the system of souls towards which the whole universe may be working. We may regard the whole process of evolution as a process of soul-making. And without love, no soul.*

---

* Those who think that a *disbelief* in immortality is justified by science and philosophy are the dupes of their own cleverness or erudition. The advance of science has freed us from crude superstition and its savage terrors, but leaves us with the larger hope—ἡ ἐλπὶς μεγάλη, καλὸς ὁ κίνδυνος, the spacious hope, glorious is the adventure.

The process of evolution, occurring not only on this planet but within the whole of the stellar systems of the universe, may be a process of indefinite multiplication of psychical and spiritual reality, and an indefinite union and systematization of that reality. It may be that the whole process of existence is a process in which God or the Absolute goes out of Himself to produce individual agents, to a certain extent separated from one another, with a very small initial amount of freedom which they can make use of and develop, and so work out their own salvation by gradually adding to that freedom—realizing the conditions under which that freedom is diminished or increased, learning by experience that they cannot be sufficient unto themselves, that they must live as parts of one another, realizing that salvation can only come to all simultaneously, that we shall all be saved together if we are saved at all. Possibly the conditions of reality itself may be such that only in this way can souls be produced. We may *imagine* conditions in which souls might spring fully developed from the Godhead, and yet that may be impossible. It is a question of what we mean by the omnipotence of God. God is omnipotent in that He can do everything in harmony with His own nature. Some things are not in harmony with His nature. It may be that the production of individual souls in initial perfection and completely adapted to one another is not in harmony with His nature.

Such a view as this seems to be assuming the time process as something real. If we regard time as ultimately real, and God as in time rather than time in God, we come up against all the contradictions that Kant has set out so fully, and a general philosophy of existence is impossible to us. So far as we regard time as ultimately real we are certainly limited to a merely scientific knowledge of the world. That is what science is—organized knowledge in terms of space and/or time. But philosophy attempts to pass beyond this position. We may, if we like, protest that it is impossible to pass beyond ; that we are in time, and cannot get out of time. I have already tried to explain how according to the doctrine of values we are on occasions lifted more or less out of time even in this temporal life. Nevertheless, the sketch which I have given of the production of souls out of the divine nature or essence, and their gradual return, is in terms of time. That is the way in which it appears to us, the only way in which we can think of it. We find that all our scientific thinking, all our scientific knowledge, while giving us an increasingly clear view of the world around us, ties us down to the self-contradictory framework of space and time. The limitation is especially apparent in the case of time.

Nevertheless, by timelessness one does not mean a *totum simul*, a mere simultaneity. Timelessness, or eternity, is not a negation of time, it is rather a fulfilment of time. Time for us, as we experience it, is more than spatialized time, more than a sequence of one thing after another. Bergson has drawn from this consideration a conclusion precisely opposite to that which I am drawing. Bergson makes time, *durée réelle*, the very stuff of reality. The time with which we deal in physics and in the other physical sciences is spatialized time. Bergson would consider that reality as such is duration, and so one finds at the centre of his system of philosophy the conception of an *élan vital* pressing forwards towards greater and greater vital complexity. This is the fundamental principle which he uses in explaining evolution, upon which may be grafted the Darwinian theory of struggle for existence and natural selection and other evolutionary factors of modern biology. The world is in process of creation, and to the question about the beginning of it all, Bergson gives a most unsatisfactory reply. He speaks about an " interruption " occurring at an unspecified date in the past in the forward progress of the spiritual principle— a falling away in the opposite direction, which is matter. In the organic world one finds this vital impulse making use of matter (its own " waste product," as it were). The vital impulse continues to mould it for its own purposes. Bergson's idea of the relation of structure and function is that function produces structure, and not structure function. His view is the opposite of the materialistic theory, according to which one starts with the simplest configuration of atoms that fall into groups or systems, the more stable systems surviving, until systems arise sufficiently complicated and stable to be capable of the function of consciousness. For Bergson the reality is spiritual energy, which asserts itself in spite of a tendency to " fall away." As there is a falling away, in a sort of condensation of the world in matter, the spiritual energy then proceeds to mould that matter and produces the various systems of function and plan, culminating in the intuitive and intellectual life of man. The objection to this theory is that it does not carry us far enough. The assumption which it has to make (viz., that of an " interruption ") practically means a retreat from the philosophic problem. To the question " Why did the interruption occur," there is no answer. On the other hand, if one holds that God exists from eternity to eternity—that the existence of God and Spirit is beyond time, then one may find—or some genius in future ages may be able to find—a place for time within that eternal system, and one may be able to explain how the temporal series has arisen.

The individual mind is an abstraction. Just as, if we look towards the future, we can see the various selves or personalities becoming more and more harmonious with one another and achieving universal values ; so, if we think back into our past, and into the past of the whole organic world and of the stellar systems, we again find ourselves arising from unity rather than from diversity. We are parts of one another from the beginning, just as we become parts of one another in the end. We are parts of one another in the beginning in a different sense, indeed, from that in which we become parts of one another in the end ; nevertheless, the beginning and the end, though separated for us by a temporal series, are parts of the same system. If we think at all we have to assume that reality is intelligible, which means that reality forms a system in which everything is relevant to everything else—we have to accept the principles of relevance and of sufficient reason.

Our thinking occurs in time, and we set out our scientific knowledge in a temporal sequence. Yet in our thinking we see that truth transcends time. The universe, the totality of things, must be a system, but it must be beyond time, a system that finds a place for time in itself. What is the meaning of time to us individually ? It has various meanings. Taken at its highest level time has the meaning of development, of a deeper and deeper penetration into the meaning of things. Time means for us deepened insight into the significance of the universe. Some may hold that " the end is progress." These have the zeal of the reformer, who wishes to leave the world better than he found it. But thought cannot stop there. Indefinite progress is intellectually almost as bad as indefinite regress. There is no meaning in a better unless one can believe in a best. This world is imperfect, and the more we appreciate these imperfections the more we tend to realize the significance of progress, and of a possible perfection. When we hear of a terrible

case of cruelty, or of cynical self-seeking, it is then that
we become specially conscious of what good means in
contrast with evil, just as it is through our own bad
actions, through our own mistakes, that we become more
aware of what we are falling away from, of the possibilities which we are missing in the way of development
of character.   And all this comes to us in sequence of
time. It can only come to us in that form in our individual
lives, and the time sequence is an essential condition of
this life. Similarly with the appreciation of beauty, we
can only wake our souls in process of time ; we need
time for it.   Likewise with truth ; we can only fully
appreciate truth through the process of manufacturing it,
hammering it out.   But some do it much more rapidly
and completely than others.   A mathematical genius
will reach mathematical truth at a much quicker rate
than will a mathematician of average ability.   Mathematics, indeed, is a good illustration of the significance
of temporal experience in revealing what is essentially
self-evident and beyond time.   The time taken in reaching
truth is relative to mathematical " sincerity," to the
extent to which the mathematician can free himself
from the influence of irrelevant factors.   So in morals,
we in our finite lives can only achieve the self-evident
through painful experience and frequent failure.   Sincerity
is an indispensable condition.   We thus gradually re-make
ourselves in the light of the moral ideal, and in so doing
gain an ever-increasing insight into the nature and
significance of that ideal.   Similarly with art—æsthetic
appreciation of music, painting, sculpture, etc.   So, too,
in religion, which is an attempt to find out the purpose
of the universe, believing that there is such a purpose,
taking it as a hypothesis, and endeavouring to identify
oneself as far as possible with that purpose, and to play
one's part within it.   Here there is the great difficulty of

optimism and pessimism. The purpose of the universe may be not beneficent, but maleficent, or again it may be a huge mistake, it may have no meaning at all, and what we think is its meaning may be simply illusion due to our own individual and restricted point of view. The argument against this is a pragmatic one, that the more sincere we are with ourselves in working out and applying the doctrine of values, the more do we realize that there is a force greater than ourselves, not only individually but also collectively, working towards a realization of these values. We advance inevitably from a religion of humanity to a religion of God.

BIBLIOGRAPHY

Ach, N. The Über den Willensakt und das Temperament. Göttingen, 1910.

Adler, A. The Neurotic Constitution. New York, 1918.

—— Individual Psychology. London, 1924.

Alexander, S. Space Time and Deity. London, 1920.

Anson, H. Spiritual Healing. London, 1923.

Archer, W. Masks or Faces ? The Psychology of Acting. London, 1888.

Aveling, F. On the Consciousness of the Universal and the Individual. London, 1911.

Baudouin, C. Suggestion and Auto-suggestion. London, 1920.

Bergson, H. Time and Free Will. London, 1910.

—— Creative Evolution. London, 1911.

—— Matter and Memory. London, 1911.

Berman, L. Glands Regulating Personality. New York, 1921.

Betz, W. Ueber Korrelation. Leipzig, 1911.

Bradley, F. H. Appearance and Reality, 2nd Edition. London, 1908.

Broad, C. D. The Mind, and its Place in Nature. London, 1925.

Brown, William. An Objective Study of Mathematical Intelligence. Biometrica. Vol. vii. Cambridge. 1910.

—— Psychology and Psychotherapy. London, 1921.

—— and Thomson, G. H. Essentials of Mental Measurement, 3rd Edition. Cambridge, 1925.

Burt, C. Mental and Scholastic Tests. London, 1921.

Carr, H. W. The Philosophy of Change. London, 1913.

Combarieu, J. La Musique, ses Lois, son Évolution. Paris, 1907.

Croce, B. What is Living and What is Dead of the Philosophy of Hegel. London, 1915.

—— Æsthetic. London, 1922.

Drever, J.   Instinct in Man.   Cambridge, 1917.
Driesch, H.   Science and Philosophy of the Organism.   London, 1908.
—— The Crisis in Psychology.   Princeton, 1925.

Edgell, Beatrice.   Mental Life.   London, 1926.
Elliot, H.   Human Character.   London, 1922.

Flugel, J. C.   Psychoanalytics Study of the Family.   London, 1922.
Fraser, Sir J.   The Golden Bough.   London, 1923.
Freud, S.   Interpretation of Dreams.   London, 1913.
—— Introductory Lectures on Psychoanalysis.   London, 1922.
—— Group Psychology and the Analysis of the Ego.   London, 1922.
—— Collected Papers, 4 Vols.   London, 1924, 1925.
—— Das Ich und das Es.   Vienna, 1923.
—— Hemmung, Symptom und Angst.   Vienna, 1926.

Gentile, G.   The Theory of Mind as Pure Act.   London, 1922.
Gordon, R. G.   Personality.   London, 1926.
Grant, Sir A.   Nicomaehean Ethics of Aristotle, 4th Edition.   London, 1885.

Hadfield, J. A.   Psychology and Morals.   London, 1922.
Haldane, J. S.   Mechanism, Life and Personality.   London, 1913.
Hart, B.   The Psychology of Insanity.   Cambridge, 1912.
Head, H.   Studies in Neurology.   Oxford, 1920.
—— Aphasia and Kindred Disorders of Speech, Cambridge, 1926.
Heath, A. G.   Moral and Social Significance of the Conception of Personality.   Oxford, 1921.

Inge, W. R.   Outspoken Essays (Second Series).   London, 1922.

James, William.   Principles of Psychology.   London, 1901.
—— Varieties of Religious Experience.   London, 1911.
Janet, Pierre.   Psychological Healing.   London, 1925.
Jennings, H. C.   The Behaviour of Lower Organisms.   New York, 1906.
Joachim, H. H.   The Nature of Truth.   Oxford, 1906.
Jones, Ernest.   Papers on Psychoanalysis, 3rd Edition.   London, 1923.

Jung, C. G.   Collected Papers on Analytical Psychology. London, 1917.
—— Psychology of the Unconscious.   New York and London, 1916.
—— Psychological Types.   London, 1923.

Keatinge, M. W.   Studies in Education.   London, 1916.
Koffka, K.   Mental Development.   *Psychologies of 1925.*   Clark University, 1926.
Köhler, W.   The Mentality of Apes.   London, 1924.

Leuba, J. H.   The Psychology of Religious Mysticism.   London, 1925.
Lodge, Sir Oliver.   The Survival of Man ; a Study in Unrecognised Human Faculty.   London, 1909.
Loeb, J.   The Mechanistic Conception of Life.   Chicago, 1912.

MacCurdy, J. T.   Problems in Dynamic Psychology.   Cambridge, 1923.
McDougall, W.   Social Psychology ; 19th Edition.   London, 1924.
—— Body and Mind.   London, 1911.
—— The Group Mind.   Cambridge, 1921.
—— Outline of Psychology.   London, 1923.
—— Outline of Abnormal Psychology.   London, 1926.
McDowall, A. S.   Evolution, Knowledge and Revelation. Cambridge, 1924.
Mackenzie, J. S.   Ultimate Values.   London, 1924.
Miller, H. C.   Functional Nerve Disease.   London, 1920.
Mitchell, T. W.   Medical Psychology and Psychical Research. London, 1922.
Moore, G. E.   Philosophical Studies.   London, 1922.
Morgan, C. Lloyd.   Emergent Evolution.   London, 1923.
Myers, C. S. and Bartlett, F. C.   Textbook of Experimental Psychology ; 3rd Edition.   Cambridge, 1926.
Myers, F. W. H.   Human Personality and its Survival of Bodily Death.   London, 1903.

Needham, J. (and others).   Science, Religion and Reality. London, 1925.

Otto, R.   The Idea of the Holy.   Oxford, 1923.

21

Pear, T H.   Remembering and Forgetting.   London, 1922.
Pearson, Karl.   The Grammar of Science ; 3rd Edition.   London, 1911.
Poincaré, H.   La Valeur de la Science.   Paris, 1908.
Pratt, J. B.   The Religious Consciousness.   New York, 1921.
Prince, Morton.   The Dissociation of a Personality.   New York, 1906.
—— The Unconscious.   Boston, 1913.
Problems of Personality (in honour of Morton Prince.)   London and New York, 1925.
Pringle-Pattison, A. Seth.   The Idea of God ; in the Light of recent Philosophy (Gifford Lectures).   Oxford, 1920.
—— The Idea of Immortality (Gifford Lectures).   Oxford, 1922.

Ribot, Th.   La Psychologie des Sentiments.   Paris, 1911.
—— La Logique des Sentiments.   Paris, 1912.
—— Essai sur les Passions.   Paris, 1910.
Rignano, E.   The Psychology of Reasoning.   London, 1923.
Rivers, W. H. R.   Instinct and the Unconscious.   Cambridge, 1920.
Roback, A. A.   Behaviorism and Psychology.   New York, 1923.
Russell, Bertrand.   The Analysis of Mind.   London, 1921.

Schiller, F. C. S.   Riddles of the Sphinx ; a Study in the Philosophy of Humanism ; 2nd Edition.   London, 1910.
Shand, A. F.   The Foundations of Character ; a Study of the Tendencies of Emotions and Sentiments.   London, 1920.
Sherrington, Sir C.   Integrative Action of the Nervous System.   London, 1906.
Sidgwick, H.   History of Ethics, 5th Edition.   London, 1902.
Smith, M. Hamblin.   The Psychology of the Criminal.   London, 1922.
Smith, W. Whately.   The Measurement of Emotion.   London, 1923.
Spearman, C.   General Intelligence objectively determined and measured.   *American Journ. Psychol.*   1904, xv, p. 201.
—— The Theory of Two Factors.   *Psychological Review,* 1914.
—— Recent Contributions to the Theory of Two Factors   *Brit. Journ. Psychol.*   1922, xiii, p. 26.

Stewart, J. A.   Plato's Doctrine of Ideas.   Oxford, 1909.
Stout, G. F.   A Manual of Psychology ; 3rd Edition.   London, 1913.
Strong, C. A.   Why the Mind has a Body.   London, 1903.

Taylor, A. E.   Elements of Metaphysics.   London, 1903.
Temple, W.   The Nature of Personality.   London, 1911.
Thomson, Godfrey H.   Instinct, Intelligence and Character ; an Educational Psychology.   London, 1925.
Thouless, R. H.   An Introduction to the Psychology of Religion.   Cambridge, 1923.

Ward, James.   The Realm of Ends ; or, Pluralism and Theism.   Cambridge, 1911.
—— Psychological Principles.   Cambridge, 1918.
Watson, J. B.   Behaviourism.   London, 1926.
Webb, C. C. J.   Divine Personality and Human Life (Gifford Lectures).   London, 1920.
Westermarck, E. A.   The Origin and Development of the Moral Ideas ; 2nd Edition.   London, 1917.
Whitehead, A. N.   The Principles of Natural Knowledge.   Cambridge, 1919.
—— The Concept of Nature.   Cambridge, 1920.
Wilson, S. A. K.   Aphasia.   London, 1925.
Windelband, W.   An Introduction to Philosophy.   London, 1921.

INDEX

Abilities, two, correlation between, 118, 119
Abnormal systems of mind resulting from past painful experiences, 74, 75
Acquisition, feeling of ownership accompanying, 61
Action, time in relation to, 286
Adler, A., fundamental instinct of self-assertion, 193
— new point of view in psychology introduced by, 12
Adolescence, problems of, 135
— sex instruction should be given before, 139
Adolescents, sex impulse in, means of escaping temptation from, 140
Affection, definition of, 244
Agoraphobia, nature of, 274, 275
Algebra, ability in, and ability in geometry, mode of measurement for, 117
— and geometry, ability in, slight connection between, 122
— geometry and arithmetic, ability in, correlation between, method, tabular statement and results, 119–124
Algebraical reasoning distinct from geometrical, 114
Amnesia, treatment by re-association of mind, 167
Amusement, emotional quality accompanying, 61
Anæsthetic revelation as a mystical experience, 283
Analysis in cure of hysteria, example, 150, 151

Analysis:
— liberation from false personality by, 188
— method of, 156, 157
— need of, in self-estimation, 302
— of patients' mind in order to obtain explanation of suggestion, 177
— psychological, followed by psychoanalysis in mental disease, 171
— — in treatment of hysteria, 169
— showing subjects of kleptomania not always free from guilt, 92
— see also *Deep analysis*
Anger accompanying combative instinct, 68
— close relation to courage (Aristotle), 218
— definition of, given by Aristotle, 212
— effect of sentiment upon, 70
— emotional quality accompanying instinct of combat, 60
Animals, behaviour of, as conscious beings, 24
— behaviour, purposive, 18
Appeal, instinct of, emotional quality accompanying, 60
Appetite accompanying instinct of food-seeking, 61
Aristotle, description and definition of virtue, 215, 216
— description of material of moral activity, 215
— ethics separated from metaphysics in philosophy of, 210
— on achievement of immortality, 285

325

Depression :
— due to physical factors, benefit derived from psychotherapy, 46, 47
— explanation of, 155
Desires, suppression of, at their source, advocated by founder of Buddhism (Gautama), 208
De-sublimation, danger of, in more emotional sides of religion, 141
Determinism, 277
— and free-will, contrasted theories of, 84
— rigid, Freud's theory of, 193
Dirt and infection, obsessional fear of, how developed, 89
Disgust, emotional quality accompanying repulsion, 60
— instinct of, how developed, 88
Dissociation, crude mental, facilitates suggestion, 175
— — — subjects of, amenable to hypnosis, 174
— — — suffered by soldiers in war, 174
— of personality and mental ability, 195
— — cases of, 195–198
— — explanation given by Freud, 198
Distress, instinct of, emotional quality accompanying, 60
Drama and psychology, connection between, now closer, 3, 4
Dramatic sense of personality, 3
Dream state, crimes of violence committed by epileptics in, 91
Driesch, definition of " entelechy," 22, 23
— definition of " psychoid," 22, 23
Duty, reason for performance cannot be explained, 293

Education, physical element in, 46
— true definition of, 133
Effort, reversed, Coué's so-called law of, 179

Effort, reversed :
— — doctrine of, 273, 274, 275
Elation, emotional quality accompanying assertion, 61
Electric lights, cluster of, attention, presentation and feeling-tone in connection with, 57, 58
— — colour and shape of, mental characteristics, 55
— — visual experience of seeing, analysed, 53, 54
Emotion and emotional disposition, distinction between, drawn by Aristotle, 214, 215
— and instinct, relation between, 59
— as auxiliary factor in suggestion, 176
— crude, mistaken for religion, 300
— in relation to music, 228–230
Emotions, complex, 61, 62
— derived, examples of, 67, 68
— — relation of, to desire, 67
— individual systems of, 63
— secondary causes of, example, 67
Empirical and value experiences contrasted, 298
Emulation, definition of, given by Aristotle, 213
Endocrine glands, disturbance of function in relation to mental disease, 161, 162
— — importance in organism of child, 128
— — in relation to consciousness of individual, 129
— — not essential to normal personality, 38
— — relation to personal consciousness, 36, 37, 38
— — — to personality, 129, 130
— — restoration to function, effect on health of personality, 39
Energy of volitional activity, 81

Mental ability, dissociation of personality and, 195
— activities, becoming conscious, 181
— — becoming conscious under certain conditions, 181
— — complex and later forms explain earlier forms, 10
— — exhibiting marks of purposive activity, 51
— blindness, causes of, 246
— capacity in groups of individuals, correlative variations of, 110
— conflict, all-importance of, 70
— — analytic, 82, 83
— — and mental difficulties, bad effect on bodily health, 39
— — occurrence of volition in, 82
— — synthetic, 82, 83
— depression, physical depression, producing or intensifying, 39
— disease, administration of thyroid extract in, 162
— — also physical, 161, 162
— — causal factor psychological in many forms of, 162
— — early treatment, 161
— — — by isolation and in mental hospitals, 171, 172
— — — by physical measures, 161, 162, 163
— — — by psychological analysis, followed by psycho-analysis, 171
— — forms of, following hysteria, 166
— — in relation to disturbance of activity of endocrine glands, 161, 162
— — — to infection and toxic absorption, 161, 162
— — originating in failure of adaptation, to special periods of life, 162, 163
— — present-day difficulty of dealing with, 45
— — responsibility and, 90

Mental disease :
— — subjects of, feeling of isolation from nature in, 283
— — sex instinct in relation to, 171
— diseases not very amenable to psychotherapy, 40
— dissociation, crude, caused by physical shock to brain, 175
— hospitals, value in early mental disease, 171, 172
— illness, disturbance of conscious life in, related to auto-intoxication or septic infection, 38
— — crimes of violence committed during, 91, 92, 93
— illnesses, explained in terms of physical disease, 40
— power, successive stages of development of, 72
— processes barred from consciousness, 182
— — complex, producing symptoms of hysteria, 150
— — correlation with physiological processes by physiologists, 7
— reaction to environment, psychological and physiological accounts of, 7, 8
— variation, science of, 110
Metaphysics, ethics separated from, in philosophy of Aristotle, 210
Mind, activity of, higher forms as opposed to lower, 1
— in relation to that of brain, physiological theory of, 26
— analytic method of approaching, 6
— and matter, relation between, ordinary views upon, 248
— and the physical organism, 33
— as a system of interest, 63
— cognitive side of, 72
— conscious, influence of memories on, 6
— — sequence of processes in time, 58

22

Responsibility and mental disease, 90
— legal definition of, 90
— moral, attitude of modern psychology towards, 93
— self-evident fact in normal persons, 85
Restraint and repression, difference between, 138
Revelation, human mechanism a mechanism of, 133
Rousseau, J. J., written confessions of, 4

Salpêtrière School, definition of hypnotic state by, 173
Schleiermacher, essential element in religious experience, 258
School-mathematics and higher mathematics compared as test of general ability, 113
Schools, sex instruction in, 139
Science, sound workers in, not emotional, 296
Scientists, great, self-effacement of, 289
Self, all-inclusive, organization of, 80
— and soul, distinction between, 297
— -abasement, instinct of, 82
— — in relation to suggestibility, 178
— -analysis, confession a form of, 4
— — and psycho-analysis, distinction between, 4
— -assertion, fundamental instinct of, 193
— -assertive instinct, source of, 81
— — — over-development of, 87, 88
— -centred nature of paranoiacs, 289
— -determination, belief in, of importance in psychotherapy 47
— -determinism, 278
— — conscience, important factor in, 188

Self :
— -estimation, need of analysis in, 302
— -hypnosis, as mystical experience, 283
— -knowledge, acquirement of, by patient, 5
— -preservation, undue development of, 87
— -regarding sentiment, 82
— — — as master-sentiment, 64
— -respect, development of strong feeling of, 83
Sensation-intensities, experimental work upon, 99
Sensory experiences of early childhood, 189
Sentiment, definition of, 70
— doctrine of, in dealing with problem of volition, 70
— self-regarding, resulting in strength of character, 71
— technical significance of, 62
Sentiments, abstract and concrete, 63
— analysis of, effect on patient, 77
— and complexes, difference between, 76
— definition, 79
— lowest units of character formation, 132
— nature of, 77
Septic foci, discovery and removal of, in treatment of early mental disease, 161, 163
— infection, disturbance of conscious life in mental illness in relation to, 38
Sex education in children, how far possible, 138
— impulse, temptation from, in adolescents, means of escaping, 140, 141
— instinct in relation to mental disease, 170, 171
— — relation to other instincts of mind, 138

Utility argument in favour of inter-actionism, 34

Value, definition of, 224
— -experiences, contrasted with empirical experiences, 298
— judgment of, how determined, 224
— level of religion higher than that of, 299
— notion of, of economic origin, 224
— personality and, 293
Vertebrates, advance of, in evolution, 237
Vicious circle affecting bodily health, starting in mind and ending in mind, 39, 40
Vigilance, Henry Head's doctrine of, 146
Violence, crimes of, committed during mental illness, 91, 92, 93
Virtue and knowledge, relation between, 220, 227
— characteristics and definition of, given by Aristotle, 216
— established, importance of process of habituation in producing, insisted on by Plato, 210
Vision, canalized, of living beings, 240
— effective, of living beings, 240
Visual consciousness, occipital area of cerebral cortex correlated with, 26
— experience, experiments dealing with, 103
Vital processes, mental in nature, 25
Volition, definitions of, 71, 72, 82, 179
— doctrine of sentiments in dealing with, 70
— efficiency of, on what dependent, 84
— method of reaching, 11
— occurrence, in mental conflict, 82

Volition :
— power of, defect in, 84
— problem of, doctrine of sentiment in dealing with, 70
Volitional activity, energy of, 81

War neurosis, desire for personal safety in subjects of, cause of hysterical symptoms, 176
— — distraught state of mind of subjects of, 177
Ward, J., distinction between process and contents of experience, 57
— theory as to acts of attention, 58
— three aspects of any moment of experience defined by, 57
Water, fear of, how developed, 87
Westermarck, E., on moral emotions, 222
Will and character, how far identical, 137
— definition of, 135
— development of, 80
— — influenced by experience in early life, 85, 86
— education of, factors contributing to, 137
— freedom of, reality of, 235
— identity of character with, 135
— -power, source of, 81
— raw material of, 86
— relation of suggestion and auto-suggestion to, 179
— see also *Volition*
Witasek, on value, 224
Word-association test, uses of, 108
Words as link between the conscious and unconscious, 184
— association and memorization in learning experiments, 58
Wrongdoing, defence of, on ground of insanity, 90 (footnote)
— described psychologically, 90
Wundt, W., *Physiological Psychology*, 97